William H. D. Adams

Curiosities of Superstition

and sketches of some unrevealed religions

William H. D. Adams

Curiosities of Superstition
and sketches of some unrevealed religions

ISBN/EAN: 9783337262785

Printed in Europe, USA, Canada, Australia, Japan

Cover: Foto ©Lupo / pixelio.de

More available books at **www.hansebooks.com**

CURIOSITIES

OF

SUPERSTITION,

AND

Sketches of some Unrebealed Religions.

BY

W. H. DAVENPORT ADAMS,

AUTHOR OF "HEROES OF THE CROSS," ETC.

"To my mind there is no study more absorbing than that of the Religions of the World,—the study, if I may so call it, of the various languages in which man has spoken to his Maker, and of that language in which his Maker 'at sundry times and in divers manners' spake to man."—MAX MÜLLER.

"Primus in orbe Deos fecit timor."—STATIUS, *Thebaid*, 661.

LONDON:
J. MASTERS AND CO., 78, NEW BOND STREET.
MDCCCLXXXII.

LONDON:
PRINTED BY J. MASTERS AND CO.,
ALBION BUILDINGS, BARTHOLOMEW CLOSE.

CONTENTS.

CHAPTER	PAGE
I. Buddhism, its Origin and Ceremonies	1
II. Magianism: the Parsees	43
III. Jewish Superstitions	68
IV. Brahmanism	84
V. Hindu Mythology, and the Vishnu Purana	99
VI. In China: Confucianism, Taouism, and Buddhism	119
VII. Among the Malays, the Slamatan Bromok, the Dyaks, the Papuan Tribes, the Ahetas	142
VIII. The Savage Races of Asia: the Samojedes; the Mongols; the Ostiaks; in Tibet	155
IX. Some African Superstitions	171
X. The Zulu Witch-finders	180
XI. Zabianism and Serpent-Worship	186
XII. Polynesian Superstitions	214
XIII. The Fiji Islanders	230
XIV. The Religion of the Maories	241
XV. The North American Indians	254
XVI. Among the Eskimos	274
XVII. A Mediæval Superstition: the Flagellants	279
XVIII. Scottish Superstitions: Halloween	288
XIX. Second Sight: Divination: Universality of Certain Superstitions: Fairies in Scotland	300

CURIOSITIES OF SUPERSTITION.

CHAPTER I.
BUDDHISM: ITS ORIGIN AND CEREMONIES.

PRAYER-WHEELS OF THE BUDDHISTS.

TRAVELLING on the borders of Chinese Tartary, in the country of the Lamas or Buddhists, Miss Gordon Cumming remarks that it was strange, every now and again, to meet some respectable-looking workman, twirling little brass cylinders, only about six inches in length, which were incessantly spinning round and round as they walked along the road. What could they be? Not pedometers, not any of the trigonometrical instruments with which the officers of the Ordnance Survey go about armed? No; she was informed that they were prayer-wheels, and that turning them was just about equivalent to the telling of beads, which in Continental lands workmen may often be seen counting as homeward along the road they plod their weary way.

The telling of beads seems to the Protestant a superfluous piece of formalism : what then are we to think of prayer by machinery? The prayers, or rather invocations, to Buddha —the Buddhists never pray, in the Christian sense—are all closely written upon strips of cloth or paper ; the same sentence being repeated some thousands of times. These strips are placed inside a cylinder, revolving on a long spindle, the end of which is the handle. From the wind-cylinder depends a small lump of metal, which, whirling round, com-

B

municates the necessary impetus to the little machine, so that it rotates with the slightest possible effort, and continues to grind any required number of acts of worship, while the owner, with the plaything in his hand, carries on his daily work. His religion requires that he should be all his time immersed in holy contemplation of the perfections of Buddha, but to a busy man no such self-absorption is possible. He is content, therefore, to say the sentences aloud at the beginning and end of his devotions, and in the interval twirls slowly, while a tiny bell marks each rotation, and reminds him if he should unconsciously quicken his pace.

Tennyson finely speaks of Prayer as that by which

"The whole round world is every way
Bound by gold chains around the feet of GOD;"

but no such efficacy can be ascribed to the cylinders of brass, copper, or gold, which are fashionable among the Buddhists. Yet we must not condemn too unreservedly : Prayer, even among Christians, is apt to degenerate into a dull, mechanical uniformity, and to become scarcely less perfunctory than that which the Tibetans grind out of their prayer-machine.

In a Lama temple, Miss Gordon Cumming once saw a colossal prayer-wheel, which might almost have sufficed for the necessities of a nation. It was turned by a great iron crank, which acted as a handle. The cylinder measured about twelve feet in height, and six to eight feet in diameter. Circular bands of gold and vermilion adorned it, each band bearing the well-known Buddhist ascription, or invocation, "To the jewel on the Lotus." Of this inscription, multiplied on strips of paper and cloth, the cylinder was full, and each time that it revolved on its axis, the devotee was accredited with having uttered the pious invocation just as often as it was repeated within the cylinder. The whole history of Superstition offers scarcely any fact more curious or suggestive than this method of prayer by machinery; and that such a grotesque extravagance should have emanated from so subtle and metaphysical a faith as Buddhism is an anomaly not easily to be explained.

Each votary who is too poor to possess a prayer-wheel of his own, attends the temple, does homage to the head

Lama, receives his benediction, and then, squatting in front of the great wheel, he turns the crank on behalf of himself and his family. But if there be a considerable number of worshippers, the priest himself works the handle, that all may participate simultaneously in the act of prayer.

The use of these machines is traced back for fully fourteen centuries, and is supposed to have originated in the belief that it was a meritorious act, and a patent cure for sin, to be continually reading or reciting portions of the sacred books of Buddha. But as many of the people could not read, a substitute had to be found, and it came to be considered sufficient if they turned over the rolled manuscripts which embodied the invaluable precepts. And as a vast amount of time and trouble was saved by this process, a further simplification became possible and popular,—the invention of wheels termed *Tehu-Chor*,—great cylindrical bands full of prayers; a cord being attached to the base of the band, which, when the cord was pulled, twirled like a children's toy. Prayer-wheels of this kind are set up in all public places in Tibet, so that the poor who do not possess little pocket Wheels of Devotion may not lose their chance of accumulating merit. In some of the monasteries the rows of small cylinders are so arranged, that the priest, or any passer-by can set them all in simultaneous motion, by just drawing his hand along them.

According to Miss Cumming, who is confirmed by other travellers, the cylinders vary in size, from tiny hand-mills, about as big as a policeman's rattle, to huge machines, eight or ten feet in diameter, worked by a heavy iron crank, or sometimes by wind or water power. The wind prayer-mills are turned by wings, which, like the cylinder, are plentifully covered with prayers. The water-mills are placed over streams, so as to dispense with human aid, and allow the running water to turn them for the general welfare of the village. Through the cylinder passes a wooden axle, which is fastened to a horizontal wheel, whose cogs are turned diagonally to the water.

"One such group of little mills we noticed," says Miss Cumming,[1] "set in a clear stream half-way between Rarung

[1] Miss Gordon Cumming, "From the Hebrides to the Himalayas," ii. 226, 227.

and Pangi, a lively, rapid river, rushing headlong down the mountain side to join the Sutlej. Having never then heard of prayer-mills, we assumed them to be for corn, as perhaps they were. At all events, we passed them without inspection, to our subsequent infinite regret. These wheels rotate with the action of the water, and so turn the cylinder, which must invariably stand upright. Sometimes several of these are placed almost across the stream, and the rudest form of temple is built over them.

"They are so placed that the wheel must invariably turn from right to left, following the course of the sun; to invert that course would not only involve ill-luck, but would amount to being a sin. Hence the exceeding unwillingness of the people we met to let us tend their little wheels, knowing from sad experience that the English sahibs rather enjoy the fun of turning them the wrong way, and so undoing the efficacy of all their morning's work.

"Some of the little pocket cylinders are very beautifully wrought; some are even inlaid with precious stones. I saw one great beauty which I coveted exceedingly. The owner would on no account sell it. I returned to the temple next morning, wishing at least to make a drawing of it, but I think he mistrusted me, for he and his plaything had both vanished, and I had to be content with a much simpler one of bronze, inlaid with copper. The people have the greatest reluctance to sell even the ugliest old mills. They cling to them as lovingly as you might do to your dear old Bible; but, as I said before, not merely from the charm of association, but from a dread lest a careless hand should turn them against the sun, and so change their past acts of merit into positive sin. So there was a great deal of talk, and many irons in the fire, before I was allowed to purchase two of these, at a price which would have supplied half the village with new ones."

The prayer-mill sometimes contains the Tibetan prayer, or litany, for the six classes of living creatures, namely, the souls in heaven, the evil spirits in the air, men, animals, souls in purgatory, and souls in hell; but, as a rule, the Lama worship begins and ends in the famous inscription to which we have already alluded—*Aum Mani Padmi Hoong* (to the jewel in the lotus.) These mystic words are raised in embossed letters on the exterior of the cylinder, and are closely written on strips of paper inside. All the sacred places are covered with them; the face of the rock, the walls of the temple; just as the Alhambra glitters with its *azulejos*, its blazoned inscriptions from the Kúran.

This mystic sentence is composed as follows: *Aum* or *Om*, equivalent to the Hebrew JAH or JEHOVAH, the most glorious title of the Almighty; *Mani*, the jewel, one of Buddha's appellations; *Padmi*, the lotus, in allusion to his lotus-throne; and *Hoong*, synonymous with *Amen*. The Buddhists regard this "six-syllabled" charm as a talisman of never-failing efficacy; but by some of the sects it is more or less varied. For instance: the Chinese Fo-ists read it as *Aum-mi-to-fuh*, which is also one of Buddha's titles; and every devout Fo-ist aims at repeating it at least three hundred thousand times in the course of his life. Some of their priests will shut themselves up in the temples for months at a time, and devote themselves to the dreary task of repetition, hour after hour, day and night. Sometimes, ten or twelve devotees will voluntarily sequester themselves, and continue all day to cry aloud in chorus; and at night they undertake the task successively, one person droning through the monotonous chant while the others sleep. Thus do they think to be heard for their much speaking! Similar excesses of formalism, however, are recorded in the history of mediæval Christianity,—in the biographies of saints and ascetics who have substituted for a practical Christianity and the active performance of social duties the dreary vanity of an unprofitable solitude, spent in the discharge of useless penances.

The Buddhist prayer which is consecrated to Buddha as the Chakravarta Rajah, or King of the Wheel, proves, on examination, to be closely related to that Sun-worship which prevailed in the early ages of the world. The wheel is, in many creeds, the symbol of the sun's chariot, that is, of the revolution of the heavenly bodies. In a sculpture, nearly two thousand years old, on the Bilsah Tepe, Buddha is represented simply by a wheel, overshadowed by the mystic *chattah*, or golden umbrella, which is a common emblem of his power. His worshippers are represented as making their offerings to the King of the Wheel. "This sacred

Wheel of the Law, or Wheel of Faith, is found again and again among the Jain and Buddhist sculptures in the caves of Ellora and Ajunta, in most cases projecting in front of Buddha's Lotus-Throne. In one instance an astronomical table is carved above the wheel. In another it is supported on either side by a stag, supposed to represent the fleetness wherewith the sun runs his daily circuit, 'going forth from the uttermost part of the heaven, and running about unto the end of it again.'"

THE HINDU TEMPLES.

Visiting the Temples at Hardwar, one of the sacred cities of India, Miss Gordon Cumming remarks upon the number of their hideous idols, painted and carved, their multitudinous brass bells, their brazen horns, their sacred courts all covered with elaborate carving, and their mythological sculptures.

She says :—"I frankly confess that there is something startling in the rapidity with which one gets quite at home amongst all this paraphernalia of heathenism, and how very soon idolatry ceases to shock the mind, and becomes merely a curious study with picturesque adjuncts. Six months previously the sight of a veritable temple with its hideous idols and devout worshippers was a thing from which one shrank in shuddering pity." But she soon became a connoisseur, and "lounged from one temple to another, inspecting jewels and exquisite stone carving, and anything wonderful the priests had to show, and quite forgot to be shocked, it was all so perfectly natural, and seemed so entirely in keeping with the tastes of the people." In this remark there is a wonderful *naïveté;* for it may reasonably be supposed that the tastes of the people would be in accord with a religion which, during its career of two thousand years, must have exercised so great an influence in forming them !

In some of the temples, according to the same writer, there are sacred bulls, carved in white marble and adorned with costly necklaces. In others the attendant priests spend the whole day in pouring single drops of precious oil on holy pebbles brought from the Nerbudda and other sacred streams, and here arranged in little trays. Amongst the privileged inhabitants are the monkeys, who frolic about incessantly with their babies in their arms, or sitting on their backs, and twining their little arms round the parental necks.

The ceremonies in the different temples are, on the whole, very similar; and the following description, taken from the Rão Mālā, applies, except in minor details, to all.

The day is marked by five services: the first at sunrise, when bells are rung in the temple, and drums or conch-shells sounded, to rouse the Du, or god, from his slumbers. After performing copious ablutions, the officiating priest enters the holy place, and swings before the idol a lamp with five or seven branches. An hour or two later, the Du is attired in raiment appropriate to the season. He wears a quilted coat in cold weather, and has a lighted brazier placed beside him; whereas, in hot weather, he is anointed with sandal-wood dust and water, clothed in fine linen, and decked out with gems and flowers. Placed close to a cool fountain, he is assiduously fanned by his attendants. In rainy weather, he is wrapped about in scarlet cloth and shawls. When he is dressed, a light breakfast of rice and milk is served up, and his votaries perform "the sixteen acts of worship." At noon a third service takes place. The Du is again rubbed with oil of sandal-wood, or sandal-dust and water, and adorned with fresh flowers. The lamps are trimmed; incense is burned; and his dinner is set before him: after which he is supposed to indulge in his noonday sleep, and profound silence is maintained throughout the temple.

At three in the afternoon a drum beats, and the god awakes! His attendants hasten to serve fruits and sweet-meats, and perform various games for his amusement. At sunset he is enshrined: his feet are basted, he is sprinkled with water, his mouth is washed, and another offering is made of sandal-wood dust, and flowers, and incense. He is once more clothed; an elaborate dinner is spread before him; betel leaves are presented; and again the many-branched candlestick is waved, while all the votaries present for the second time perform "the sixteen acts of worship."

The last service takes place at night, when the image is supposed to sup on bread and water. After receiving the usual oblations of incense and flowers, he is undressed, and if he be movable, put to bed, or if not, is warmly covered with shawls and quilts.

Not the least remarkable objects in the Hindu temples are their great statues of bulls in marble or in metal. It is worthy of note that "in the great Brazen Laver, which Solomon was commanded to make for the use of the Temple at Jerusalem, the symbols selected for the adornment of that consecrated Molten Sea should have been those which in later ages were to hold so prominent a place in the symbolism of faiths so widely spread as those of Brahma and Buddha. That huge laver was supported by twelve oxen of cast metal, three looking to each point of the compass, while the brim of the great sea itself was all wrought with flowers of lilies, much the same as the pattern of lotus or water-lily with which the shrine of Buddha is invariably edged." The bull is another symbol which seems to connect the creed of the Hindu with the old nature-worship; for the vernal equinox takes place when the sun enters the sign of Taurus, and this event was always and everywhere a signal for feasting and rejoicing.

But, as Max Müller observes, the ancient religion of the Aryan inhabitants of India started, like the religion of Greece and Rome, of the Germans, Slavs, and Celts, with a simple and intelligible mythological phraseology.[1] In the Veda, the names of all the so-called gods or Devas undisguisedly betray their original physical character and meaning. Under the name of Agni (ignis) was praised and invoked the fire; the earth by that of Prithvî (the brave); the sky by the name of Dyu (Zeus, Jupiter), and afterwards of Indra; the firmament and the waters by the name of Οὐρανός. Under many appellations was the sun invoked, such as Sûrya, Savitri, Vishnu, or Mitra; and the dawn by the titles of Ushas, Urvasî, Ahanâ, and Sûrya. Nor was the moon forgotten: for though not often mentioned under its usual name of Kandra, reference is made to it under its more sacred appellation of Soma; and a particular denomina-

---

[1] Max Müller, Buddhism and Buddhist Pilgrims, pp. 5, 6.

tion was reserved for each of its phases. There is hardly any fact of nature, if it could impress the human mind in any way with the ideas of a higher power, of order, eternity, or beneficence,—whether the woods, or the rivers, or the trees, or the mountains,—without a name and representative in the early Hindu Pantheon. No doubt there existed in the human mind, from the very beginning, something, whether we call it a suspicion, an innate idea, an intuition, or a sense of the Divine. What distinguishes man from the rest of the animal creation is chiefly his ineradicable feeling of dependence and reliance upon some higher power; that consciousness of bondage, from which the very name of "religion" was derived. "It is He that hath made us, and not we ourselves." The presence of that power was felt everywhere, and nowhere more clearly and strongly than in the rising and setting of the sun, in the change of day and night, of spring and winter, of birth and death. But although the Divine Presence was felt everywhere, it was impossible, in that early period of thought, and with a language incapable as yet of defining anything but material objects, to conceive the idea of GOD in its purity and fulness, or to assign to it an adequate and worthy expression.

It must also be remembered that the influence of the genius and forces of Nature would necessarily be greater in an age when the human mind was occupied by few objects of thought, than now when it ranges over the whole world of art and science. Moreover, to the eye of ignorance everything seems large and portentous, or dim and inscrutable. The fire from heaven, the reverberating thunder, the gale that crashed down the mountain ravines and felled great trees before it, the planetary bodies steadily revolving in their courses, the stream with its glow and its ripple, the dense shadows of the haunted forest, the recurring rush and roll of the sea,—all these were things which for early man had a constant novelty and strangeness, and seemed incessantly to claim his reverent consideration. He could not account for them : whether a bane or a delight they were equally unintelligible. They represented, therefore, some Power which he could regard only with awe and reverence. And of that Power the sun would necessarily be the chief type and symbol. All life and love seemed dependent upon it. The trees throve, and the flowers bloomed, and the banks rippled, and the birds sang, and the harvests ripened, through the sun. It was the source of light and heat, of the vigour and activity of nature. While it shone men's hearts leaped with joy, and the wheels of labour revolved with pleasant toil; but when it disappeared, and the darkness usurped the heavens, the spirits sank, and humanity felt in the change of scene a presentiment and presage of the darkness of death. All vitality, all motion centred in the sun. "It was like a deep furrow," says Max Müller, "which that heavenly luminary drew, in its silent procession from east to west, over the fallow mind of the gazing multitude; and in the impression left there by the first rising and setting of the sun, there lay the dark seed of a faith in a more than human being, the first intimation of a life without beginning, of a world without end." Who can wonder that the Chaldean, and the Celt, alike ascended to the high places, and paid their worship of symbolic fires to the great fountain of life and light, the central force of the universe? Who can wonder that all the Aryan tribes made it, so to speak, the nucleus of their religious systems? The Hindu peasant, centuries ago, addressed it in his heart in much the same language which Gawain Douglas afterwards employed. As its glorious orb rose above the gleaming horizon, he sent forth to it a message of welcome:

> "Welcome, the lord of light and lamp of day;
> Welcome, fosterer of tender herbis green;
> Welcome, quickener of flourished flowers' sheen;
> Welcome, support of every root and vein;
> Welcome, comfort of all kind fruits and grain;
> Welcome, the bird's green beild upon the brier;
> Welcome, master and ruler of the year;
> Welcome, welfare of husbands at the ploughs;
> Welcome, repairer of woods, trees, and boughs;
> Welcome, depainter of the bloomit meads;
> Welcome, the life of everything that spreads."

And because it was all this, and more, the Hindu saw in it something greater than a mere luminary,—a planetary body; he endowed it with Divine attributes, he made it a god, he gave it his worship, and by an elaborate symbolism kept it ever before him.

A necessary consequence of this deification of the sun

was the deification of the other bodies that shared with him the firmament; but as they were inferior in splendour and utility, they naturally became recognized as inferior gods. And when once the religious feeling of humanity had gone thus far, its further development became only a question of time. The homage given to the stars was soon extended to the winds and streams and groves. A legion of gods sprang into existence, and for a while they seemed to satisfy the needs and aspirations of humanity. But as the thoughts of men expanded, as their intellect ripened with the ages, and grew strong enough to doubt, and bold enough to question the conclusions of the common faith, a revolt took place against "the contradictions of a mythological phraseology, though it had been hallowed by sacred customs and traditions." Men grew tired of so complex and cumbrous a religious system, and having observed a definite fundamental unity of nature in spite of the diversity of its operations, they came to believe in a similar unity of the Divine Power. The idea of a supreme authority once entertained, men soon understood that supremacy meant oneness; that if there were a God over all, He must be one and indivisible. One of the earliest proclamations of this sublime truth is found in the Rig-Veda, which says :[1]—

"That which is one the sages speak of in many ways— they call it Agni, Yama, Malarisvan."

And again :[2]—

"In the beginning there came the Source of golden light —He was the only true Lord of all that is—He stablished the earth and this sky :—Who is God to whom we shall offer our sacrifice?

"He who gives life, He who gives strength; whose blessing all the bright gods desire; whose shadow is immortality; whose shadow is death :—Who is the God to whom we shall offer our sacrifice?

"He who through His power is the only King of the breathing and awakening world; He who governs all, man and beast :—Who is the God to whom we shall offer our sacrifice?

"He whose power these snowy mountains, whose power

[1] Rig-Veda, i. 164, 46.
[2] Rig-Veda, x. 121, by Max Müller.

the sea proclaims, with the distant river—He whose these regions are, as it were, His two arms :—Who is the God to whom we shall offer our sacrifice?

" He through whom the sky is bright and the earth firm —He through whom heaven was stablished—nay, the highest heaven—He who measured out the light in the air :—Who is the God to whom we shall offer our sacrifice?

" He to whom heaven and earth, standing firm by His will, look up, trembling inwardly—He over whom the rising sun shines forth :—Who is the God to whom we shall offer our sacrifice?

" Wherever the mighty water-clouds went, where they placed the reed and lit the fire, thence even He, who is the only life of the bright gods :—Who is the GOD to whom we shall offer our sacrifice?

" He, who of His might looked even over the water-clouds, the clouds which gave strength and lit the sacrifice, He *who is God above all gods :*—Who is the God to whom we shall offer our sacrifice?

" May He not destroy us—He the creator of the earth ; or He, the righteous, who created Heaven ; He who also created the bright and mighty waters :—Who is the God to whom we shall offer our sacrifice?"

The creed of a plurality of gods was one that carried in itself the seeds of its destruction. But there was another cause of weakness in their mortal attributes. Deriving their existence from the life of nature, they were subject to the accidents which that life involved. Thus, the sun at noonday might glow with splendour, but at night it was conquered by the shadows, and in winter it seemed to yield to some stronger Power. The moon waxed and waned, and was frequently eclipsed. As nature is subject to change, so also must be the gods that represent its forces and aspects. Such instability, such inherent weakness could not long satisfy the human mind ; having risen to the height of the idea of one God, it next demanded that that God should be immutable. What rest, what contentment would it find in the supposition of deities as changeful as the winds? Tossed about by the currents of passion and feeling, buffeted by adverse circumstances, the soul yearns intensely for something fixed, something absolute, something unaffected by vicissitude, and finds it in the Divine Being, the same to-day as yesterday, and the same to-morrow as to-day.

These two opposite principles did not come into immediate collision; the priests of heathendom laboured long and earnestly to avert such a catastrophe. In Greece they succeeded by transferring the mortal or changeable element from "the gods" to "the heroes."[1] The human details in the characters and lives of Zeus and Apollon were transferred to the demi-gods or heroes represented as the sons or favourites of the gods. The two-fold character of Herakles as a god and a hero is recognized even by Herodotus; and indeed, some of the epithets applied to him sufficiently indicate his solar and originally divine personality. But to make some of the solar myths of which Herakles was the centre intelligible and conceivable, it became needful to depict Herakles as a mere human being, and to raise him to the seat of the Immortals only after he had endured toils and sufferings incompatible with the dignity of an Olympian divinity.

In Peru the same treatment was adopted, but with different results. A thinking, or, as he was called, a free-thinking Inca, remarked that the sun's perpetual travelling—he knew nothing, of course, of the Copernican theory—was a sign of servitude, and he threw doubts on the divine nature of aught so restless as the great luminary appeared to him to be. These doubts led to a tradition, which, even if unhistorical was not wholly untrue, that in Peru had existed an earlier worship—that of an Invisible Deity, the Creator of the World—Pachacamac.

" In Greece, also, there are signs of a similar craving after the 'Unknown God.' A supreme God was wanted, and Zeus, the stripling of Creta, was raised to that rank. He became God above all gods—$ἀπάντων\ κύριος$, as Pindar calls him. Yet more was wanted than a mere Zeus; and then a supreme Fate or Spell was imagined before which all the gods, and even Zeus, had to bow. And even this Fate was not allowed to remain supreme, and there was something in the destinies of man which was called $ὑπέρμορον$ or ' beyond

---

[1] The thought in this paragraph, and several of the expressions, are from Max Müller.

Fate.' The most awful solution, however, of the problem belongs to Teutonic mythology. Here, also, some heroes were introduced; but their death was only the beginning of the final catastrophe. 'All gods must die.' Such is the last word of that religion which had grown up in the forests of Germany, and found a last refuge among the glaciers and volcanoes of Iceland. The death of Sigurd, the descendant of Odin, could not avert the death of Balder, the son of Odin, and the death of Balder was soon to be followed by the death of Odin himself, and of all the immortal gods."

Such a catastrophe was inevitable, so that Prometheus, the man of forethought, could safely predict the fall of Zeus.[1]

A similar issue was worked out in India, but with this difference; that the seeming triumph of reason threatened to end in the destruction of all religious belief. At the outset no vehement contention took place. On the basis of the old mythology arose two new formations,—the Brahmanical philosophy and the Brahmanical ceremonial; the former opening up all avenues of philosophical inquiry, the latter immuring religious sentiment and sympathy within the narrowest possible barriers. Both, however, claimed to find their origin and antiquity in the sacred book of the Veda.

It was in the sixteenth or fifteenth century before CHRIST that the Brahmans, a branch of the white Aryans, passed into Hindustan from the north-west, and mixed with a more numerous race of coloured and barbarous aborigines. Among their immigrants the sacerdotal and the royal or noble classes already occupied an authoritative and a distinct position; and soon after their settlement in India, the lower classes, by a natural process, sank into the markedly inferior condition of the aborigines. Thus was established a singularly rigorous system of caste,—the priesthood and

---

[1] So in Shelley's lyrical drama of " Prometheus Unbound :"—
"*Mercury* (addressing Prometheus.)   Once more answer me :
   Thou knowest not the period of Jove's power?
Prometheus.   I know but this, that it must come.
Mercury.   Alas!
   Thou canst not count thy years to come of pain.
Prometheus.   They last while Jove must reign; nor more nor less
   Or I desire or fear."

the aristocracy combining to oppress and keep down the two inferior orders of the Brahmans and the aborigines. Intermarriage was strictly forbidden, and every device adopted which could be made useful in strengthening and perpetuating the class-distinction.

This revolution in the social world assisted the revolution in the religious; and the educated classes rapidly abandoned their nature worship in favour of the idea of an infinite and everlasting Godhead, which soared far above the feeblenesses and sins of humanity. To become one with this Godhead by throwing off the personality linked with a mind that was mean and miserable, thenceforth constituted the religious aspiration of the Brahman. And in attaining this object he was instructed to seek the help of the Brahmanical priesthood ; nay, he was taught that without that help he would never succeed, and for this purpose a complex and comprehensive ceremonial was enjoined upon him. From his cradle to his grave it dogged his footsteps. Put forward as a stay and support, it was really a clog, an encumbrance. Not an event in his life could take place for which a formula of praise or prayer was not invented. Thanksgiving and sacrifice were alike minutely regulated. For the benefit of the inferior castes the old Pantheon of gods and demons had been retained, and the priesthood allotted to each his share of the worshipper's offerings and oblations. Each was represented as insisting so strongly on certain observances, and punishing so heavily any neglect or violation of them, that the votary feared to approach their shrine unless under the protection and guidance of their priests. Otherwise he might unwittingly rush into all kinds of sins. They alone knew what food might be eaten, what dress might be worn, what god might be addressed, what sacrifice paid. An error in pronunciation, a mistake about clarified butter, an unauthorised arrangement of raiment or hair, might involve the unassisted worshipper in pains and penalties of the most awful character. Never was so complete and absolute a ceremonial system known as that by which the Hindu priesthood obtained an entire mastery over the Hindu people. Never was any law more minute in its provisions, or more Draconic in the severity with which it punished their violation.

Yet, strange to say, this ceremonial did not interfere with liberty of thought. Any amount of heresy was compatible with its observance. A man might think as he liked so long as he complied with its various conditions. In some of the Brahmanical schools of thought the names of the devs or gods were never heard; in others their existence was ignored, was virtually contradicted. Thus, one philosophical system maintained the existence of a single Supreme Being, and asserted that everything else which seemed to exist was but a dream and an illusion which might and would be dispelled by a true knowledge of the One God. Another contended for two principles,—first, a Mind, subjective and self-existent; second, Matter endowed with qualities; and explained that the world with its cloud and sunshine, its sorrows and joys, was the result of the subjective self, reflected in the mirror of Matter, and that the freedom of the soul could be secured only by diverting the gaze from the shows and phantasms of Nature, and becoming absorbed in the knowledge of the true and absolute self. A third system allowed the existence of atoms, and referred every effect, including the elements and the mind, gods, men, and animals to their fortuitous concourse. This was identical with the Lucretian system, which in its turn was related to the Epicurean. Hence it has been said that the history of the philosophy of India is an abridgment of the history of philosophy. Each of these systems was traced back to the sacred books of the Vedas, Brâhmanas and Upanishads; and those who believed in any one of them was considered as orthodox as the most devout worshipper of Agni,—if the latter were saved by works and faith, the former was saved by faith and knowledge,—a distinction not unknown in the Christian philosophy.[1]

Out of this condition of the Hindu mind arose Buddhism, springing from it as naturally as the flower from the seed.

The remarkable man[2] who founded this wide-spread religion is reputed to have been a prince of the name of

---

[1] Max Müller, pp. 13, 14.
[2] Professor Wilson propounded a theory to the effect that there never was any such man as Buddha, but the theory has found few supporters.

Siddhartha, son of Suddhodana, king of Kapilavastu, a territory supposed to have been situated on the borders of Oudh and Nipal. He is often called Sakya, after his family, and also Gautama, from the great "Solar" race of which the family was a branch.[1] Having at an early age exhibited an ascetic and contemplative tendency, his father fearing he might be induced to abandon his high station as Kshatriga, found him a wife in a princess of great personal charms, and involved him in all the pomp and luxury of a magnificent court. But Siddhartha drank of the cup only to taste the bitter in the draught; and each year's experience of the world convinced him of its inability to satisfy the aspirations of the soul; so that, like Solomon, he would exclaim, " Vanity, vanity, all is vanity." The joys of life could not render him forgetful of its sorrows. The thought would force itself upon him that at any moment he might be afflicted with some loathsome or torturing disease; that his friends might be suddenly snatched away; that however sunny and bright the present, it could not prevent the inevitable approach of old age, with its grey hairs, its wrinkled brow, and its tottering limbs; and that the moral of the whole show was to be sought in the darkness of the grave. Unable to endure any longer the mental conflict begotten of his keen sense of the realities as compared with the illusions of the world, he stole from the guarded palace, and at the age of 29 or 30, went forth as a beggar, or religious mendicant, to study in the schools of the Brahman priests. He underwent their penances; he mastered their philosophy; but dissatisfied with their cumbrous code of superstitious ceremonial, he withdrew into the forest, and adopted a course of religious asceticism.

This lasted for six or seven years, but brought him no repose. Then he resolved on returning once more to human companionship. Beset by the Spirit of Evil he fought long and bravely against temptation, and having triumphed, prepared to attain the secret of happiness by giving himself up to abstruse meditation. Week after week he was absorbed in thought, continually investigating the origin of

[1] The name "Sakya" is made into "Sakya-muni,"—*muni* in Sanskrit meaning "solitary," (Greek, μόνος,) alluding to his solitary habits; and to Gautama is often prefixed "Sramana," or "ascetic."

things, and the mystery of existence. All the evils under which he, in common with his fellow-men, groaned, he traced back to birth. Were we not born, we could not suffer. But whence comes birth or continued existence ? . . . We have no room, however, to dwell on his processes of thought ; enough to say that he came to the conclusion that the ultimate cause of existence is ignorance, and that the removal of ignorance means, therefore, the termination of existence, and of all the pain and sorrow which existence implies and induces. Realising this absolute unconsciousness of the outer world in his own self, he claimed and assumed the name of the Buddha, or " Enlightened."

The scene of his victory over life and the world received the name of Bodhimanda, (the seat of intelligence,) and the tree under which the religious reformer sat in his hour of moral and intellectual triumph was called Bodhidruma, (the tree of intelligence,) whence Bo-tree. The Buddhists believe that it marks the centre of the earth. Hiouen-thsang, the Chinese pilgrim, professes to have found the Bodhidruma, or some tree that passed for it, twelve hundred years after Buddha's death, at a spot near Gaya Proper, in Bahar, where still may be seen an old dagoba, or temple, and some considerable ruins.

Having at last attained to a knowledge of the causes of human suffering, and of the method of removing and counteracting them, the Buddha felt that the task was imposed upon him of communicating that knowledge to others. He began " to turn the wheel of the law,"—that is to preach,— at Benares ; and among his earliest disciples was Bimbisara, the ruler of Magadha. His career as a teacher extended over forty years, during which period he travelled over almost every part of Northern India, making a large number of converts, and firmly establishing his religious system. He died at Kusinagara in Oudh, in 543 B.C., at the age of eighty, and his body being burned, the relics were distributed among numerous claimants, who raised monumental tumuli, or topes, for their preservation.

All the expositions and teachings of the Buddha were oral, and the task of committing them to writing was undertaken by the chief of his disciples shortly after his death. These canonical books are divided into three classes, forming the "Tripitaka," or "three-fold basket." In the first class we find the *Soutras,* or Sermons of the Buddha; in the second, the *Vinaya,* or book of discipline; in the third, the *Abhidharma,* or philosophy. After a period of a century or so, the Buddhist leaders met and revised the Tripitaka, and a third revision took place in 250 or 240 B.C., since which date the text has remained without alteration.

The doctrine of Buddha has been defined as a development of four main principles, (or "Sublime Verities.") 1st. That every kind of existence is painful and transitory; 2nd. That all existence is the result of passion; 3rd. That, therefore, the extinction of passion is the one means of escape from existence and from the misery necessarily attendant upon it; 4th. That all obstacles to this existence must be swept away.

But what is meant by existence? That separation from the general Being of the world which is involved in individual life, and in the opposition of the subject which thinks, and the object which is thought about. And what is meant by its extinction? Not so much annihilation, as the becoming one with nature, wherein that form of consciousness which separates subject and object is set aside. This extinction Buddha called Nirvâna, or "the blowing out of the lamp;" it does not necessarily mean the annihilation of consciousness altogether, but only of a finite form of it, which may be as the light of a lamp compared with the light of day.

Buddha's doctrine has been stigmatised as Atheism and Nihilism, and was unquestionably liable on its metaphysical side to both charges. It was Atheistic, not because it denied, for it simply ignored, the existence of such gods as Indra and Brahma, but because, like the Sankhya philosophy, it admitted but one subjective Self, and considered creation as an illusion of that Self, imaging itself for a while in the mirror of Nature. If there were no reality in nature, there would be no real Creator.

Says Max Müller,[1] stating with his usual clearness a problem which has perplexed most students of the history of religion : "How a religion which taught the annihilation of all existence, of all thought, of all individuality and per-

[1] Max Müller, pp. 14, 15.

sonality, as the highest object of all endeavours, could have laid hold of the minds of millions of human beings, and how at the same time, by enforcing the duties of morality, justice, kindness, and self-sacrifice, it could have exercised a decided beneficial influence, not only on the natives of India, but on the lowest barbarians of Central Asia, is one of the riddles which no philosophy yet has been able to solve. The morality which it teaches is not a morality of expediency and rewards. Virtue is not enjoined because it necessarily leads to happiness. No; virtue is to be practised, but happiness is to be shunned, and the only reward for virtue is, that it subdues the passions, and thus prepares the human mind for that knowledge which is to end in complete annihilation."

Probably no religious system has ever attained a widespread influence over the minds of men which has held out so few of those inducements most alluring to human nature. The idea of complete annihilation might recommend itself to a philosopher, but would hardly have been regarded as likely to attract the masses. We suppose the explanation is to be found in the particularity of ritual enjoined by the Buddhist priests, this particularity of ritual having always had a fascination for the multitude.

"'There are ten commandments which Buddha imposes on his disciples. They are—not to kill, not to steal, not to commit adultery, not to lie, not to get intoxicated, to abstain from unseasonable meals, to abstain from public spectacles, to abstain from expensive dresses, not to have a large bed, not to receive silver or gold. The duties of those who embraced a religious life were most severe. They were not allowed to wear any dress except rags collected in cemeteries, and these rags they had to sew together with their own hands; a yellow cloak was to be thrown over these rags. Their food was to be extremely simple, and they were not to possess anything except what they could get by collecting alms from door to door in their wooden bowl. They had but one meal in the morning, and were not allowed to touch any food after midday. They were to live in forests, not in cities, and their only shelter was to be the shadow of a tree. There they were to sit, to spread their carpet, but not to lie down, even during sleep.

They were allowed to enter the nearest city or village in order to beg, but they had to return to their forest before night, and the only change which was allowed, or rather prescribed, was, when they had to spend some nights in the cemeteries, there to meditate on the vanity of all things. And what was the object of all this asceticism? Simply to guide each individual towards that path which would finally bring him to Nirvâna, to utter extinction or annihilation. The very definition of virtue was that it helped man to cross over to the other shore, and that other shore was not death, but the cessation of all being. Thus charity was considered a virtue; modesty, patience, courage, contemplation, and science, all were virtues, but they were practised only as a means of arriving at deliverance."

Buddha himself was an incarnation of the virtues. His charity, for example, was melting as day. When he saw a tigress standing, and unable to feed her cubs, he offered up his body to be devoured by them. The Chinese pilgrim, visiting the spot on the banks of the Indus where this miracle was supposed to have occurred, remarks that the soil was still red with the blood of Buddha, as were also the trees and flowers.

Then as to his modesty, it was as supreme as that of a virgin who has never seen men. One day Prasenagit, his royal disciple and protector, besought him to work some miracles in order to silence his adversaries, the Brahmans. Buddha complied, and performed the required miracles; but at the same time he exclaimed, "Great King, I do not teach the law to my pupils, telling them, Go, ye saints, and before the eyes of the Brahmans and householders perform, by means of your supernatural powers, miracles greater than any man can perform. I tell them, when I teach the law, Live, ye saints, hiding your good works and showing your sins." And yet, all this self-sacrificing charity, all this self-sacrificing humility by which the life of Buddha was distinguished throughout, and which he preached to the multitudes that came to listen to him, had but one object, and that object was final annihilation.[1]

Annihilation! what drearier prospect can be opened to the heart, or soul, or mind of man? The utter cessation of

[1] Max Müller, pp. 15, 16, 17.

that individuality of which the meanest and wretchedest among us feels proudly conscious; of the thoughts which animate, the desires which warm, the dreams that delight, the hopes that stimulate, the affections that inspire! Do we indeed suffer all the sorrows and uncertainties of life,—do we indeed strive, and endure, and struggle,—do we, indeed, learn to labour and to wait, to bear the burden of the day and the torture of the night, for no other purpose, with no other prospect, than when the brief fever is over, to pass away into nothingness? With so much difficulty can the mind reconcile itself to such a dreary hypothesis that the creed of almost every race and people has contemplated a future stage of existence, even when it has failed to attain to anything like a clear and full conviction of the immortality of the soul. The law of compensation seems to demand that a future life shall redress the inequalities of the present.

Yet this doctrine of Annihilation was preached by Buddha, and apparently accepted by the millions who became his disciples. But did they really accept it as he preached it? No; the truth is, they read into it, as it were, their own innate, unconquerable belief in a hereafter, and converted his Nirvâna into a Paradise, which they embellished with the bright colours of imagination. It can hardly be doubted that this was not the meaning or intention of Buddha himself. Look, for a moment, at his "Four Verities." The first of these, as we have already stated, asserts the existence of pain; the second, that the cause of pain is sin; the third, that the cessation of pain may be secured by Nirvâna; the fourth, that the way to this Nirvâna consists of eight things: right faith or orthodoxy, right judgment or logic, right language or veracity, right purpose or honesty, right practice or religious life, right obedience or lawful life, right memory, and right meditation.

These precepts may be understood as the usual laws of an elevated morality, pointing to and terminating in a state of meditation on the highest object of thought, such as has been enjoined by several philosophical or religious systems; —such as was revived in France and Germany in the seventeenth century under the name of Pietism. There is nothing in this teaching incompatible with a belief in the immortality of the soul and the existence of a GOD. But with the Buddhist Nirvâna it is otherwise. Its motive principle, by the way, is a mean and cowardly one, for it makes happiness depend upon the cessation of pain; represents as the highest purpose of human effort the escape from pain. The Buddhist insists that life is a prolonged misery; that birth is the cause of all evil; and he adds that even death cannot deliver him from this evil, because he believes in transmigration, or an eternal cycle of existence. To escape from it we must free ourselves from the bondage, not of life only, but of existence; and this must be done "by extirpating the cause of existence."

But what *is* that cause?

The Buddhist teacher, involving himself in a cloud of metaphysics, answers, that it is attachment; an inclination towards something, having its root in thirst or desire. " Desire presupposes perception of the object desired; perception presupposes contact; contact, at least a sentient contact, presupposes the senses; and as the senses can only perform what has form and name, or what is distinct, distinction is the real cause of all the effects which end in existence, birth, and pain. Now this conception is itself the result of conceptions or ideas; but these ideas, so far from being, as in Greek philosophy, the true and everlasting forms of the Absolute, are in themselves mere illusions, the effects of ignorance. Ignorance, therefore, is really the primary cause of all that seems to exist. To know that ignorance, as the root of all evil, is the same as to destroy it, and with it all effects that flowed from it."

In Buddha's own case we may see how such teaching operated upon the individual.

He entered into the first stage of meditation when he became conscious of freedom from sin, acquired a knowledge of the nature of all things, and yearned after nothing but Nirvâna. But he was still open to the sensation of pleasure, and could employ his powers of discrimination and reasoning.

In the second stage he ceased to use those powers, and nothing remained but the desire of Nirvâna, and the satisfaction inherent to his intellectual perfection.

In the third stage indifference succeeded to satisfaction;

but self-consciousness remained, and a certain amount of physical gratification.

These, too, faded away in the fourth stage, along with memory, and all sense of pain; and before the neophyte opened the doors of Nirvâna.

After having gone through the four stages once, Buddha began them a second time, but died before he attained the fourth stage.

After passing through the four stages of meditation, every Buddhist enters into the infinity of space; thence rises into the infinity of intelligence; to soar, afterwards, into the region of Nothing. But even there he finds no repose; something still remains—the idea of the Nothing in which he rejoices. This is annihilated in the fourth and last region, and then he enjoys absolute, perfect rest, "undisturbed by nothing, or what is not nothing."

Buddha taught that this Nirvâna—which to most persons will seem a metaphysical incomprehensibility—could be attained by all men. As there is no difference between the body of a prince and the body of a beggar, so is there none between their spirits. Every man is equally capable of coming to a knowledge of the truth, and if he but *will* to do so, of working out his own emancipation.

It is important to observe the absence of any theological element in Buddhism. Its founder seems never to have spoken of God, and his Nirvâna is wholly different from the Brahmanic idea of absorption into the Divine Essence. Of the gods of the people he taught that they were, like men, subject to the law of Metempsychosis, or Transmigration, and therefore that as they were unable to deliver, they were unworthy to be worshipped. A recent writer thinks it would be incorrect to speak of Buddha either as a theist or an atheist, and asserts that he simply describes a condition of absolute rest as an escape from the popular metempsychosis, which may be interpreted either in a theistic or an atheistic sense. But a careful examination of his system shows, we think, that it was wholly alien to a belief in a Supreme Spirit.

"Buddhism," says Barthélémy Saint-Hilaire, "has no God; it has not even the confused and vague notion of a Universal Spirit, in which the human soul, according to the orthodox doctrine of Brahmanism, and the Sânkhya philosophy, may be absorbed. Nor does it admit Nature, in the proper sense of the word, and it ignores that profound division between spirit and matter which forms the system and the glory of Kapila. It confounds man with all that surrounds him, all the while preaching to him the laws of virtue. Buddhism, therefore, cannot unite the human soul, which it does not even mention, with a God, whom it ignores; nor with nature, which it does not know better. Nothing remained but to annihilate the soul; and in order to be quite sure that the soul may not re-appear under some new guise in this world, which has been cursed as the abode of illusion and misery, Buddhism destroys its very elements, and never wearies of glorying in this achievement. What more is wanted? if this be not the Absolute Nothing, what is Nirvâna?"

Repellent as seems to us the central doctrine of Buddhism, it extended rapidly. This extension was due, however, to the simplicity of the ritual which Buddha enjoined; the pure morality which he advocated; the equality of all men on which he insisted; and the spirit of love, tenderness, gentleness, compassion, and toleration which he inspired. Hence it came to pass that his disciples multiplied in the north-western territories of Hindustan, and his creed found acceptance, at a later period, probably about three centuries before CHRIST, all over India. In Ceylon it was adopted at a very early period; but it was not until the second century before CHRIST that it made its way into China and Tibet. From Ceylon it spread into Birmah and Siam, and the islands of the Indian Archipelago, and from China it penetrated into Japan. It is now the religion of more than one fifth of the whole human race.

Its influence has been very considerable, and may distinctly be traced in some of the Gnostic teaching and in the Alexandrine or Neo-Platonic philosophy. It modified the old Brahmanic religion, which, acting under its impulse, threw off its human sacrifices and more barbarous rites. The festival of Juggernaut, which for the time places in abeyance all caste distinctions, and adopts many Buddhist symbols, shows that the Brahmans, even when they drove it out of

India, were compelled to retain some of its relics, just as they were under the necessity of recognising Buddha as one of the Avatars of their god Vishnu. Buddhism may be described as "the parent of Indian architecture," which, fashioned at first on the Greek patterns, speedily assumed a character of its own, as may be seen in its colossal temples.

But, as is the case with all religious systems of purely human origin, Buddhism gradually fell away from the standard of its founder. The heart craves an object of worship, a something or some one on which or on whom to rest its hopes and fears, and the Buddhists, untaught to reverence a Supreme Being, transferred their adoration to Buddha himself, whose life and work they involved in a cloud of myth and legend. His relics came to be worshipped, and reliquary towers for their preservation were everywhere erected.

The enthusiasm which fired the Buddhists, and largely contributed to the rapid extension of their creed, for Buddhism, unlike Brahmanism, is a proselytising religion, finds a striking illustration in the career of Hiouen-thsang, the Chinese pilgrim, who, in the middle of the seventh century, crossed the deserts and mountains which separate China from India, and visited the principal cities of the Indian Peninsula.

HIOUEN-THSANG, A BUDDHIST PILGRIM.[1]

Hiouen-thsang was born in a provincial town of China, in one of the revolutionary and anarchical periods of the Chinese Empire. His father, having quitted the public service, was able to devote his leisure to the education of his four children, one of whom, Hiouen-thsang, was distinguished at an early age by his genius and his thirst for knowledge. After receiving instruction at a Buddhist monastery, he was admitted as a monk, when only thirteen years old. During the next seven years, he travelled about with his brethren from place to place, in order to profit by the

---

[1] The following sketch is founded on M. Stanislas Julien's "Voyages des Pélerins Buddhistes," and on Max Müller's review of that valuable work.

lectures of the most eminent professors; but his peaceful studies were frequently interrupted by the horrors of war, and he was forced to seek refuge in the more remote provinces of the empire.

At the age of twenty he took priest's orders, having already become famous for his multifarious learning. He had studied the chief canonical book of the Buddhist faith, the records of Buddha's life and teaching, the system of ethics and metaphysics, and had completely mastered the works of K'ung-fu-tze and Lao-tse. But, like many inquiring minds, he was tortured by doubt. For six years more he prosecuted his studies in the principal places of learning in China, and was frequently solicited to teach when he had come to learn. Baffled in all his efforts to satisfy his anxious and restless intellect, he resolved at last on paying a visit to India, the parent-land of Buddhism, where he knew he should find the original of the works, which, in their Chinese translation, had proved so dubious and excited so much mistrust. From the records of his pilgrim predecessors he was aware of the dangers of his journey; yet the glory, as he says, of recovering the Law, which was to be a guide to all men, and the means of their salvation, seemed to him worthy of attainment. In common with several other priests, he applied for the Imperial permission to travel out of China. It was refused, and his companions lost heart. But Hiouen-thsang was made of sterner stuff. His mother had often told him how, before his birth, she had had visions of her future offspring travelling to the Far West in search of the law; and he himself had been similarly encouraged.

Having no worldly pleasures to enfeeble him, and believing only in one object as worth living for, he resolved to face danger and difficulty; made his way to the Hoang-Ho, and the place of departure of the caravans for the West, and, eluding the vigilance of the Governor, succeeded in crossing the frontier. He was without friends or helpers; but after spending the night in fervent prayer, found a guide in a person who, next morning, unexpectedly presented himself. For some distance this guide conducted him faithfully, but abandoned him when they reached the Desert. There were still five watch-towers to be passed, and the uncertain track through the Desert was indicated only by skeletons and the hoof-marks of horses. Bravely went the pilgrim on his way, and though misled by the " mirage" of the Desert, he safely reached the first tower. There he narrowly escaped death from the arrows of the watchman, but the officer in command was himself a devout Buddhist, and he not only allowed Hiouen-thsang to proceed, but gave him letters of recommendation to the governors of the other towers. At the last tower, however, he was refused leave to pass, and neither bribes nor entreaties proved of any avail. He was compelled to retrace his steps, and make a long détour, in the course of which he lost his way. His water-bag burst, and for the first time his courage wavered. Should he not return? But no; he had taken an oath never to make a step backward until he had reached India. It were better to die with his face to the West, than return to the East and live.

For four nights and five days he traversed the Desert, without a drop of water to quench his thirst, with no other refreshment than that which he derived from his prayers; and that these should afford any hope or consolation seems strange enough, when we remember that Buddhism held out to him no hope of a God or a Saviour. " It is incredible in how exhausted an atmosphere the Divine spark within us will glimmer on, and even warm the dark chambers of the human heart." Comforted by his prayers, he resumed his onward march, and in due time arrived at a large lake in the country of the Oigom Tatars, by whom he was received with an abundant hospitality. One of the Tatar Khans insisted that he should reside with him and teach his people; and as he would listen to no remonstrances or explanations, Hiouen-thsang was driven to a desperate expedient. The king, he said, might fetter his body, but had no power over his mind and will; and he refused all food, with a view to put an end to a life which he no longer regarded as of value. In this resolution he persisted for three days, and the Khan, afraid that he would perish, was compelled at last to yield. But he extracted from him a promise that on his return to China he would visit him, and abide with him for three years. At last, after a month's detention, during which the Khan and his court daily attended the lectures of the pious monk, he resumed his journey, attended by a strong escort, and furnished with letters of introduction to the twenty-four princes whose dominions he must cross.

His route lay through what is now called Dsungary, across the Musur-dabaghan mountains, the northern chain of the Belur-tag, the valley of the Yaxartes, Bactria, and Kabulistan. The pilgrim's description of the scenes through which he passed is interesting and vivid; he was a keen observer, and gifted with considerable powers of expression.

Of the Musur-dabaghan mountains he says:—

"The crest of these heights rises to the sky. Since the beginning of the world the snow has been accumulating, and it is now transformed into masses of ice, which never melt, either in spring or summer. Hard shining sheets of snow are spread out until they vanish into the infinite, and mingle with the clouds. If one looks at them, one's eyes are dazzled by the splendour. Frozen peaks impend over both sides of the wood, some hundred feet in height, and some twenty or thirty feet in thickness. It is not without difficulty and danger that the traveller can clear them or climb over them. Sudden gusts of hurricane and tornadoes of snow attack the pilgrims. Even with double shoes, and in thick furs, one cannot help trembling and shivering."

But as Max Müller justly observes, what is more important in the early portion of our traveller's narrative than any descriptions of scenery, is his account of the high degree of civilisation that then obtained among the tribes of Central Asia. Historians have learned to believe in the early civilisation of Egypt, Babylon, China, India; but they will have to abandon all their old ideas of barbarism and barbarians now that they find the Tatar hordes possessing, in the seventh century, " the chief arts and institutions of an advanced society." The theory of M. Oppert, who gives to a Turanian or Scythian race the original invention of the cuneiform letters and a civilisation anterior to that of Babylon and Nineveh, ceases to be improbable; since no new wave of civilisation could have touched these countries between the cuneiform period of their literature and history and the epoch of Hiouen-thsang's visit.[1]

" In the kingdom of Okini, on the western portion of China, Hiouen-thsang found an active commerce, gold,

[1] Max Müller, p. 36.

silver, and copper coinage; monasteries, where the chief works of Buddhism were studied, and an alphabet derived from Sanskrit. As he travelled on he met with mines, with agriculture, including pears, plums, peaches, almonds, grapes, pomegranates, rice, and wheat. The inhabitants were dressed in silk and woollen materials. There were musicians in the chief cities who played on the flute and the guitar. Buddhism was the prevailing religion, but there were traces of an earlier worship, the Bactrian fire-worship. The country was everywhere studded with halls, monasteries, monuments and statues. Samarkand formed at that early time a kind of Athens, and its manners were copied by all the tribes in the neighbourhood. Balkh, the old capital of Bactria, was still an important place on the Oxus, well-fortified, and full of sacred buildings. And the details which our traveller gives of the exact circumference of the cities, the number of their inhabitants, the products of the soil, the articles of trade, can leave no doubt in our minds that he relates what he had seen and heard himself. A new page in the history of the world is here opened, and new ruins pointed out, which would reward the pickaxe of a Layard."

Hiouen-thsang passed into India by way of Kabul. Shortly before he reached Pou-lou-cha-pou-lo, the Sanskrit Purushapura, the modern Peshawer, he was informed of a remarkable cave, where Buddha had converted a dragon, and had promised to leave it his shadow, in order that, whenever the fierce passions of its dragon-nature should awake, it might be reminded of its vows by the presence of its master's shadowy features. The promise was fulfilled, and the dragon-cave became a favourite resort for pilgrims. Our traveller was warned that the roads to the cave were haunted by robbers, so that for three years no pilgrim had been known to return from it. But he replied that it would be difficult during a hundred thousand Kalpas to meet once with the true shadow of Buddha, and that having come so near it in his pilgrimage, he could not pass on without paying the tribute of his adoration.

He left his companions in their security, and having, with some difficulty, obtained a guide, proceeded on his way. They had accomplished but a few miles when they were attacked by five robbers. Hiouen-thsang showed them his shaven head and priestly robes. " Master," said one of the fraternity, "where are you going?" " I desire," replied Hiouen-thsang, " to adore the shadow of Buddha." " Master," said the robber, " do you not know that these roads are full of bandits?" " Robbers are men," was the answer, " and as for me, when I am going to adore the shadow of Buddha, though the roads might be full of wild beasts, I shall walk on fearless. And inasmuch as I will not fear you, because you are men, you will not be insensible to pity." These words, in their simple faith, produced a strange effect upon the robbers, who opened their minds to the enlightenment of the wise man's teaching.

Hiouen-thsang resumed his journey, with his guide, and passed a stream which rushed tumultuously between the walls of a precipitous ravine. In the rock was a door opening into a depth of darkness. With a fervent prayer the pilgrim entered boldly, advanced towards the east, then moved fifty steps backwards, and began his devotions. He made one hundred salutations, but saw nothing. This he conceived to be a punishment for his sins; he reproached himself despairingly and wept bitter tears, because he was denied the happiness of seeing Buddha's shadow. At last, after many prayers and invocations, he saw on the eastern wall a dim patch of light. But it passed away. With mingled joy and pain he continued to pray, and again he saw a light, and again it vanished swiftly. Then, in his ecstasy of loving devotion, he vowed that he would never leave the place until he had seen the " Venerable of the age." After two hundred prayers, he saw the cave suddenly fill with radiance, and the shadow of Buddha, of a brilliant white colour, rose majestically on the wall, as when the clouds are riven, and all at once flashes on the wondering eye the marvellous image of the " Mountain of Light." The features of the divine countenance were illuminated with a dazzling glow. Hiouen-thsang was absorbed in wondering contemplation, and from an object so sublime and incomparable he could not turn his eyes away.

After he awoke from his trance, he called in six men, and bade them kindle a fire in the cave, that he might burn incense; but as the glitter of the flame made the shadow of Buddha disappear, he ordered it to be extinguished. Five of the attendants saw the shadow, but the sixth saw nothing; and the guide, when Hiouen-thsang told him of the vision, could only express his astonishment. "Master," he said, "without the sincerity of your faith and the energy of your vows, you could not have seen such a miracle."

Such is the account which Hiouen-thsang's biographers give of his visit to Buddha's cave; but Max Müller remarks, to the credit of Hiouen-thsang himself, that in the *Si-yu-hi*, which contains his own diary, the story is told much more simply. After describing the cave, he merely adds :—" Formerly, the shadow of Buddha was seen in the cave, bright, like his natural appearance, and with all the marks of his divine beauty. One might have said, it was Buddha himself. For some centuries, however, it has not been possible to see it completely. Though one does perceive something, it is only a feeble and doubtful resemblance. If a man prays with sincere faith, and if he have received from above a secret impression, he sees the shadow clearly, but cannot enjoy the sight for any length of time."

From Peshawer the undaunted pilgrim proceeded to Kashmir, visited the principal towns of Central India, and arrived at last in Magadha, the Holy land of the Buddhists. There, for a space of five years, he devoted himself to the study of Sanskrit and Buddhist literature; he explored every place which was consecrated by memories of the past. Passing through Bengal, he travelled southward, with the view of visiting Ceylon, the chief seat of Buddhism. But, unable to carry out his design, he crossed the peninsula from east to west, ascended the Malabar coast, reached the Indus, and after numerous excursions to scenes of interest in North-Western India, returned to Magadha to enjoy, with his old friends, the delights of learned leisure and intellectual companionship.

Eventually, his return to China became necessary, and traversing the Punjab, Kabulistan, and Bactria, he struck the river Oxus, following its course nearly up to its springhead on the remote Pamir tableland; and after a residence of some duration in the three chief towns of Turkistan, Khasgar, Yarkand, and Khoten, he found himself again, after sixteen years of varied experience, in his native land. By this time he had attained a world-wide reputation, and he was received by the Emperor with the honours usually accorded to a military hero. His entry into the capital was marked by public rejoicings; the streets were decked with gay carpets, festoons of flowers, and waving banners. The splendour of martial pomp was not wanting; the civic magistrates lent the dignity of their presence to the scene; and all the monks of the district issued forth in solemn procession.

If this were a triumph of unusual character, not less unaccustomed were the trophies which figured in it.

First, 150 grains of Buddha's dust;

Second, a golden statue of Buddha;

Third, another statue of sandal-wood;

Fourth, a statue of sandal-wood, representing Buddha as descending from heaven;

Fifth, a statue of silver;

Sixth, a golden statue, representing Buddha victorious over the dragon;

Seventh, a statue of sandal-wood, representing Buddha as a preacher; and

Eighth, a collection of 657 Buddhist works in 520 volumes.

Admitted to an audience of the Emperor in the Phœnix Palace, he was offered, but declined, a high position in the Government. "The doctrine of Confucius," he said, "is still the soul of the administration;" and he preferred to devote his remaining years to the study of the Law of Buddha. The Emperor invited him to write a narrative of his travels, and placed at his disposal a monastery where he might employ himself in peaceful and happy seclusion in translating the works he had brought back from India. He quickly wrote and published his travels, but the translation of the Sanskrit MSS. occupied the rest of his life. It is said that the number of the works he translated, with the assistance of a large staff of monks, amounted to 740, in 1335 volumes. Often he might be seen pondering a passage of difficulty, when suddenly a flash of inspiration would seem to enlighten his mind. His soul was cheered, as when a man walking in darkness sees all at once the sun piercing the clouds and shining in its full brightness; and, unwilling to trust to his own understanding, he used to attribute his knowledge to a secret inspiration of Buddha and the Bôdhisattvas.

When his last hour approached, he divided all his property among the poor, invited his friends to come and see him, and take a cheerful farewell of the impure body of Hiouen-thsang. "I desire," he said, "that whatever merits I may have gained by good works may fall upon other people. May I be born again with them in the heaven of the blessed, be admitted to the family of Mi-le, and serve the Buddha of the future, who is full of kindness and affection. When I descend again upon earth to pass through other forms of existence, I desire at every new birth to fulfil my duties towards Buddha, and arrive at the last at the highest and most perfect intelligence." He died in the year 664.

The life of Hiouen-thsang, and his narrative of travel, have been translated into French by M. Stanislas Julien.[1] The foregoing particulars have been borrowed from a review of M. Julien's work, by Max Müller, which originally appeared in the "Times" of April 17 and 20, 1857.

We translate from Stanislas Julien's "Vie et Voyages de Hiouen-thsang" the Chinese narrative of the pilgrim's last days:—

"After completing his translation of the Pradjñâ, the Master of the Law became conscious that his strength was failing, and that his end was near at hand. Accordingly he spoke to his disciples: 'If I came into the palace of Yu-hoa-kong, it was, as you know, on account of the sacred book of the Pradjñâ. Now that the work is finished, I feel that my thread of life is run out. When after death you remove me to my last resting-place, see that everything be done in a modest and simple manner. You will wrap my

[1] Voyages des Pélerins Bouddhistes. Vol. I. Histoire de la Vie de Hiouen-thsang, et ses Voyages dans l'Inde, depuis l'an 629 jusqu'en 645, par Hoeï-li et Yen-thsong; traduite du Chinois par Stanislas Julien.
Vol. II. Mémoires sur les Contrées Occidentales, traduits du Sanscrit en Chinois, en l'an 648, par Hiouen-thsang, et du Chinois en Français, par Stanislas Julien. Paris, 1853—1857. B. Duprat.

body in a mat, and deposit it in some calm and solitary spot in the bosom of a valley. Carefully avoid the neighbourhood of palace or convent ; a body so impure as mine should be separated from it by a great distance.'

" On hearing these words, his disciples broke out into sobs and cries. Drying their tears, they said to him : ' Master, you have still a reserve of strength and vigour ; your countenance is in no wise altered ; why do you give sudden utterance to such miserable words?'

" ' I know it through and in myself,' replied the Master of the Law ; ' how would it be possible for you to understand my presentiments ?'

" On the first day of the first moon in the spring of the first year *Lin-te* (664), the neighbouring interpreters and all the religious of the convent, came to solicit him, with the most pressing earnestness, to translate the collection of the *Ratnakoûta soûtra.*

" The Master of the Law, yielding to their fervid persistency, made an effort to overcome his weakness, and translated a few lines. Then, closing the Hindu text, he said : ' This collection is as great as that of the *Pradjñâ,* but I feel I have not sufficient strength to complete such an enterprise. My last moments have arrived, and my life can be only of short duration. To-day I would fain visit the valley of Lantchi, to offer my last homages to the statues of the innumerable Buddhas.'

" Accordingly, he set forth with his disciples. The monks, at his departure, did not cease to shed tears.

" After this pious excursion he returned to the convent. Thenceforward he ceased to translate, and occupied himself solely in his religious duties.

" On the eighth day, one of his disciples, the monk Hiouen-Khio, originally of Kao-tch'ang, related to the Master of the Law a dream which he had had. He had seen a *Fesu-thou* (or *Stoûpa,*) of imposing aspect and prodigious height, crumble suddenly to the ground. Awakened by the fall, he ran to inform the Master of the Law. ' The event does not concern you,' said Hiouen-thsang; ' it is the presage of my approaching end.'

" On the evening of the ninth day, as he crossed the bridge of a canal in the rear of his residence, he fell, and injured his leg. From that moment his strength declined perceptibly.

"On the sixteenth day he cried out, as if awaking from a dream : 'Before my eyes I see an immense lotus-flower, charming in its freshness and purity.'

"He had another dream on the seventeenth day, in which he saw hundreds and thousands of men of tall stature, who, decorated with garments of embroidered silk, with flowers of marvellous beauty, and jewels of great price, issued from the sleeping-chamber of the Master of the Law, and proceeded to set out, both internally and externally, the hall consecrated to the translation of the holy books. Afterwards, in the rear of that hall, on a wooded mountain, they everywhere planted rich banners of the most vivid colours, and created an harmonious music. He saw moreover, without the gate, an innumerable multitude of splendid chariots loaded with perfumed viands and fruits of more than a thousand kinds, as beautiful in form as in colour; no fruits were there of terrestrial growth! The people brought them to him, one after the other, and offered him a profusion; but he refused them, saying : 'Such viands as these belong only to those who have obtained the superior intelligence. Hiouenthsang has not yet arrived at that sublime rank : how could he dare to receive them?' In spite of his energetic refusal they continued to serve him without intermission.

"The disciples who watched by him happening to make some slight sound, he opened his eyes suddenly, and related his dream to the sub-director (*Karmmadana*), a certain Hoeï-te."

"'And from these omens,' added the Master, 'it seems to me that such merits as I have been able to acquire during my life have not fallen into oblivion, and I believe, with an entire faith, that it is not in vain one practises the doctrine of the Buddha.'

"Immediately, he ordered the master Kia-chang to make a written list of the titles of the sacred books and the treatises which he had translated, forming altogether seven hundred and forty works and thirteen hundred and thirty-five volumes (*livres*). He wrote down also the *Kôti* (ten millions) of paintings of the Buddha, as well as the thousand images of *Mi-le* (*Mâitrêya bôdhisattva*), painted on silk, which he had caused to be executed. There were, moreover, the *Kôtis* (one hundred millions) of statuettes of uniform colour. He had also caused to be written a thousand copies of the following sacred books:

Nong-touan-pan-jo-king (*Vadjra tchhêdika pradjñâ parâmitâ soûtra*).
Yo-sse-jou-laï-pou-youen-kong-te-king (*Arya bhagavati bhâichadja gourou poûrwa pranidhâna nâma mahâ yâna soûtra*).
Lou-men-t'o-lo-ni-king (*Chat moukhi dhârani*)."

He had ministered to the wants of upwards of twenty thousand persons among the faithful and heretical; he had kindled a hundred thousand lamps, and purchased thousands upon thousands (*ocean*) of creatures.

When Kia-chang had finished this long catalogue of good works, he was ordered to read it aloud. After hearing it, the religious crossed their hands and loaded the Master with congratulations. Then he said to them:—" The moment of my death approaches; already my mind grows feeble and seems to be on the point of quitting me. Distribute at once in alms my clothes and goods; let statues be fabricated; and order the religious to recite some prayers."

On the twenty-third day, a meal was given to the poor, at which alms were distributed. On the same day, he ordered a moulder named Song-kia-tchi, to raise, in the Kia-cheou-tien palace, a statue of the Intelligence (Buddha); after which he invited the population of the convent, the translators, and his disciples, to bid "a joyous farewell to that impure and contemptible body of Hiouen-thsang, who, having finished his work, merited no longer existence. I desire," he added, "to see poured back upon other men the merits which I have acquired by any good works; to be born with them in the heaven of the Touchitas; to be admitted into the family of *Mi-le* (*Mâitrêya*); and to serve the Buddha, full of tenderness and affection. When I shall return to earth to pass through other existences, I desire, at each new birth, to discharge with boundless zeal my duties towards the Buddha, and finally to arrive at the Transcendent Intelligence (*Anouttara samyak sambôdhi*)."

After having made these adieux, he was silent, and engaged in meditation; then with his dying tongue he faltered forth his bitter regret that he did not enjoy more of the "world of the eyes" (the faculty of seeing), of the "world of the thought" (the faculty of thinking), of "the world of the knowledge which springs from observation" (the knowledge of sensible objects); of the "world of the knowledge which springs from the mind"—*l'esprit* (the perception of spiritual things); and that he did not possess the fulness of the Intelligence. Finally, he pronounced two *gubhas*, which he caused to be repeated to the persons near him:—

"Adoration to *Maitrêya Tathagata*, gifted with a sublime intelligence! I desire, with all men, to see your affectionate visage.

"Adoration to *Maitrêya Tathagata!* I desire, when I quit this life, to be born again in the midst of the multitude who surround you."

The Master of the Law, after having long fixed his gaze upon Te-hoeï, the sub-director of the convent (*Karmmadana*), raised his right hand to his chin and his left upon his breast; then he stretched out his legs, crossed them, and lay down on the right side.

He remained thus, immovable, without taking anything, until the fifth day of the second moon. In the middle of the night his disciples asked him:

"Master, have you at length obtained to be born in the midst of the assembly of *Maitrêya?*"

"Yes," he replied, with a failing voice. And having spoken, his breathing grew rapidly weaker, and in a few moments, his soul passed away.

His servants, feeling quietly, found that his feet were already cold, but that the back part of the head retained its warmth.

On the seventh day (of the second moon) his countenance had not undergone any alteration, and his body exhaled no odour.

The religious of the convent having passed several days in prayers, it was not until the morning of the ninth day that the sad news reached the capital.

The Master of the Law was seven *tchi* high; his face was of a fresh complexion. His eyebrows were wide apart, his eyes brilliant. His air was grave and majestic, and his features were full of grace and vivacity. The quality or tone (*timbre*) of his voice was pure and penetrating, and his language at times soared to a lofty eloquence, so noble and so harmonious that one could not refuse to listen. When he was surrounded by his disciples, or animated by the presence of an illustrious guest, he would often speak for half-a-day, while his hearers sat riveted in an immovable attitude. His favourite attire was a robe of fine cotton stuff, proportioned to his height and figure; his gait was light and easy; he looked straight before him, throwing his glances neither to the right nor to the left. He was majestic as those great rivers which embrace the earth; calm and shining as the lotus which springs in the midst of the waters. A severe observer of discipline, he was unchanged and unchangeable. Nothing could equal his affectionate benevolence and tender pity, the fervour of his zeal or his inviolable attachment to the practices of the Law. He was reserved in his friendship, made no hasty bonds, and when once he had entered his convent, nothing but an imperial decree could have drawn him from his pious retreat.

On the third day of the second moon (of the period *Lin-te*, —664), the Master of the Law had sent Hiu-hiouen-pi to inform the Emperor of the wound he had received, and of the malady it had induced.

On the seventh day of the same month the Emperor, by a decree, ordered one of the imperial physicians to take with him medicaments and attend upon the Master of the Law, but by the time he arrived, the Master was already dead. Teou-sse-lun, governor of Fang-tcheou, announced by a report this melancholy event.

At the news, the Emperor shed tears copiously, and cried aloud in his sorrow, declaring that he had just lost the treasure of the empire. For several days he suspended the usual audiences.

All the civil and military functionaries abandoned themselves to groans and tears: the Emperor himself was unable to repress his sobs or moderate his grief. On the next day but one, he spoke to his great officers as follows:

" What a misfortune for my empire is the loss of Thsang, the Master of the Law! It may well be said that the great family of Cakya has seen its sole support shattered beneath it, and that all men remain without master and without guide. Do they not resemble the mariner who sees himself sinking into the abyss, when the storm has destroyed his oars and his shallop? the traveller astray in the midst of the darkness, whose lamp dies out at the entrance to a bottomless gulf?"

When he had uttered these words, the Emperor groaned again, and sighed many times.

On the twenty-sixth day of the same month, the Emperor issued the following decree:

"In accordance with a report addressed to me by Teousse-lun on the death of the Master of the Law, Hiouen-thsang, of the convent *Yu-hoa-sse*, I order that his funeral take place at the expense of the State."

On the sixth day of the third moon, he issued a new decree as follows:

"By the death of Thsang, the Master of the Law, the translation of the sacred books is stopped. In conformity to the ancient ordinances, the magistrates will cause the translations already completed to be copied carefully: as for the (Indian) manuscripts which have not yet been translated, they will be handed over in their entirety to the director of the convent *Ts'e-'en-sse* (of the Great Beneficence,) who will watch over their safety. The disciples of Hiouen-thsang and the translators' company, who previously did not belong to the convent *Yu-hoa-sse*, will all return to their respective convents."

On the fifth day of the third moon appeared the following decree:

"On the day of the funeral of the Master of the Law, Hiouen-thsang, I permit the male and female religious of the capital to accompany him *with banners and parasols* to his last resting-place. The Master of the Law shone by his noble conduct and his eminent virtues, and was the idol of his age. Wherefore, now he is no more, it is just that I should diffuse again abundant benefits to honour the memory of a man who has had no equal in past times."

His disciples, faithful to his last wishes, formed a litter of coarse mats, removed his body to the capital, and deposited it in the convent of the Great Beneficence, in the middle of the hall devoted to the labours of translation. United by the sentiment of a common sorrow, they uttered such cries as might have shaken the earth. The religious and the laics of the capital hastened to the spot, and poured out tears mingled with sobs and cries. Every day the crowd was swollen by fresh arrivals.

On the fourteenth day of the fourth month, preparations were made for his interment in the capital of the West. The male and female religious, and a multitude of the men of the people, prepared upwards of five hundred objects necessary for the celebration of his obsequies; parasols of smooth (*unia*) silk, banners and standards, the tent and the litter of the *Ni-ouan* (Nirvâna;) the inner coffin of gold, the outer one of silver, the *so-lo* trees (*salas*,) and disposed them in the middle of the streets to be traversed by the procession. The plaintive cadences of the funereal music, and the mournful dirges of the bearers resounded even to Heaven. The inhabitants of the capital and of the districts situated within a radius of five hundred *li* (fifty leagues,) who formed the procession, exceeded one million in number. Though the obsequies were celebrated with pomp, the coffin of the Master nevertheless was borne upon a litter composed of rude coarse mats. The silk manufacturers of the East had employed three thousand pieces of different colours in making the chariot of the Nirvâna, which they had ornamented with flowers and garlands, loaded with precious stones. They had asked permission to place the body of the Master of the Law upon this resplendent catafalque; but afraid of infringing his dying command, his disciples had refused. So it went first, bearing the Master's three robes and his religious mantle, of the value of one hundred ounces of silver; next came the litter constructed of coarse mats. Not one of the assistants but shed copious tears or was almost choked with grief!

Upwards of thirty thousand religious and laics spent the night near his tomb.

On the morning of the fifteenth day the grave was closed; then, at the place of sepulture, an immense distribution of alms was made, and the crowd afterwards dispersed in silence.

On the eighth day of the fourth moon of the second

year of the Tsong-tchang period (669,) the Emperor decreed that the tomb of the Master of the Law should be transported into a plain, situated to the west of the *Fan-tch'ouen* valley, and that a tower should be erected in his honour.[1]

[1] Hoeï-li terminates the last book of his biography of the Master with a long and pompous panegyric of Hiouen-thsang. This *morceau*, which forms (says Stanislas Julien,) twenty-five pages in the Imperial edition and ten in the *Nan-king*, offers an analysis of the life and voyages of the Master of the Law; but it contains no new fact or one of any interest in relation to the history and geography of India or the Buddhist literature. No English version has appeared of M. Julien's elaborate translation of the Chinese History of Hiouen-thsang.

CHAPTER II.

MAGIANISM: THE PARSEES.

THE ZENDAVESTA.[1]

WHEN the pure morality of Christianity is adduced as a proof of its high origin, one of the favourite devices of Modern Unbelief is to claim an equally high standard for the morality inculcated by the primitive creeds, and to rain praises upon the ethical systems embodied in the Soûtras of the Buddhists, the Rig-Veda of the Brahmans, or the Zendavesta of the Parsees. In making this claim our philosophers probably calculate on the little knowledge which the multitude possess of any creeds but their own. They are well aware that, to the popular mind, the teaching of Buddha or Zoroaster is necessarily a sealed book, and that the whole extent of its purport is known only to a few scholars. Hence, when they come to support their thesis by quotations, they are able to select those isolated passages which shine with the lustre of genuine diamonds, and produce an absolutely false impression of the general character of the writings in which they occur ; thin veins of precious metal shining here and there through masses of worthless ore. No doubt the Veda contains numerous utterances of the highest beauty, in which the soul's devotion to a Supreme Power is expressed with a lyrical fervour inferior only to that of the Sweet Singer of Israel. No doubt the Zendavesta, or the books of K'ung-fu-tze, like the works of later and maturer intellects—a Xenophon and a Plato, a Seneca and a Marcus Aurelius—are enriched with thoughts of the

[1] More correctly, Avesta-Zend.

loftiest description, and frequently breathe the most exalted aspirations. But what we have to remember is, that these are wholly exceptional; that they are the most arduous efforts of each self-absorbed thinker, and the indications of his boldest flights. At other times the wing grows feeble; at other times the music is faint and even discordant; the bird can do no more than creep along the ground. In the sayings of our LORD, however, or in the writings of His Apostles, the tone is always sustained, clear, definite. There is no uncertainty or hesitation. Nothing mean or unworthy is woven in their texture. No concessions are made to man's coarser desires or grosser passions. The system set before us is rounded in perfection, and shows not a flaw from beginning to end. We feel that He who speaks, whether in His own Person or through His disciples, speaks as never man spoke before; and that the Voice which fills our ears and stirs our hearts is, in deed and in truth, a Voice from Heaven.

We propose to furnish in this chapter a general view of the construction and teaching of the Parsee Scriptures, with the view of showing the signal inferiority of the creed it embodies to Christianity in all that can elevate the mind and satisfy the soul. At the same time we admit that the Parsee creed, and all similar creeds, possess an intrinsic value, apart from their ethical deficiencies, as illustrating the recognition of an Almighty Will, an Eternal and Supreme Force, by all the higher races of mankind. They show us the hopes, fears, and desires of great tribes and peoples which existed in the days before men wrote history; and they show us how their wisest teachers groped in the dark, and stumbled in the thorny path,—favoured occasionally, it is true, with a wonderful glimpse of light, and striking now and again into the pleasant places, but never rejoicing in the glory which rose upon earth with the Sun of Righteousness, never treading in that narrow but secure way which leads to Eternal Life. We see in them the great minds of the early world, like children on the seashore, perplexed by a music which they could not comprehend, and astonished by a power which they were unable to define. Yet happier and wiser they than the cold materialist of a later age, who resolves all mysteries, all phenomena, into the working of a blind inflexible Law, and takes out of creation its light, beauty, and joy by denying the existence of an all-powerful and all-loving Creator.

The religion professed by the ancient Persians, and still accepted by the Parsees of Western India, and by a scattered population in Yezd and Kerman, is taught in the books known as the Zend-Avesta. This title comes from the Sassanian term *Avesta* or *Apusta*, that is, the text;[1] and *Zend*, or *Zand*, that is, the commentary upon it. The meaning of the latter word, however, seems to have varied at different periods. Originally it signified the interpretation of the sacred texts handed down from Zoroaster (or Zarathustra) and his disciples. In course of time the interpretation came to be esteemed not less authoritative and sacred than the original text, and both were called *Avesta*. But the language in which they were written having died out, they became unintelligible to the majority of the people, and a new *Zend* or commentary was required before they could be understood. The new "Zend" was the work of the most learned priests of the Sassanian period, and consisted of a translation of the double "Avesta" into the vernacular language then in vogue.[2] And as this translation is the only key which the priests of modern Persia possess to the old creed as taught by Zarathustra, it has usurped the place of the original Zend, and is now the recognised official commentary.

But, anciently, the word "Zend" implied something more than a simple interpretation of the "Avesta," or sacred texts. That interpretation was the source of certain new doctrines, the whole of which were considered orthodox, and designated *Zandi-agahi*, or Zend doctrines; doctrines which, it can hardly be doubted, supplied Plutarch and some other of the Greeks with ethical suggestions. The name *Pazend*, which frequently occurs in connection with *Avesta* and *Zend*, denotes a further exposition of Zarathustrian teaching, as contained in the Vendidad, to which we shall shortly refer.

Thus far we have been indebted to Dr. Haug's account

[1] Sanscrit, *Avasthâ*. This is Haug's conjecture.
[2] The Pazend language was identical with the Parsi, i.e., the ancient Persian.

of the origin of the Zendavesta. His views are confirmed by Westergaard, who asserts that the sacred books belong to two epochs; that is, that they are written in one age, and collected and systematised in another, in much the same way as, according to Wolf, the Homeric poems were produced and assumed their present form. All the earlier traditions ascribe their origin to Zarathustra; but modern philologists affirm that they could not have sprung from any single mind, because they present no defined or self-consistent system of religious belief or moral economy. Like the hymns of the Vedas, and the strains of the Norse Edda, the several portions of the Zendavesta, so they say, must have been composed by different bards, each of whom coloured his particular theme according to the hues of his lively imagination. This theory, however, though it may have an element of truth in it, is hardly the whole truth. The Zendavesta is unquestionably wanting in unity and completeness. But it seems to us that traces of a dominant mind are everywhere visible; that the various parts are held together as on a thread by the teaching of Zarathustra himself; and that the additions made by later and inferior writers are not such as wholly to obscure the original work.

It is to the celebrated Frenchman, Anquetil Duperron, that the scholars of the West owe their knowledge of these remarkable books. Happening to see a facsimile of a few pages written in Zend characters, he resolved on setting out for India in order to purchase manuscripts of all the sacred books of the Zarathustrian religion, to acquire a thorough insight into their signification, and to obtain a knowledge of the rites and religious observances of the Parsees. His means being limited, he entered himself as a sailor on board a ship of the Dutch Indian Company, and worked his way out to Bombay in 1754. With money supplied by the French Government to assist him in his ingenious researches, he bribed one of the most learned *dustoors* or priests, Dustoor Darat, or Surat, to procure the treasures he desired, and to instruct him in the Zend and Pehlvi languages. As soon as he had acquired the requisite proficiency, he addressed himself to the task of translating the whole of the Zendavesta into French. This was in 1759. Returning to Europe, he convinced himself of the genuineness of his purchases by comparing them with MSS. in the Bodleian Library; and, after several years of arduous labour, produced the first European version in 1771. At the outset, the authenticity of his work was challenged both in England and Germany; but all doubts have been set at rest by the inquiries of Rask and others; and thus, through the fanciful enterprise of a young Frenchman, the veil has been lifted which for so long a period shrouded the mysterious religion of the Magi.

We do not, however, possess the whole of the Avesta. It is asserted by an Arabian writer that Zarathustra himself covered with his verses no fewer than twelve thousand parchments, and who shall compute the extent of the literature accumulated by his disciples? Whether this literature perished at the epoch of the Macedonian conquest of Persia, or whether it was destroyed by Alexander the Great, or whether it gradually perished as the influence of the Greek philosophy prevailed over the Zarathustrian theology, it is impossible to determine. The remains of the sacred books, however, with short summaries of their contents, have been handed down to us. Originally they were twenty-one in number, called *Nosks*, and each *Nosk* consisting of "Avesta" and "Zend"—text and commentary. The number twenty-one corresponded to the number of words composing the "Honovar," or most sacred prayer, of the Zarathustrians. It is, we may add, a magical number, being the result of the multiplication of the sacred numbers, *three* and *seven*.

Of these divisions the *précis* now extant, and collected for the first time by the Danish scholar Westergaard, comprise the following books: First, the *Yasna*, which sets before us the devotions proper to be offered in connection with the sacrificial ceremonies. This Yasna is divided into seventy-two chapters, representing the six Yahânhârs, or "seasons" during which Ahura-Mazda, the Good Principle, created the world. The reader will here note the coincidence between the six creative seasons of the Magian seer, and the six creative days of the Hebrew lawgiver. The Yasna consists of two parts, the older of which is written in what is called the Gâtha dialect, and had acquired a peculiar sanctity prior to the date of composition of the other books. It may be described as a treasury of songs, hymns, and metrical prayers, which embody a variety of abstruse reflections upon subjects of metaphysical inquiry, and are much better adapted to stimulate the intellect of the student than to foster the devotion of the worshipper. They are rhymeless, like the poetical effusions of Cædmon, and in their metrical structure bear a curious resemblance to the Vedic hymns. Of these collections, or Gâthas, there are five, and their leading title seems to be : "The Revealed Thought, the Revealed Word, and the Revealed Deed of Zarathustra the Holy." It is added that the Archangels first sang the Gâthas. Their general purport is an exposition of the work and teaching of the great founder of Magianism, who is represented as inveighing against a belief in the *devas*, or gods, and exhorting his disciples to lift up their hearts only to Ahura-Mazda, the Supreme Goodness.

Now it seems necessary to correct a popular error, that the Zendavesta is largely liturgical : an error confirmed by the assertion of Gibbon, who says : " Every mode of religion, to make a deep and lasting impression on the human mind, must exercise our obedience, by enjoining practices of devotion for which we can assign no reason ; and must acquire our esteem by inculcating moral duties analogous to the dictates of our own hearts. The religion of Zoroaster was abundantly provided with the former, and possessed a sufficient portion of the latter." But Zarathustra himself, in one of his best-known precepts, warns his followers that " he who sows the ground with care and diligence, acquires a greater stock of religious merit than he would gain by the repetition of ten thousand prayers." It is the tendency of all ethico-religious systems, at least in their earliest stage of development, to discourage purely liturgical observances, and to enjoin on the disciple a state of self-concentration and self-absorption varied only by physical activity. Unaided by a divine Revelation, their founders never rise higher than the passive virtues of endurance and patience. As time passes away, and the new creed falls into the hands of a special school of expounders, minute rites and rigid practices are accumulated in order to impose upon the neophyte, and deepen the influence of those who alone possess a clue to their meaning. The formalities which encumber the Zarathustrian worship were invented long after the death of the master, and no indication of them appears in the oldest section of the Zendavesta. They are to be found chiefly in the much later pages of the *Sadder*, where fifteen different genuflexions and prayers are required of the devout Persian every time he cuts his finger-nails!

To return to the Yasna. The Gâthas, of which we have been speaking, were not improbably composed by Zarathustra himself, and may be held to express his belief and his thoughts in his own words. The second part, or "Younger Yasna," is of a much later date and less lofty tone. The invention of some of the Master's disciples or priests, it re-establishes the Polytheism which Zarathustra so strenuously condemned; and furnishes the believer with a manual of prayers and incantations (in prose) to the genii of the woods and streams and hills, the powers of fire and earth and water, and all the invisible spirits which haunt the luminous air.

We come next to the *Visparad*, a collection of prayers in three-and-twenty chapters, written in Zend, and of a similar tenour to those in the younger Yasna. These prayers refer to the preparation of the sacred water, and the consecration of certain offerings—such as the sacred bread—which are carried round about the sacred fire, and after having been exhibited to it, are eaten by the priest and by the votary on whose behalf the ceremony is performed.

The *Yashts* (Yêsti)—that is, worship by prayers and sacrifices—fall to be considered in the third place. Of these devotions, which are consecrated to the praise and worship of one Divine Being, and of a certain limited group of inferior deities, twenty-four are extant. In using them the votary endeavours, by a wearisome enumeration of the glorious achievements of the deity he is addressing, and of the miracles he has wrought, to induce him to come and enjoy the meal prepared for him, and then to bestow on his fervid worshipper a blessing not inferior to the boons bestowed on his children in bygone times. So far as concerns the legendary history of the ancient Iranians, and in connection with their belief in the pantheon of Magianism, the Yashts are of great value, and indeed, from this point of view, are the most precious portion of the Zendavesta.

While the three parts already described exhibit more or less of a liturgical character, the fourth division, known as

E

the *Vendidad*, forms a collection of customs, observances, laws, pains, and penalties, the growth of a period much later than that of Zarathustra, when Ritual began its encroachments on Religion. It is the essence of all *genuine* Ritual that it should illustrate and explain Doctrine, but this is never found to be the case in the primitive creeds. In all such it becomes merely the ingenious invention of a subtle priesthood, by which its members established their influence over an ignorant community. In the eyes of the unlearned its complex character invested it with an air of mystery; they were led to look upon the "form" as of greater importance than the "spirit," and to attribute a strange, a wonderful potency to rites and ceremonies which they could not understand. While it is the special feature of the faith of CHRIST that it appeals in its sweet simplicity to every heart, and that it requires of the believer to present himself before the altar with the innocence and trustfulness of a little child; that it seeks not to confuse by a multiplicity of minute observances, and even sums up its leading tenets in two brief and easily intelligible commandments; Magianism, conscious of its inherent defects, unable to fall back on the redeeming sacrifice of a SAVIOUR, deficient in any enduring principle of vitality, sought to build up its structure on a foundation of ceremonies and formalities. And when it could not feed the soul with the bread of truth, it dazzled the senses by imposing spectacles, and confused the imagination with a cumbrous code of the most complicated ritualistic frivolities; so that the Persian worship, with its incantations and devices, laid the foundation of the later Magic.

Turning our attention now to that portion of the Zendavesta which is called the Vendidad, we find that it is divided into twenty-two Fargards, or chapters.

In the first of these we find an account of the creation by Ahura-Mazda, of sixteen holy regions, sinless spotless Edens, localities of perfect bliss; each of which is destroyed in succession by Ahriman, the Spirit of Evil,—a fable evidently suggested by the Mosaic history of Paradise. The second treats of a certain king, Yimo Vivaugham, who introduced agriculture into the land of Iran. The third sets forth the various means by which Zoma, or the Earth, may be rendered happy.

You must beware of excavating deep holes in it, for through these the *devs*, or demons, pass to and fro between hell and earth ; nor must you bury within it the dead bodies of men or dogs, or other animals. The fourth chapter enumerates six categories of crime, and the several punishments connected with them. The fifth and sixth are occupied with a description of various kinds of impurity. The seventh and eighth contain liturgical directions in reference to the disposal of the carcases of men and dogs ;[1] and it is stated that whoever eats of flesh so unclean can never be purified, but that hell will undoubtedly be his portion. Even the house in which a man or a dog dies must immediately be purified by the use of incense or sweet-smelling odours ; a sanitary precaution of some importance in hot climates. In the ninth occurs an elaborate detail of the rite of purification denominated the *Barathium*, to be performed by, and on behalf of a person who shall have been unwittingly defiled by touching the dead. The tenth and eleventh are not less minute in their directions what word must be repeated twice, and thrice, and four times at the different Gâthas, in order that Ahriman and his lieutenants may be expelled from men and women who have been in contact with the dead, and from houses, cities, and provinces into which they have obtained an entrance.

The twelfth Fargard treats of various funeral ceremonies, and repeats a number of injunctions relative to the cleansing of places, of clothes and other articles, polluted by lifeless bodies. It concludes with elaborate warnings against a two-footed *dev*, called Ashmog. The thirteenth and fourteenth run riot in praise of the noble qualities of dogs, and severe in their rebuke of the " superior animals" who ill-use them. The fifteenth reads like a Commination Service, in its denunciation of certain crimes which can never be undone even by the profoundest penitential offices, and are punished by Ahura-Mazda with eternal condemnation. The seventeenth, like the sixteenth, is tediously liturgical, and discusses such minutiæ as the arrangement of the hair of the head, the extraction of bad or gray hairs, and the cutting of

---

[1] Dogs are here associated with man on account of their high value in an early stage of civilisation. Zarathustra protected them by special ordinances and penalties.

nails. If these operations are performed without certain prescribed ceremonies, the devs come upon earth, and parasitical organisms are produced to the great discomfort and injury of man. The eighteenth lays down the distinctions which should characterise an *Athrava*, or priest. He must wear the *padan*, a mouth-cover, of two fingers' breadth; must carry an instrument for disposing of parasitical insects; devote his nights to study, keep alive the sacred fire, and succour the distressed. The nineteenth chapter recounts the perils to which Zarathustra was exposed, when he had left the south on his mission, from the murderous assaults of Ahriman and his host, who hastened up from the north; the north, to an inhabitant of the warm sunny south, naturally appearing the fit home and haunt of the Spirit of Evil. The twentieth is devoted to the praise of Taneslied, who is represented as having swept away disease, death, bloodshed, war, evil-doers, falsehood, and all kinds of wickedness. The twenty-first enjoins the salutations to be paid to the sacred Bull, and extols some of its illustrious qualities. Finally, the twenty-second narrates the mission of Zarathustra, and describes the evil he will dispel through the influence of the Word; Ahura-Mazda having ordered him to establish his worship in the region called Airya-Mava, or Irman, so that it may become bright, pure, and happy as the abode of Ahura-Mazda himself, free from sin, and, consequently, free from sorrow and suffering.

From this brief summary it will be seen that the religion of the Parsees in its present form is a definite Dualism, recognizing the existence of two distinct principles, Good and Evil, impersonated by spirits of equal power, named Ahura-Mazda, (or Spento-Manyus,) and Ahriman, (or Angro-Manyus.) But no such doctrine was taught by Zarathustra himself. His creed, like all the earliest creeds, was purely Monotheistic. He set before men, as the sole object of their love and adoration, one Supreme Being, Ahura-Mazda, the great "Life-Giver" or the "Living Wisdom," as the name is variously explained. Nor was his conception of this one God altogether unworthy of the Founder of a Religion. He does not represent Him, indeed, as the "Father," loving, sympathetic, compassionate, and so full of condescension, that He is willing to give His Son to die for the salvation of erring Humanity; for he did not enjoy that fuller revelation of the Divine Nature which was vouchsafed to the Hebrew race. But he shows Him as the "Lord over all lords, the Forgiving, the Omniscient." He is ineffably pure, the source of all Truth, the Holy God. In the Khordah Avesta, Zarathustra is introduced as inquiring: "Tell me the name, O pure Ahura-Mazda, which is Thy greatest, best, and fairest name?" Ahura-Mazda replies: "My name is He who may be questioned: the Gatherer of the people: the Most Pure: He who takes account of the actions of men. My name is God (Ahura); My name is the Great Wise One (Mazdas.) I am the All-Seeing, the Desirer of Good for My creatures, He who cannot be deceived: the Protector: the Tormentor of tormentors: He who smiteth once and only once: the Creator of All."

His happiness, like His holiness, is without spot or blemish; every blessing is His that man can imagine—health and wealth, virtue, wisdom, prosperity, immortality; and these blessings He is willing to bestow on His creatures if in thought and word and deed they eschew impurity. But we nowhere read that He will assist them in the struggle against sin by creating in them a new heart, or by vouchsafing the grace of His Holy Spirit. The mystery of the Atonement was beyond the reach of the soul and intellect even of Zarathustra; and the highest conception of God to which he could attain was that of a Being of perfect Goodness, sitting enthroned in a strange awful loneliness, with no other feeling than that of approval of Good and disapproval of Evil. He is, of course, the supreme type of Power: all that *is* flows from Him, as light from the Sun: He creates both the shadow and the brightness of the human existence, good and ill, fortune and misfortune. So far above all human intelligence is He placed, that images of Him are forbidden, though He is understood to be symbolised by the sun and by fire. He can be served only by prayers and offerings, by a life of purity and truth, by abstinence from sinful passions, by the banishment of sinful thoughts. Thus Herodotus says of the Zarathustrians, that they reject the use of temples, of altars, and of statues. "They smile," he says, "at the folly of those nations who imagine that the Gods are descended from, or have any affinity with, human nature. The loftiest mountain-tops are the places chosen for their sacrifices. Hymns and prayers are their principal forms of worship. And the Supreme God, who fills the vast sphere of Heaven, is the object to whom they are addressed."

The service of Ahura-Mazda consisted, then, as we see, in the performance of good works, in the cultivation of virtue, and in the due offering up of prayer and praise. It was an intellectual worship that Zarathustra prescribed; a worship that might assist in the development of a high morality, but could not inculcate a deep and true religious feeling. Of contrition for sin, of humbling oneself before GOD, of self-sacrifice and self-abnegation, of love, and faith, and hope, the creed of Zarathustra took no account. And here, as well as elsewhere, we observe its vast inferiority to the religion of CHRIST. It made no provision for the awakening and fostering of those tender emotions of profound humility, thankful adoration, and unutterable gratitude which are awakened in the Christian's heart by the name of JESUS. It could never have called forth such an utterance of the son's glad submission to the will of the FATHER as we find, for example, in the ejaculatory verse of Ben Jonson:

> "Hear me, O GOD!
> A broken heart
> Is my best part:
> Use still Thy rod,
> That I may prove
> Therein Thy love.
>
> "If Thou hadst not
> Been stern to me,
> But left me free,
> I had forgot
> Myself and Thee.
>
> "For sin's so sweet,
> As minds ill-bent
> Rarely repent,
> Until they meet
> Their punishment."

Such lines as these indicate a relation between man and

his GOD which could never obtain between the Zarathustrian and his Ahura-Mazda. His was a cold, unimpassioned, logical creed, warmed by no single heart-throb of Divine love and mercy; a creed which demanded human worship for a sinless God, but did not invite human faith in a loving Redeemer; and, consequently, a creed which left untouched the deepest springs and most responsive chords of our humanity.

Both the excellencies and the short-comings of Magianism are shown in the confessions and prayers included in the Zendavesta. For example, there is much that is elevated and noble in the following, yet its tone is curiously Pharisaical, and may be contrasted with that of Ben Jonson's verses. Instead of being the aspiration of a sinful soul after forgiveness, and a reaching forth towards love and light, it is the self-eulogium of a mind confident in its own sustaining power, and to appreciate its weakness we need only to contrast it with the fervour of a David or a S. Paul. We remember that the Hebrew king exclaimed: " My heart panteth, my strength faileth me: as for the light of mine eyes, it also is gone from me," and how the Apostle confessed himself " the chief of sinners." With no such aching consciousness of weakness does the Zarathustrian bow himself before God. There is all the pride of self-righteousness in his prayer. Thus:

" I remain standing fast in the statutes of the law which Ahura-Mazda gave to Zarathustra. As long as life endures I will stand fast in good thoughts in my soul, in good words in my speech, in good deeds in my actions. With all good am I in harmony, with all evil am I at variance. With the punishments of the future life I am content. I have taken hold of good thoughts, words, and works. I have forsaken evil thoughts, words, and works. May the power of Ahriman be broken! may the reign of Ahura-Mazda increase!"

And again:

" I am steadfast in this faith, and turn myself not away from it, for the sake of a happy life, or for the sake of a longer life, nor for power, nor for a kingdom. If I must give up my body for the sake of my soul, I give it willingly. I believe firmly in the good Mazda-yusaian faith; in the

Resurrection; in the bridge of souls,[1] in the invariable reward of good deeds and punishment of bad deeds, in the everlasting continuance of paradise and the annihilation of hell; and I believe that, at the last, Ahura-Mazda will be victorious, and Ahrimanes will perish with the Devs, and all the children of darkness. . . . . I am full of hope that I shall attain to Paradise and the shining Garathânan, where all majesty dwelleth. I make this confession in the hope that I may hereafter become more zealous to accomplish good works and keep myself more from sin; and that my good deeds may serve for the diminution of evil and the increase of good till the rising again."

We know the form of prayer taught us by JESUS CHRIST; how simple it is, how complete, how absolute in its renunciation of self, how comprehensive in its charity. "Thy will be done" . . . . "Forgive us our trespasses as we forgive them who trespass against us" . . . "Lead us not into temptation." Such are its leading thoughts: submission before GOD, charity before Man; both implying and demanding the conquest and humiliation of self. Let us contrast it with a Zarathustrian prayer:

"In the name of God the Giver and Forgiver, Rich in Love, praise be to Ahura-Mazda, the God with the name . . . 'Who always was, always is, and always will be.' . . . . Ahura-Mazda the Wise, the Creator, the Over-seeing God, pure, good, and just! With all strength bring I thank-offerings and praise to the Lord, the completer of good works, who made men greater than all earthly beings, and through the gift of speech created them to rule over the creatures and to war against the evil spirits. Praise to the omniscience of God who has sent through the holy Zarathustra power and knowledge of the law. All good do I accept at Thy command, O God, and think, speak, and do it. I believe in the pure law, and by every good work I seek forgiveness for sins. I keep pure the six powers—thought, speech, act, memory, reason, understanding. According to Thy will am I able to fulfil (these resolutions.) O Accomplisher of Good, to Thy honour are good thoughts, good words, and good works. I enter on the shining way

[1] The bridge *Chinavat* by which the souls of the good crossed into Paradise; a fancy afterwards adopted by Muhámad.

to Paradise. May the terror of hell not overcome me! May I pass the bridge Chinavat and attain to Paradise, the bright and odoriferous, where are all joys. Praise to the Lord who awards those who accomplish good deeds according to His will, who purifies the obedient, and at last purifies the wicked in hell. All praise be to the Creator, Ahura-Mazda, the All-Wise, the Mighty, the Rich in Love."

Prayer, according to Zarathustra, is not the humbling of the soul before its Creator, not the aspirations of the spirit towards the Source of all Love and Mercy, not the desire of the creature to be at peace with GOD, but the renunciation of will,—a noble and worthy aim in itself, but not fulfilling the Christian idea of prayer. To do good and to shun evil is, no doubt, the motive of the Christian life; but prayer is something more and something higher, the sacrifice of an humble and a contrite heart.

> "Heaven is the magazine wherein GOD puts
> Both good and evil; prayer's the key that shuts
> And opens this great treasure; 'tis a key
> Whose wards are Faith, and Hope, and Charity.
> Wouldst thou prevent a judgment due to sin?
> Turn but the key and thou mayst lock it in.
> Or wouldst thou have a blessing fall upon thee!
> Open the door and it will shower on thee."[1]

But no such conception as this is discernible throughout the length and breadth of the Parsee Scriptures, which here, as elsewhere, and in relation to other matters, attain a lofty, but not the loftiest, level; rise above earth, but do not soar to Heaven. They seem instinct with echoes of the original revelation vouchsafed to man, but those echoes are faint and imperfect; whereas, in the Hebrew creed, the voices of GOD are repeated with a fulness and a power which leaves the heart nothing to desire. In this vast superiority we cannot fail to see a strong and striking proof of its authenticity. If it be found difficult to account for the moral excellence and æsthetic beauty of Zarathustrianism without tracing it back in some indirect way to a Divine origin; how shall we explain the sublimity and grandeur of the Hebrew Theism, unless we admit that it is all it pro-

[1] Quarles.

fesses to be,—is, in very truth, the expression of the will of the everliving GOD?

We have spoken of Zarathustra's religion as originally monotheistic; its purity, however, was not long preserved, and the cause of its corruption lay in itself. Zarathustra could not deny the existence of Evil, and to explain it was driven to concoct an extraordinary hypothesis. As in every electrified object there are two poles, a positive and a negative, so, according to the Prophet, in Ahura-Mazda, and in all rational beings, man included, are present a good and holy Will, and its shadow or negative,—a higher and a lower nature,—the Positive and the Negative Mind. How Zarathustra reconciled this idea with his conception of Ahura-Mazda, as Perfect Goodness, we are unable to comprehend. At all events, it contained the germs of the future Dualism of the Persian religion. The Negative Mind soon came to be separated from the good and holy Will, and was quickly personified as an independent evil being, a Power of Night and Darkness, Ahriman (Angro-Manyus,) equal in might to Ahura-Mazda, and disputing with him the possession of the world. Thus arose the myth of the constant struggle between the two powers, as between Day and Night; the servants of Ahura-Mazda being sent forth to encounter, resist, and overcome the slaves and works of Ahriman, thereby bringing about the end of all things, when Ahriman himself should be vanquished and reconciled.

In course of time the difficulties of this dual theory were detected by acute intellects, and at the Sassanian Revival an attempt was made to dispose of them by introducing the doctrine of Monotheism under a new form, that of a Great Primal Cause (Zervana Akarana), the Boundless Time or Uncreated Whole, such as we trace in the later Greek poetry, and apparently rather a "metaphysical abstraction." like the Greek 'Ανάγκη, or the Roman Nemesis, than "an active and presiding deity." Thence proceeded both the Good and the Evil Principles; the two antagonist creators who balanced against each other in perpetual conflict a race of spiritual and material beings, light and darkness, good and evil. The wise benevolence of Ahura-Mazda formed men capable of virtuous impulses, and endowed each with everything that could contribute to his happiness. He preserved by his watchful providence the harmonious movements of the planets, and the temperate combination of the elements. But the malice of Ahriman has long since pierced Ahura-Mazda's "egg;" in other words, violated the sweet accord and bounteous beauty of His works. Since that fatal irruption, the most minute articles of good and evil are alternately commingled and agitated together; the most poisonous herbs spring up among the most wholesome plants; the warfare of deluges, earthquakes, and conflagrations disturbs the serenity of nature; and humanity is subjected to all the blighting influences of sin, suffering, and sorrow. While the rest of mankind were led away captive in the chains of their terrible enemy, the faithful Persian alone remained constant in his faith in Ahura-Mazda, and fought under his banner of light, looking forward to a triumphant day when Good should prevail over all the world.

It seems to us impossible to doubt that, in this later development of the Zoroastrian faith, its priests and teachers were largely indebted to the Sacred Writings, though into what they borrowed they introduced much original and fanciful speculation.

A Parsee, with a firm faith in Ahura-Mazda, and conscious of having obeyed the law, offered up prayer and praise, and renounced, in intention at least, evil thoughts and deeds and words, lay down on his death bed in a certain hope and expectation of the Eternal life. We have seen that the Zendavesta appointed a variety of penances, by the performance of which the believer obtained immediate pardon for ordinary transgressions; and therefore, full of the self-righteousness which his creed was so well adapted to inculcate, he faced the passage of the Dark River without fear. He knew not of any need to implore the mercy of a Redeemer, to humble himself in sackcloth and ashes, to base his hope on the infinite love of GOD made man, on the glorious sacrifice of the Cross; his soul passed straight to Paradise, as an arrow flies towards its mark. In the Khordah Avesta we can follow the stages of its journey:—
On the first night after death the soul dwelt near the head of the inanimate body it had just deserted, and sat there praying, rejoicing in as much joy as is vouchsafed to the whole living world. And so did it dwell on the second night,

praying. And so did it dwell on the third night, praying. But when the third night verged upon dawn, the soul of the pure man went forward. A wind, sweeter than all other winds, blew to meet it from the south. And in that wind came to embrace the pilgrim *his own law*, under the figure of a maiden beautiful and shining, fair as the fairest of created beings. The pilgrim then took the first step in his celestial progress, and arrived in the paradise *Hamata;* he took the second, and reached the paradise *Hûkhta;* he took the third, and arrived at the paradise *Hvarsta.* The beatified wanderer made yet another step, and gained the presence of the Eternal Light. There was he addressed by an already beatified soul : " How art thou, O pure deceased, who hast come from the perishable world hither to the imperishable ?" Ahura-Mazda here interrupted : " Ask him not, for he has come on the fearful trembling way, the separation of soul and body. Bring him hither of the food of the full fatness, that is, of the filling food for those who think, speak, and do good, for the pure after death."

A recent writer says of this notion of a progressive advance to the " Eternal Light," of the welcome received from the blessed, and from the gentle words of Ahura-Mazda himself; and of the conducting angel who represents the man's own earthly faith and life, (like Bunyan's Mr. Good-Conscience meeting old Honest beside the River of Death,) " all these," he says, " are beautiful thoughts." Surely fanciful, rather than beautiful ; and better adapted to amuse religious sentimentalists than to satisfy healthy and earnest believers. The obvious reference to the three days and nights spent by our LORD " in prison" appears to indicate that this is a comparatively modern portion of the Zendavesta, founded upon some vague knowledge of the mystery of the Resurrection.

While the pure soul proceeded, as we have seen, by three stages or gradations to the Paradise of Light and Sweetness, the evil and unclean soul, on the other hand, descended, also by three stages, to the terrors of Douzakh, the dark abode of Ahriman and the Devs. There it suffered according to its sinfulness until the general day of Resurrection. At that great epoch these nights of indescribable woe will be undergone by all who have not expiated their earthly offences; woe so terrible, that the Blessed, looking down upon it from their celestial battlements, will be moved to tears of pity. And then the massive mountains and the solid rocks shall be melted by the heat, and streams of liquid gold shall flow, in which both the pure and evil shall receive a regenerating bath. Ahriman and his devs shall share in the universal happiness, and all created life shall swell the song of praise sent up in honour of Ahura-Mazda.

While we are unable to doubt that in the Zendavesta, as it has come down to us, may be traced the direct influence of the Hebrew creed, and that ideas and principles of a still later date were borrowed more or less closely from Christianity, we can as little doubt that Zarathustrianism had no inconsiderable effect on the Jewish popular belief. The Jewish prophets, after the Captivity, would seem to have adopted much of what may be called their poetic language and machinery from the writings of the Magian teachers. The Talmud contains unmistakable evidence of its indebtedness to the same source. The Angelology of the Jewish doctors originated, probably during the captivity of the Tribes in Babylonia, in the Magian superstitions; and it was then that the complete angelic hierarchy was evolved, with its seven great archangels corresponding to the seven Amchaspands of the Zendavesta. It was then that for the first time the Jewish popular creed recognised the existence of two antagonistic hosts of spiritual beings, arrayed against each other in everlasting battle. Then was developed the fancy of a guardian angel attending every individual to shelter him from the malignant hostility of his Dev or demon. So that much of the mythology which Milton employs so effectively in "Paradise Lost," having borrowed it from the traditions and legends of the Hebrew race, came originally from the far East, and was invented by the followers of Zarathustra. The Miltonic and popular conception of Satan, so unlike the Biblical representation of the great Destroyer, was largely coloured from the Magian sketch of Ahriman, the Power of Darkness.

It is certain that the grand and lofty Hebrew revelation of the One GOD was modified and debased by its contact with the Magian teaching. It has been well remarked that wherever any approximation had been made to this sublime truth of the existence of the one great First Cause, either "awful religious reverence" or "philosophic abstraction" had removed the Creative Power absolutely out of the range of human sense, and supposed that the intercourse of the Divinity with man, the moral government, and even the actual creative work, had been carried on by the intermediate agency of, in Oriental phrase, an Emanation, or, in Platonic language, of the "Wisdom," "Reason," or "Intelligence" of the Supreme. The Jews, under the influence of their intercourse with the Persians, adopted that conception, and, departing from the path laid down for them by Revelation, interposed one or more intermediate beings as the channels of communication between GOD and man. The Apostle seizes on the popular fancy, and endeavours to restore from it the original truth, when he tells his readers that the "Word" of which they spoke so vaguely and presumptuously was none other than GOD Himself,—the SON of GOD, but equal with the FATHER,—the brightness of His glory and the express image of His person. He showed them that the mediation between the lofty spiritual nature of GOD and the intellectual and moral being of Man was not to be accomplished through any independent agency, but by the revelation of GOD Himself in the person and presence of His beloved SON. That this, the essential and central truth of Christianity, was one which the unassisted human intellect could never have developed we know, from the fact that it is found in no creed of admittedly human origin, and that it is never clearly set forth even in any religious system which has borrowed from Christianity.

We can imagine the ability of man to shape out for himself an idea of some awful Power, some mighty First Cause, which created and ordered the universe, and controlled and shaped its destinies. Looking around upon creation, he might, perhaps, without any severe intellectual effort, attain to the thought of a Creator. This conception once realised, he might in due time come to believe that the Creator could be pleased or angered by the doings of His creatures ; and that the anger of One so powerful would be something to dread and avoid. But the idea of this grand and terrible

Creator sending from Heaven His own Son to take upon Himself humanity, and thereby save the creature from the just wrath it had provoked, and the dread retribution it had deserved,—an idea, so glorious and consoling, could never, we believe, have been grasped by the loftiest human intellect, unless aided by a revelation from above.

The exact relation of Zarathustrianism to Christianity it is somewhat difficult to define, because a cloud of doubt and uncertainty hangs over the compilation of the later portions of the Zendavesta. While the great antiquity of the Gâthas cannot be disputed, while there is clear evidence that they contain much of the original teaching of Zarathustra,—teaching nobler and more exalted than that of his followers,—it seems not less certain that the doctrines of the Resurrection and the Future Life were borrowed from the Hebrews. What then is left to justify a comparison with Christianity? The keynote of its scheme is intellectual pride; that of the Christian religion, spiritual abasement. The former urges on its disciples the necessity of good thoughts, words, and deeds in order to please Ahura-Mazda; the latter, as a proof of faith in the mission of its Founder. The former teaches an excellent code of morals, so far as relates to the individual; the latter lays down one golden rule, " Do unto others as thou wouldest they should do unto thee." The former enforces the law of self-control; the latter of self-renunciation. It is impossible to pretend that Magianism shows the same insight into man's wants, failings, passions, temptations, as Christianity shows; or provides a system so capable of adaptation to every age, and rank, and character.

We see no reason to doubt the authenticity and antiquity of the Zendavesta; but it is somewhat surprising that scholars who make haste to accept *it* as genuine, should show so much scepticism in reference to the Christian Scriptures. Surely, as regards the latter, the evidence of genuineness is infinitely stronger than as regards the former. We know that they were implicitly accepted by men who lived almost in the very time of those who recorded them; on the other hand, of Zarathustra and his contemporaries or successors we know absolutely nothing. Some authorities represent him to have flourished as early as 2200 B.C.; others as late as 500 B.C. Some consider him to have been the founder of a dynasty; others invest him with a supernatural personality. But at the best he remains *nominis umbra;* as indistinct and shadowy, as in his teaching he is cold and clear. Of the authenticity of his writings the principal proofs are those derivable from the writings themselves. But if we allow that such proofs are admissible, what shall we say of those to be found in the Gospels and Epistles? As their morality is so much more elevated than that of the Zendavesta, so is the certainty of their Divine origin infinitely more assured. The class of testimony which asserts the authenticity of the one not less convincingly affirms the genuineness of the other. And if the Gospels are all that they purport to be, how can we avoid the conclusion that they are truthful also in the witness they bear to the life and character of CHRIST?

We may point to a remarkable contrast between Magianism and Christianity,—that the former has undergone an almost complete revolution of meaning and doctrine, while, in spite of sectarian glosses, the latter remains virtually unaltered. The faith once for all delivered to the saints is held by believers to-day in all its original purity. We repeat the Creed just as it fell from the rapt lips of martyrs, saints and confessors. But the monotheism of Zarathustra has been broken up into a curious Dualism; and upon the religious system of the Gâthas has been accumulated such a burden of ritual, of novel teaching, of borrowed dogmas, and alien mysteries, that the acutest students are almost baffled in their endeavours to distinguish the false from the true, and the new from the old. It is almost impossible to determine what belongs to the Zarathustrian original, and what to perversions or adaptations from the Jewish Scriptures.

It is an indisputable testimony to the living force and divine genius of Christianity, that it occupies a void which no one of the primitive religions has ever been able to fill. We find it difficult to conceive that any man who has once been a Christian could voluntarily embrace Zarathustrianism or Buddhism, and attempt to satisfy his soul with it, any more than with the philosophy of the Stoics. We are tempted to ask, indeed, whether either could at any time have satisfied the cravings of humanity. We know that all their ethical schemes could not lift the sages of Greece and Rome out of the deep, the intense sadness which possessed them, nor respond to their yearnings after a something they could neither describe nor define. Their state of thought and feeling has been expressed by a modern poet, Matthew Arnold, with what seems to us a wonderful fidelity :—

> " Nor only in the intent
> To attach blame elsewhere,
> Do we at will invent
> Stern powers who make their care
> To embitter human life, malignant deities.
>
> " But next, we would reverse
> The scheme ourselves have spun,
> And what we made to curse
> We now would lean upon,
> And feign kind gods who perfect what man vainly tries. . . .
>
> " We pause, we hush our heart,
> And then address the gods :
> 'The world hath failed to impart
> The joy our youth forebodes,
> Failed to fill up the void which in our breasts we bear !'"

Their principles of thought were pure, but they felt that there existed a purity which was beyond their reach; their standard of conduct was high, but they were inwardly conscious that it ought to be higher. On that golden "ladder of sunbeams" which rises from earth to the angel-guarded battlements of heaven, they had ascended a few timid steps, but above and beyond they could see a glory to which it was not given them to rise. Hence it has often been said, and justly, that the men were greater than their system; and such, so far as Magianism was concerned, may well have been the case with the loftier minds of Bactria and Persia. But it can never be pretended that the Christian is greater than Christianity. Let him be ever so holy in his living, ever so exalted in his aspirations, he will not seek for something *beyond* and *out of* Christianity, because he feels and knows that he cannot exhaust all its capabilities; that it soars far higher than he can ever soar. It has truths which the profoundest psychologist cannot fathom; it opens up visions which the boldest imagination cannot comprehend; it contains a wealth of emotion and sympathy which the most passionate soul can never exhaust. After we have said and done all we can, after we have mastered all that has been said and done by other men, we still find in the life and character of CHRIST that which may well engage, and yet never weary our attention. And here we touch upon a feature which no human system of religion or morality has ever matched. Strip the Zendavesta, if you will, of all its later and less worthy adjuncts, and yet it cannot, any more than the Rig-Veda, present us with the divine beauty of the Man of Sorrows. But this it is which fills, soothes, blesses, inspires the aching, restless, craving human heart. When it can no longer satisfy itself with the cold moralities of philosophy, when it pines for a deeper and a warmer life, when it is weary with problems which it cannot solve, and disappointed in hopes which it has seen fade away like dreams of the night, it turns to the Cross and is comforted. The mysteries which perplexed it vanish in the light that emanates from the Divine history of the SON of GOD. The awe with which it regards the passionless abstraction of a great First Cause, a supreme entity of Power and Wisdom without Love, passes into reverent admiration and joyous thanksgiving when it looks up into the face of the Good Shepherd, and reposes in the shadow of the Vine, and learns how that He Who was with the FATHER before the beginning, has suffered even as we suffer, has borne the heavy burden of the flesh even as we have borne it, and now sits on the right hand of GOD,—not an idea, not a principle, not a Spirit, but a PERSON, bidding all who believe to come unto Him and be at rest.

This, indeed, is the cardinal merit of Christianity,—it has given us CHRIST.

GOD forbid that we should deny a certain value even to the "unconscious prophecies of heathendom," or refuse to see something of the spirit of CHRIST in the teaching of the ancient sages and philosophers; but when an attempt is made to raise Magianism to an equal rank with Christianity, and the cold intellectual utterances of the Zendavesta to rank with the living voices of Holy Writ, it is essential to point out how vast, how impassable is the gulf between them; how little Magianism did or could do to elevate man's spiritual nature; and how largely Christianity surpasses it, in and through the manifestation of the Divine love in the mystery of GOD made Man.

CHAPTER III.

JEWISH SUPERSTITIONS.

THE TALMUD.

THE Talmud, (from the Hebrew *lamad*, to learn,) is the name given to the great code of the Jewish civil and canonical law. It is divided, like the Zendavesta, into two parts, the Mishna and the Gemara; the former being, as it were, the text, and the latter the commentary and supplement. Of late years public attention has been exceptionally drawn to it by the writings of the late Emanuel Deutsch, and it has obtained, as we think, a wholly undeserved amount of panegyric.

Deutsch, an enthusiast in his attachment to the land and religion of his forefathers, put it forward as a wondrous treasure, the real value of which had been wholly overlooked. It contained, he seemed to say, a complete *corpus juris;* and, as an encyclopædia of law, should be compared with the corresponding collections of Roman or of English law, with the Pandects of Justinian and the Commentaries of Blackstone. Herein lies the excuse for rules that have been considered unduly subtle, or in other ways offensive to modern taste. But it contains something more than a body of law; it is also a collection of Jewish poetry and legend, of Jewish science, and Jewish metaphysical speculation. The Mishna is a development of the laws contained in the Pentateuch. The members of the Sanhedrim, who were chiefly concerned in the formation of this law, were obliged (so argues Deutsch) to be accomplished men. It was necessary that they should possess some knowledge of physical science, or at least of zoology, botany, and geography in their then condition. It was necessary also that they should be good linguists, having some acquaintance with Latin and Greek, as well as with Aramaic, Syriac, and Hebrew. Disreputable men were kept out, and all were compelled to be married men and fathers of families. "The origin of the Talmud," he says, "is coeval with the return from the Babylonish captivity." And though it is the glory of Christianity to have carried into the heart of humanity at large the golden germs of thought previously hidden in the schools of the learned, yet numerous precepts, supposed to be purely Christian, lie enshrined in the pages of the Talmud. It would be difficult to find a penal legislation more distinctly humane. As for its myths, its allegories, its apparent absurdities, they should be read in the spirit in which Christians read Bunyan's "Pilgrim's Progress." The Talmud insists upon the pre-existence of the soul, on the dogmas of Immortality and the Resurrection, it denies the doctrine of everlasting damnation; it excludes no human being from the world to come. And as the Talmud, continues Deutsch, although redacted at a later period, is, in point of time, prior to the New Testament, the beautiful maxims of the former cannot have been borrowed from the latter. In a word, it is a collection which took nearly a thousand years to form, and has been commented upon for a thousand years since. It breathes charity to all men. If we except a few items of coarseness, such as must occur in every legal code, it is all good; at least, it is never bad; it deserves all possible respect and even reverence. Such, in a condensed form, is the account of the Talmud which Deutsch asks us to accept.

But it cannot be admitted that the defects of the Talmud are trivial, any more than that the spirit of the Rabbins towards Christianity was tolerant. Nor can it be admitted that the Talmud owes nothing to the Christian Scriptures.

On the first point hear what Professor Hurwitz says:— "The Talmud contains many things which every enlightened, nay, every pious Jew, must sincerely wish had never appeared there, or should at least long ago have been expunged from its pages. Some of these Agadatha are objectionable *per se;* others, indeed, are susceptible of explanations, but without them are calculated to produce false and erroneous impressions." So much may be said, we think, of the legends in the Talmud ; such as the size of Leviathan and the way in which he is to be killed and cooked for the chosen people, and the marriage of Adam with Lilith before the creation of Eve, with the diabolic progeny which sprang from them.

Another point to be considered is the influence of the Alexandrian books, commonly known by us as the Apocrypha. Of these the Books of Wisdom and Ecclesiasticus at any rate exhibit the reflections of singularly devout and thoughtful minds, which had exercised themselves in the contemplation of the writings of Moses and the prophets in combination with no inconsiderable tincture of Greek philosophy. It would be a question of great interest to see how far ideas suggested in those very remarkable compositions have found their way into the Talmud.

As regards the sentiments of the Rabbins towards Christianity : in the reign of Domitian, (that is, about A.D. 90,) the Sanhedrim took measures against the Minim, that is to say, the degenerated; for so they called the Jews who had been converted to Christianity. The Rabbi Tarphon said : —" The Gospels and all the books of the Minim deserve to be burnt, for Paganism is less dangerous : the Pagans misunderstand the truths of Judaism from ignorance, the Minim deny them with full knowledge of the case. Better to seek an asylum in a Pagan temple than in the synagogues of the Minim." The Sanhedrim of Jamnia and other similar bodies adopted the like tone. And it was men like these who helped to form the Talmud.

Not the less it remains true, that every powerful movement which has occurred in the world's history has shown a part of its power in the way it has influenced opponents. The Reformation, as the Ultramontane De Maistre is compelled to admit, wrought a very perceptible change even among Roman Catholics. The French Revolution of 1793 did not leave Legitimists in the position they had occupied before its outbreak. Now Christianity is the greatest movement the world has ever seen. Dean Merivale in his excellent " History of the Romans under the Empire," states with no less eloquence than truth the immense indirect influence which it had begun to exercise on heathen thought by the end even of the first century. We can trace it in Pagan literature. But Deutsch and similar Talmudophilists would have us believe that it had no influence whatever upon the Talmud, and that whenever we find kindred thoughts in the teaching of Christianity, and in the teaching of their favourite work, it is the Gospel which is indebted to the Talmud and not the Talmud to the Gospel.

But for our part we wholly dissent from this extraordinary theory, which, indeed, cannot be supported by any chronological evidence. There are occasions, of course, in which dates become of comparatively trifling importance. A man feels troubled, for example, with the enigmas of life, and finds light and consolation in reading the book of Job ; that most beautiful book—*quel bellissimo libro*, as the Italian poet Giusti called it. Some friend, finding him thus engaged, begins to argue in favour of Bishop Warburton's view, that it is a composition of comparatively late date, perhaps of the age of Jeremiah, and not (as used to be generally supposed) as early as the time of Moses. In such a case a man may well reply, that without any wish to discourage critical inquiry in its proper place, he is content for the present to go on reading for his soul's health, to accept the words before him as a message from above, and to feel sure that whenever GOD gave it, it was given at the time when it was most needed. But in the case of the Talmud dates are of real and living importance, though we own that it is difficult to fix them with accuracy. We believe, however, with one of Deutsch's critics, that Christian elements *have* found their way into the Talmud, though doubtless, pre-Christian ideas, similar to those which are met with in the Books of Wisdom and Ecclesiasticus, are also to be found there. Is it not true that the Mishna was brought into its present form by Rabbi Jehudah, surnamed the Holy, about A.D. 200, and that the Gemara was not completed until A.D. 500? Deutsch, indeed, appeals to the article in the "Novellæ Constitutiones" (or *Novels*, as they are commonly called) of Justinian against the Talmud. The reference is correct enough, but the *Novels* belong to the later parts of Justinian's reign, and were not promulgated before the year 534.

It is well known that at the present time there are three

parties among the Jews who differ widely as to the amount of respect which ought to be paid to the legislation contained within the pages of the Talmud. Two out of these parties would greatly modify it, or actually sweep it away. We believe that its influence upon practice is not destined to endure; and that though there *is* a book which will continue so to influence life, that book is not the Talmud, but the Bible. The Talmud has its curiosities and even beauties, as well as its gross absurdities and defects; but, after all, it will be found, we believe, that it often reflects but too truly the mind of those of whom it was said, "Ye have made the commandment of GOD of none effect by your traditions."

With these preliminary observations, we pass on to a more particular description of the Talmud.

There are two Talmuds, the one called the Talmud of the Occidentals, or the "Jerusalem" Talmud, and the other the "Babylonian" Talmud. The former of these originally included the whole of the first five *Sedarim* (or portions,) but now consists of only thirty-nine treatises. Its final redaction is supposed to have taken place towards the close of the fourth Christian century, but the authorities engaged in the work cannot now be determined. But it is certainly distinguished by more accuracy of expression and precision of statement than the second or Babylonian, or "our" Talmud, which makes use of its predecessor, and was not completed for a century later. Its editor is generally considered to be Rabbi Ashi, president of the Academy of Syro in Babylon (A.D. 365—427.) Both the Mishna, though revised in A.D. 219, and the "Palestine" Gemara, had become greatly corrupted through the interpolation of gross traditions and the critical judgments of different schools, when Rabbi Ashi, with the assistance of his friend and disciple, Abina, undertook the labour of sifting the old from the new, and introducing order into chaos.

Ashi was appointed to the headship of the school of Sora at the age of twenty-three, and under his rule Sora became the head-quarters of Rabbinism in the East. When he entered on the redaction of the Mishna and Gemara, he began by assembling yearly at the great feasts the most learned Hebrews, and examining them with respect to their traditional practices and expositions. He then called together his disciples every spring, and gave out to them a particular treatise of the Mishna; in the autumn they again came before him with all the information relative to it they had collected in the interval. This he personally investigated, and reduced into shape. The Mishna being composed of sixty-three treatises, he was thus engaged for upwards of thirty years. The final revision occupied him twenty-two years. At the time of his death (in his seventy-fifth year) the work was all but completed; the last touches were given by his friend, Rabbi Abina.

The Mosaic is the written law of the Jews; the Mishna, the oral. The latter is the very basis of Judaism, is its civil, religious, and juridico-political code,—an explanation and amplification of the Mosaic. It was developed out of the authoritative decisions of the schools and of certain distinct and well-authenticated traditions which were traced back to Sinai itself. Thus there were two chief sections, or parts: *Halacoth*, the rabbinical decisions, and *Haggadah*, the traditional narratives and popular illustrations. Of the great bulk of the former the reputed author is Hillel, the head of the Sanhedrim in the early part of Herod the Great's reign, but, probably, he only collected them. Maimonides arranges them under five heads:—

a. Mosaic and Scriptural;
b. Mosaic and traditional;
c. Dicta and decisions generally received, but doubtful;
d. Decisions of the wise, given by them as "hedges of the law;" and
e. Counsels of prudence, which it was well to follow, though they had no legal authority.

The Haggadic narratives are generally of a light and amusing character, though occasionally a deep significance underlies them, converting them into allegories and fables and parables well worthy the attention of the student, though he may not think so highly of them as Frankel, who exclaims: "They are as vivid flashes: or as those spirits of light in Jewish myth, that flow forth in daily myriads from GOD's throne, and then vanish to make way for others."

The Halacoth and Haggadoth accumulated rapidly after

the Captivity, representing in due time "a body of traditional exposition of high authority, which increased rapidly, and required the life-long study of a numerous body of Sopherim, or Scribes, to digest and hand on without loss to succeeding generations." Soon it outgrew the grasp of even the strongest memory and the profoundest application, and it became evident that, unless put upon record, all that was valuable would perish, and only that be preserved which chanced to be in accordance with popular sentiment. To the digest made by Hillel, Simon ben Gamaliel added the worthiest of the later material; and his son, Jehudah the Holy, entered on a complete redaction and revision, which he published in A.D. 219. Hillel, grandfather of the Gamaliel at whose feet S. Paul sat, had arranged the traditional Halacoth under eighteen heads; Jehudah re-arranged them into six Sedarim, or sections :—

1. *Zeraïm* (Seeds,) on Agriculture;
2. *Moed* (Feast,) on the Sabbath, Festivals, and Fasts;
3. *Nashim* (Women,) on Marriage, Divorce, &c., including the laws on Vows and the Nazirship;
4. *Nizikin* (Damages,) chiefly civil and penal law, including the ethical treatise Aboth;
5. *Kadashim* (Sacred things,) Sacrifices, &c., a description of the Temple at Jerusalem, &c.;
6. *Tehoroth* (Purifications,) on pure and impure persons and things.

We now see that, about A.D. 221 Jehudah the Holy created the Mishna, we have already seen that three centuries later, the same exhaustive work of redaction and revision was done for the Gemara,—the two forming what is now known as the Talmud. The two "editors" received each his peculiar title of honour; Jehudah was styled Rabbina, Ashi Rabban.

Of the language of the Babylon Talmud it is said that it is debased with foreign and barbarous terms and grammatical solecisms to a much greater extent than the "Jerusalem Talmud." Mr. Blunt asserts that "the Haggadic narratives resemble more closely the vernacular Aramaic, showing their origin in ordinary folk lore. The Halacoth are in Mishnic Hebrew, carrying evidence of higher date. The style is so exceedingly concise as to make the sense that it contains a microscopic study. The difficulties indeed of the Gemara are so great, that no one need think to master them thoroughly who has not drawn in Gemara with his mother's milk. The study of the Talmud presumes a thorough knowledge also of the Hebrew Bible, a single word often indicating an entire passage. The wonderful moral confusion of the Talmud, the mixed character of which may be detected in every page, is nowhere more strikingly exemplified than in the prayer put by the Gemarist into the mouth of Rabbi Nechoniah ben Hakakana, on entering the school, or Beth Midrash, and quitting it again in the evening."

The morning prayer was as follows:—

"I beseech Thee that no scandal may occur through fault of mine, and that I err not in matters of Halacah, so as to cause my colleagues to exult. May I not call impurity pure, or purity impure; and may my colleagues not blunder in matters of Halacah, that I may have no cause to triumph over them."

The spirit of this prayer, in its meekness and modesty, is truly commendable, and presents a striking contrast to that of the evening prayer:—

"I thank Thee that Thou hast given me my portion among those who have a seat in the Beth Midrash, and that Thou hast not cast my lot among those who sit in the corner. I early rise, and they early rise; but I rise to the service of the law, they to vanity. I labour, and they also labour, but I labour and receive a recompense; they labour, but receive nothing. I hasten, and they also hasten; but I hasten in the direction of the world to come, they hasten towards the pit of destruction."

It is impossible to believe that both these prayers come from the same source; "sweet waters and bitter" do not alike flow from the fountain of Marah.

With respect to the general character of the Talmud, with all its weakness and strength, its beauty and deformity, its poetry and commonplace, its tender wisdom and glaring absurdity, we cannot do better than quote the moderate opinion of the writer already cited, as infinitely more trustworthy than the dithyrambic utterances of Deutsch and his imitators. He says:—

"In its origin it was the result of an almost necessary development. Starting with the axiom that the law of Moses is binding on the children of Abraham in every generation, its precepts have been applied to the changing habits and customs of the Jews in different ages and under various climates, by a literal interpretation when possible, otherwise on the *ci-près* principle, rarely by giving a new direction to its enactments, as instanced under the Hillel *régime*. It is this application of the Law to the needs of Jewish Society, by a process slow and gradual, that has made each successive stage of development, in Jewish opinion, more valuable than its predecessors. Thus if the Law has been likened to water, the Mishna, which gives a later direction to its precepts, is as wine; and the Gemara, declaring as it does the sense in which the Mishnic Hilkoth are to be taken, is as hippocras. It is not that the Law is less, or that the traditional decisions and expository matter are more sacred, but the latest phase of judicial interpretation is the most binding; and where the rule of action is clear and decisive, no antecedent utterance need trouble the inquirer. Yet the Talmud has always been antiquated. It has never known the sunshine of youth. It has still been the mouldering, moss-grown ruin. In its origin it presupposed vital action where there was nothing but death; Temple service with the Temple hopelessly in ruins, 'not one stone upon another;' sacrificial rites that were impossible without an altar, and for which certain prayers were substituted, carefully numbered out, and made binding on the individual in lieu of public offering. . . . Nothing can be more completely out of place than strict Talmudism amid the complications of modern society; it is impossible to make its precepts consist with the social and political duties of the highly educated Jew. Our LORD, Who came not to destroy the Law, but to fulfil it, has pointed out those modes of dealing with the Law in its higher and more spiritual bearings, that in the end must be accepted by Israel as his truest wisdom."

Mr. Deutsch gives the following account of the six sections of the Mishna :—

"Section I. *Seeds:* of Agrarian laws, commencing with a chapter on Prayers. In this section the various tithes and donations due to the Priests, the Levites, and the poor, from the products of the lands, and further the Sabbatical year, and the prohibited mixtures in plants, animals, and garments, are treated of.

"Section II. *Feasts:* of Sabbaths, Feast and Fast days, the work prohibited, the ceremonies ordained, the sacrifices to be offered, on them. Special chapters are devoted to the Feast of the Exodus from Egypt, to the New Year's Day, to the Day of Atonement (one of the most impressive portions of the whole book,) to the Feast of Tabernacles, and to that of Haman.

"Section III. *Women:* of betrothal, marriage, divorce, &c.; also of vows.

"Section IV. *Damages:* including a great part of the civil and criminal law. It treats of a law of trades, of buying and selling, and the ordinary monetary transactions. Further, of the greatest crime known to the law, viz., idolatry. Next of witnesses, of oaths, of legal punishments, and of the Sanhedrim itself. This section concludes with the so-called 'Sentences of the Fathers,' containing some of the sublimest ethical dicta known in the history of religious philosophy.

"Section V. *Sacred Things:* of sacrifices, the first-born, &c. ; also of the measurements of the Temple (Middoth).

"Section VI. *Purifications:* of the various Levitical and other Hygienic laws, of impure things and persons, their purification, &c."[1]

In defence of the Haggadah, with all its incongruities, puerilities, and absurdities, it is only just to hear what Deutsch, its enthusiastic apostle, has to say. And first he applies to it the rhyming apology which Bunyan put forward on behalf of his great allegory,—which, by the way, Mr. Deutsch surely misrepresents and misunderstands when he speaks of it as Haggadistic :—

> ". . . Wouldst thou divert thyself from melancholy?
> Wouldst thou be pleasant, yet be far from folly?
> Wouldst thou read riddles and their explanation?
> Or else be drowned in thy contemplation?
> Dost thou love picking meat? Or wouldst thou see
> A man in the clouds, and hear him speak to thee?

[1] Emanuel Deutsch, " Literary Remains," (edit. 1874, pp. 32, 33.)

> Wouldst thou be in a dream, and yet not sleep?
> Or wouldst thou in a moment laugh and weep?
> Wouldst lose thyself, and catch no harm?
> And find thyself again without a charm?
> Wouldst read thyself, and read thou know'st not what
> And yet know whether thou art blest or not
> By reading the same lines? O then come hither,
> And lay this book, thy head and heart together."

Mr. Deutsch thus seeks to disarm antagonists by a skilful concession. He does not wonder—not he—that the so-called "Rabbinical stories," submitted at intervals to the English public, should have met with an unflattering reception. The Talmud, which has always at hand a drastic word, says of their collectors :—" They dived into an ocean, and brought up a potsherd." But then, he says, these follies form only a small item in the vast mass of allegories, parables, and the like, that compose the Haggadah. And, besides, they are partly ill-chosen, partly ill-translated, and partly did not even belong to the Talmud, but to some recent Jewish story books. Herder—to name the most famous critic of the "Poetry of Peoples"—has spoken most eulogistically of what he saw of the genuine specimens. And, indeed, "not only is the entire world of pious biblical legend which Islam has said and sung in its many tongues to the delight of the wise and simple for twelve centuries, now to be found either in embryo or fully developed in the Haggadah, but much that is familiar among ourselves in the circles of mediæval sagas, in Dante, in Boccaccio, in Cervantes, in Milton, in Bunyan, has consciously or unconsciously flowed out of this wondrous realm, the Haggadah. That much of it is overstrained, even according to Eastern notions, we do not deny. But," argues Mr. Deutsch, "there are feeble passages even in Homer and Shakespeare." To this it may be replied, that in Homer and Shakespeare such passages are rare, and do not form the bulk of their writings; and, moreover, that for the Iliad or for Hamlet we do not claim the position of authority which is claimed for the Talmud.

Let us glance briefly at the cosmogony of the Talmud. It assumes that the universe has been developed by means of a series of cataclysms; that world was destroyed after world, until GOD made "this world, and saw that it was very good." It assumes also that the kosmos was wrought out of some original substance, itself created by GOD. "One or three things were before this world,—Water, Fire, and Wind; Water begat the darkness, Fire begat light, and Wind begat the spirit of Wisdom."

"The *how* of the creation was not mere matter of speculation. The co-operation of angels, whose existence was warranted by Scripture, and a whole hierarchy of whom had been built up under Persian influences, was distinctly denied. In a discussion about the day of their creation, it is agreed on all hands that there were no angels at first, lest men might say, 'Michael spanned out the firmament on the south, and Gabriel to the north.'" There is a distinct foreshadowing of the Gnostic Demiurgos—that antique link between the Divine Spirit and the world of matter—to be found in the Talmud. What with Plato were the Ideas, with Philo the Logos, with the Kabbalists the "World of Aziluth," what the Gnostics called more emphatically the wisdom (σοφία), or power (δύναμις), and Plotinus the νοῦς, that the Talmudical authors call Metation. There is a good deal, in the post-captivity Talmud, about the Angels, borrowed from the Persian. The Archangels or Angelic princes are seven in number, and their Hebrew names and functions correspond almost exactly to those of their Persian prototypes. There are also hosts of ministering angels, the Persian *Yazatas*, whose functions, besides that of being messengers, were twofold,—to praise GOD, and to be guardians of man. In their first capacity they are daily created by GOD'S breath out of a stream of fire that rolls its waves under the supernal throne. In their second, two of them accompany every man, and for every new good deed man acquires a new guardian angel, who always watches over his steps. When a righteous man dies, three hosts of angels descend from the celestial battlements to meet him. One says, (in the words of Scripture,) " He shall go in peace ;" the second takes up the strain and says, "Who has walked in righteousness ;" and the third concludes, "Let him come in peace and rest upon his bed." In like manner, when the wicked man passes away, three hosts of wicked angels are ready to escort him, but their address is not couched in any spirit of consolation or encouragement.

There are various indications in the Talmud of a belief in the resurrection and immortality of the soul. The resurrection, it teaches, is to be brought about by the mystic influence of the "Dew of life" in Jerusalem. It does not uphold the dogma of everlasting damnation, though it allows that the punishment of apostates, idolaters, and traitors will endure for "generations upon generations."

In conclusion, it is but fair that we should present the brighter and better aspect of this extraordinary book, its ethical side, and afford some illustrations of the moral and religious philosophy which pervades it,—which is its salt, and preserves its savour. The following sayings have been translated by Deutsch.[1] Many of them bear a striking resemblance to the great and glorious sayings of the Gospels; and to us it seems impossible to doubt that they evidence the influence of the former. It is true that the Talmud as a whole preceded the New Testament, but as its redaction took place at a much later period, we see nothing absurd in the hypothesis that its redactors had felt the spell of the Christian teaching, and occasionally introduced some of its rare and precious threads of purest silk into the coarse woof woven by traditionalists, scholiasts, and commentators :—

The house that does not open to the poor shall open to the physician; even the birds in the air despise the miser. He who gives charity in secret is greater than Moses himself. Honour the sons of the poor, it is they who bring science into splendour.

Let the honour of thy neighbour be to thee like thine own. Rather be thrown into a fiery furnace than bring any one to public shame.

Hospitality is the most important part of divine worship. There are three crowns : of the law, the priesthood, the kingship; but the crown of a good name is greater than they all.

Iron breaks the stone, fire melts iron, water extinguishes fire, the clouds drink up the water, a storm drives away the clouds, man withstands the storm, fear unmans man, wine dispels fear, sleep drives away wine, and death sweeps

[1] E. Deutsch, Literary Remains, p. 55, sqq.

all away—even sleep. But Solomon the Wise says, Charity saves from death.

The dog sticks to you on account of the crumbs in your pocket.

The camel wanted to have horns, and they took away his ears.

The soldiers fight, and the kings are the heroes.

He in whose family there has been one hanged should not say to his neighbour, Pray hang this little fish up for me.

The cock and the owl both await the daylight. The light, says the cock, brings delight to me; but what are *you* waiting for?

When the thief has no opportunity for stealing, he considers himself an honest man.

If thy friends agree in calling thee an ass, go and get a halter round thee.

Fools are no proof.

One eats, another says grace.

He who is ashamed will not easily commit sin. There is a great difference between him who is ashamed before his own self, and him who is only ashamed before others. It is a good sign in man to be capable of being ashamed. One contrition in man's heart is better than many flagellations.

How can you escape sin? Think of three things,—whence thou camest, whither thou goest, and to whom thou wilt have to account for all thy deeds,—even to the King of kings, the All-holy, praised be He.

Love your wife like yourself, honour her more than yourself. Whosoever lives unmarried lives without joy, without comfort, without blessing. Descend a step in choosing a wife. If thy wife is small, bend down to her and whisper into her ear. He who forsakes the love of his youth, GOD'S altar weeps for him. He who sees his wife die before him, has, as it were, been present at the destruction of the sanctuary itself, around him the world grows dark. It is woman alone through whom GOD'S blessings are vouchsafed to a house. She teaches the children, speeds the husband to the place of worship and instruction, welcomes him when he returns, keeps the house godly and pure, and GOD's blessings rest upon all these things. He who marries for money, his children shall be a curse to him.

After the thief runs the theft; after the beggar, poverty.

While thy foot is shod, smash the thorn.

When the ox is down, many are the butchers.

Luck makes rich, luck makes wise.

If you wish to hang yourself, choose a big tree.

When the pitcher falls upon the stone, woe unto the pitcher; when the stone falls upon the pitcher, woe unto the pitcher; whatever befalls, woe unto the pitcher.

Youth is a garland of roses, age a crown of thorns.

Be thou the cursed, not he who curses. Be of them that are persecuted, not of them that persecute. Look at Scripture, there is not a single bird more persecuted than the dove, yet GOD has chosen her to be offered up on His altar. The bull is hunted by the lion, the sheep by the wolf, the goat by the tiger. And GOD said, "Bring Me a sacrifice not from them that persecute, but from them that are persecuted."

"Hath GOD pleasure in the meat and blood of sacrifices?" asks the prophet. No; He has not so much ordained as permitted them. It is for yourselves, He says, not for Me that you offer, Like a king, who sees his son carousing daily with all manner of evil companions: You shall henceforth eat and drink entirely at your will at my own table, he says. They offered sacrifices to demons and devils, for they loved sacrificing, and would not do without it. And the LORD said, "Bring your offerings to Me, you shall then at least offer to the true GOD."

Even when the gates of heaven are shut to prayer, they are open to tears.

The reward of good works is like dates, sweet and late to ripen.

Life is a passing shadow, says the Scripture. Is it the shadow of a tower, of a tree? A shadow that prevails for a while? No, it is the shadow of a bird in his flight,—away speeds the bird, and there is neither bird nor shadow.

Repent one day before thy death. There was a king who bade all his servants to a great repast, but did not indicate the hour; some went home and put on their best garments, and stood at the door of the palace; others said, There is ample time, the king will let us know beforehand. But the king summoned them of a sudden; and those that came in their best garments were well received, but the foolish ones, who came in their slovenliness, were turned away in disgrace. Repent to-day, lest to-morrow you might be called.

He who has more learning than good works is like a tree with many branches but few roots, which the first wind throws on its face; whilst he whose works are greater than his knowledge, is like a tree with many roots but fewer branches, but which all the winds of heaven cannot uproot.

CHAPTER IV.

BRAHMANISM.

THE BRAHMANS.

IN the "Book of Sir Marco Polo" occurs a quaint description of the *Abraiaman* or Brahmans, which, though inaccurate in some of its details, seems worth quotation here :—

You must know, he says, that these Abraiaman are the best merchants in the world [an obvious misconception!] and the most truthful, for they would not tell a lie for anything on earth. If a foreign merchant who does not know the ways of the country apply to them, and place his goods in their hands, they will take charge of them most loyally, selling them to the best advantage, seeking jealously the profit of the foreigner, and asking no commission except what he pleases to bestow. They eat no flesh, drink no wine, and live a life of great chastity; nor would they on any account take what belongs to another, for so their law commands. And they are all distinguished by wearing a thread of cotton over one shoulder and tied under the other arm, so that it crosses the breast and the back.

They have a rich and powerful king, who is eager to purchase precious stones and large pearls; and he sends these Abraiaman merchants into the kingdom of Maabar called Soli, which is the best and noblest Province of India, and where the best pearls are found, to fetch him as many of these as they can get, and he pays them double the cost price for all. So in this way he has a vast treasure of such valuables.

These Abraiaman are idolaters; and they give greater

heed to signs and omens than any people that exist. I will mention one of their customs as an example. To every day of the week they assign a special augury. Suppose some purchase is on foot; he who proposes to become the buyer takes note, when he rises in the morning, of his shadow in the sun, which ought, he says, on that day to be of such and such a length; and should his shadow be of the proper length for that day he completes his purchase; if it be not, he will on no account do so, but waits till his shadow reaches the prescribed measurement. For there is a certain length fixed for every day in the week; and the merchant will not complete any business unless he finds his shadow of the length set down for that particular day. Also to each day in the week they assign one hour as unlucky, which they term *Choiach*. For example, on Monday the hour of Half-tierce (7 to 8 a.m.), on Tuesday that of Tierce, (9 to 10 a.m.), on Wednesday Nones (12 to 1 p.m.), and so on.

Again, if one of them be in the house, and, while meditating a purchase, should see a tarantula (such as is very common in that country) on the wall, provided that it advance from a quarter which he deems lucky, he will complete his purchase at once; but if it come from a quarter which he considers unlucky, he will not do so on any inducement. Moreover, if, on going forth, he hear any one sneeze, he will proceed if he consider it a good omen; but, if the reverse, he will straightway sit down in his place for as long as he thinks it well to tarry. Or if, in travelling along the road, he see a swallow fly past, should its direction be lucky he will proceed, but, if not, he will turn back again : in fact, they are worse, in these vagaries, than so many Patarins ! (i.e. heretics.)

These Abraiaman are very long-lived, owing to their extreme abstinence in eating. And they never allow themselves to let blood in any part of the body. They have capital teeth, which is due to a certain herb they chew; it greatly improves their appearance, and is also very good for the health.

There is another class of people called *Chugi* [Jogi], who are indeed properly Abraiaman, but they form a religious order devoted to the Idols. They are extremely long-lived, every man of them living to 150 or 200 years. They eat very little, but what they do eat is good; rice and milk chiefly. And these people make use of a very strange beverage; for they brew a potion of mixed sulphur and quicksilver, and drink it twice every month. This, they say, gives them long life; and they are used to take it from their childhood.

Certain members of this Order lead the most ascetic life imaginable, going completely naked; they worship the Ox. Most of them wear a small image of an ox, in brass, pewter, or gold, tied over the forehead. Moreover, they take cow-dung, and burn it, and make a powder of it; and then they make it into an ointment, with which they daub themselves as devoutly as Christians use holy water. Further, if they meet any person who treats them well, they daub a little of this powder on the middle of his forehead.

They do not eat from bowls or trenchers, but place their food on leaves of the Apple of Paradise and other large leaves; these, however, they use dry, never green. For they say the green leaves have a soul in them, and so it would be a sin. And they would rather die than do what their Law pronounces to be sin. If any one ask how it comes that they are not ashamed to go about in their nudity, they say :—" We go naked because naked we came into the world, and we desire to have nothing about us that is of this world. Moreover, we have no sin of the flesh to be conscious of, and therefore we are not ashamed of our nakedness, any more than you are to show your hand or your face. You who are conscious of the sins of the flesh do well to be ashamed, and to cover your nakedness."

On no account would they kill an animal, not even a fly, or a flea, or a louse, or anything in fact that has life; for they say all these have souls, and it would be sinful to do so. They eat no vegetables in a green state, only when they are dry. And they sleep on the ground, naked, without a rag of clothing over them or under them; so that it is a marvel they do not all die, instead of living so long as I have told you. They fast every day in the year, and drink nothing but water. And when a novice has to be received among them they keep him awhile in their convent, and make him follow their rule of life.

They are such cruel and perfidious idolaters that it is very devilry ! They say that they burn the bodies of the dead, because if they were not burnt, worms would generate and consume them ; and when no more food remained for them, they would die, and the souls belonging to those bodies would bear the sin and the punishment of their death.

In another part of his immortal work, Marco Polo speaks of the fish-charmers of Ceylon as Brahmans (or *Abraiaman.*) The pearl-fishers, he says, pay one twentieth part of all that they take to these men, who charm the great fishes, and prevent them from injuring the divers whilst engaged in seeking pearls under water. Their charm holds good only for the day; at night they dissolve it, so that the fishes can work mischief at their will. These Abraiaman, he adds, know also how to charm beasts and birds and every living thing.

Commenting on this statement, Colonel Yule observes that the modern snake-charmers do not seem entitled to the distinctive appellation of Abraiaman, or Brahmans, though they may have been so in former days. At the diamond-mines of the Northern Circars Brahmans are employed in the similar task of propitiating the tutelary genii. The snake-charmers are called in Tamul *Kadal-kalti*, "Sea-binders," and in Hindustani, *Haibanda*, or "Shark-binders." At Aripo they belong to one family, supposed to enjoy monopoly of the charm. The chief operator is (or was, not many years ago) paid by Government, and he also received two oysters from each boat daily during the fishery. Turnoub, on his visit, found the incumbent of the office to be a Roman Catholic Christian, but that did not seem to affect the exercise or the validity of his practices. It is remarkable that when Turnoub wrote, not more than one authenticated accident from sharks had taken place, during the whole period of the British occupation.

Among the shepherds, or hillmen, in the neighbourhood of Rampore (or "City of Rama,")—the Paharis, as they are called,—a curious custom lingers, which resembles the strange old Highland ceremony of the sunwise turn, or Deisul, round any particular object, partly for luck, partly as a survival of the sun-worship of the men of old. Sometimes the villagers gather their flocks into one great herd, and, walking at the head, lead them slowly round the village, following the solar course. Gradually they quicken their pace to a run, and in this fashion perambulate the village thrice or even oftener.

This sunwise turn is practised in other cases, as in sickness or accident. Sheep and goats are solemnly paraded round the sufferer; after which they lose their heads. If the sufferer be wealthy, the number so sacrificed to the demons is often considerable. But the Paharis very firmly hold that though the lesser spirits may be thus propitiated, no sacrifice is acceptable to the Supreme Deity; that all He claims is devout worship.

They believe in the existence of three and thirty millions of good and evil spirits, but their special adoration seems to be reserved for the spirit which watches over their particular village, and in their temples they reserve for him a kind of ark or shrine, wherein his veiled image is carefully preserved. Every day this ark is slung upon long poles, and taken out for an airing; and once a year it is borne through the country side in solemn procession, and the people assemble and dance before it, as the Israelites of old danced before the tabernacle. The said ark is gaily decorated with bright-coloured hangings, and upon it is set a brazen head, with four or more faces, overshadowed by yaks' tails, like huge plumes of dark or scarlet wool. Sometimes the whole structure is adorned with faces of polished metal, which gleam and reflect like mirrors in the sun. Moreover, it is usually draped all around with a deep fringe of silky white yaks' tails, depending almost to the ground, and concealing the bodies of the bearers, so that the tabernacle seems to crawl along upon its own feet.

To the service of the temple certain people are set apart in every village. In the morning they sound an alarm in honour of the god with bell, and conch, and cymbal, and again in the evening with a similar din they announce the close of day. Ablutions are ignored by the villagers in their own case, but they will have their goddess washed and dressed daily. They burn incense before her, and serve her with offerings of leaves of wild mint.

Occasionally, all the tribes assemble at a religious festival, and each village sends forth its ark, with the men and women attired in their brightest colours, and glittering with all their jewels. The various processions, with dance and song and gambol, proceed towards the appointed rendezvous; one of their little temples, of rudely carved cedarwood, situated in the calm shade of a group of forest-trees. Near this temple is usually prepared a neatly-levelled space, covered with green turf, or, perhaps, paved; and here the Khudas, or arks, are solemnly deposited. For three days the festivities are kept up, and the sound of singing and dancing seems continuous. Every now and then each village-company raises its Khuda from the ground, and carries it in a little circle, sunwise, while the nodding plumes seem to keep time to the rude chant of the simple worshippers, and an outer ring of men, joining hands, follow the rhythm in fantastic dance. Then the idol is set down; the people prepare their homage; the dance goes on; and the women, in a long undulating chain, sunwise revolve around the mystic Khuda.

Each woman, throwing one arm around her neighbour's waist, keeps the other free, and waves a plume-like chowni or yak's tail, as she bows to the Khuda. They do not all wave simultaneously, but in swift succession, so as to produce the effect of a continuous graceful motion. If one of the women retire, from fatigue, another slips into her place: sometimes the men form the circle, then both men and women join, always carrying on the same evolutions, the same circular motion. At nightfall the huge fires are kindled, and the lurid gleams of pine-wood torches flicker athwart the darkness, while the echoes ring incessantly with the monotonous clang of great trumpet-shells and tomtoms.

When they have expended all their energies the revellers bring the festival to a close, and each village-company bears back its patron-goddess to her own little sanctuary.

Whether, as some surmise, this ceremony is associated with any tradition of Noah's Ark, we cannot pretend to determine. But it is certain that some legends of the Flood still linger among the hillmen. There is a popular myth which tells of a mighty ship built by Manu and the Seven Sages, in which they stored the seed of all kinds of life, and of its being rescued by Brahma when the Deluge overwhelmed the primitive earth. Brahma, it says, drew the great vessel for many days until he reached a high peak of the Himalayas, where he moored it securely. In memory whereof, the peak has ever since borne the name of *Naubandhana*.

Mr. W. Simpson, who has seen much of India and the Indians, describes an Ark-festival which he witnessed in a Himalayan valley. After indulging in the usual ceremonial ablutions, the people of the district assembled at the village of Coatee to do honour to its patron-goddess. The Khuda was brought out, and with dance and music, conducted in noisy procession through the deep shades of the forest and its lonesome glens, until they reached a certain grove, in which a small temple was situated. The Khuda was then deposited on the paved space in front; and an aged priest washed all the brazen faces with mint leaves and water previous to offering up incense, flowers, fruit, and bread.

A number of playful young kids were next brought forward. The priest sprinkled them with water. On the ground lay a large flat brazen dish, and one of the villagers stood beside it with a sacred hatchet, rudely ornamented. At a single blow he struck off the head of a kid. The priest's assistant raised the head, and muttering certain words, presented it to the Khuda. Dipping his finger into the blood, he flicked some drops upon the carven image, and placed the head with the other offerings. Meanwhile, the kid's body had been so disposed that all its blood dripped into the brazen vessel; and when two or three animals had been sacrificed and the dish was full, one of the men lifted it up, and, first presenting it to the Khuda, turned round, and swang the body against the whitewashed wall of the temple, so as to empty it of blood. This ceremony was thrice repeated.

The festival is known as the *Akrot-ka-pooja*, or Walnut Festival, from the pastime that follows the sacrificial scene. The priest, with a few companions, takes his place in the balcony of the temple, and all the young men present pelt them liberally with walnuts and green pine-cones, which the group in the balcony rapidly collect and return in plentiful volleys. For about half-an-hour this severe encounter lasts, when the assailed descend, and once more mingle with the crowd.

By this time the sacrificial kids have been cooked, and the people seating themselves on the paved space in front of the Khuda, cakes and flesh are served out among them. In opposition to the usual Eastern custom, the women are helped before the men. It is now time for the homeward journey, but the mysterious oscillation of the Khuda is understood to signify its desire to visit the neighbouring village of Cheenee; and thither the multitude at once proceed, dancing, singing, shouting, while the forest glades resound with the trumpets and the tomtoms, and a few of the nimbler-footed speed ahead to give notice to the authorities at Cheenee of the honour in store for them. When near the latter village, the procession is met by the goddess of Cheenee, with her retinue, and an exchange of courtesies takes place. Next morning, the goddess of Kothi, or Coatee, returns to her own charge.

SHAMANISM : DEVIL-DANCING.

In many parts of Central and Southern India the rite of Devil-Dancing is practised, and Bishop Caldwell gives a striking description of it as it exists among the Shawars of Tinnevelly :[1]

"When the preparations are completed and the devil-dance is about to commence, the music is at first comparatively slow; the dancer seems impassive and sullen, and he either stands still or moves about in gloomy silence. Gradually, as the music becomes quicker and louder, his excitement begins to rise. Sometimes, to help him to work himself up into a frenzy, he uses medicated draughts, cuts and lacerates himself till the blood flows, lashes himself with a huge whip, presses a burning torch to his breast, drinks the blood which flows from his own wounds, or drains the blood of the sacrifice, putting the throat of the decapitated goat to his mouth. Then, as if he had acquired new life, he begins to brandish his staff of bells, and to dance with a

[1] The Tinnevelly Shawars, by R. Caldwell, Madras, 1849.

quick but wild unsteady step. Suddenly the afflatus descends; there is no mistaking that glare, or those frantic leaps. He snorts, he swears, he gyrates. The demon has now taken bodily possession of him, and though he retains the power of utterance and motion, both are under the demon's control, and his separate consciousness is in abeyance. The bystanders signalize the event by raising a long shout, attended with a peculiar vibratory noise, caused by the motion of the hand and tongue, or the tongue alone. The devil-dancer is now worshipped as a present deity, and every bystander consults him respecting his diseases, his wants, the welfare of his absent relatives, the offerings to be made for the accomplishment of his wishes, and, in short, everything for which superhuman knowledge is supposed to be available."

Before we quit this subject, it may be for the interest and convenience of the reader, if we offer a brief account of the doctrines and rites of Brahmism. This movement against the old Hindu faith, initiated by Rammohun Roy, and developed by Babu Keshub Chunda Sen, owes its origin, however unconsciously, to the influence of Christianity, which the Hindu mind, on awaking from its long sleep of centuries, found, as it were, by its side, and the pure and elevated character of which it could not but recognise.

Rammohun Roy was born in the district of Moorshadabad in 1772, and was upwards of forty years of age when he undertook the part of a religious reformer. A man of considerable natural powers, he had cultivated them carefully, acquired a thorough knowledge of Sanskrit and Arabic, and accompanied his meditations on the Sastras, or Hindu religious books, with a close study of the English Scriptures. Removing to Calcutta in 1814, he endeavoured to engage his friends in the same pursuits, and as this effort led him naturally to new inquiries, he soon came to abandon his belief in traditional Hinduism. A cry of 'infidel!' was immediately raised against him; he became the subject of an incessant hostility; was on one occasion mobbed in the streets of Calcutta; and owed his life to the protection of the British Government. Persecution, however, could not quench his thirst after knowledge. He applied himself to the study of Greek and Hebrew, that by reading the Bible in its original languages, he might penetrate more thoroughly into the spirit of Hebrew and Christian devotion.

Having dismissed the authority of the Puranas, he rested his faith on the Vedas, the oldest of the Hindu sacred books, in the conviction (an erroneous one) that the old creed of Hinduism was monotheistic, and the belief (a justifiable one) that the Puranas represented the degeneracy of a later age. Strange to say, he did not detect the Pantheism that overflows the Vedas: in the Upanishads or treatises attached to them, he fancied that he saw a pure Deism, and to diffuse this among his countrymen, he published numerous translations and organised a society of believers, who recited texts from the Vedas, and chanted Christian hymns. In 1830 he went further; founding a prayer-meeting, which proved the seed of what is now known as the Brahma Samáj. The building erected for the purpose of holding the meetings was, according to the trust deed, to be open to people of all sorts and conditions, "who shall behave and conduct themselves in an orderly, sober, religious, and devout manner, for the worship and adoration of the Eternal, Unsearchable, and Immutable Being, who is the Author and Preserver of the Universe, but not under and by any other name, designation, or title, peculiarly used for and applied to any particular Being or Beings by any man or set of men whatsoever." It provided also, in direct opposition to the practices of Hinduism, that no graven image, sculpture, carving, picture, painting, portrait, or likeness of anything, should "be admitted within the walls of this building;" that no animal sacrifices should take place there; that no eating or drinking, feasting or rioting, should be permitted; that evil speaking against the beliefs of men should be prohibited; and that no prayer, or sermon, or teaching should be allowed, unless it had "a tendency to the contemplation of the Author and Preserver of the Universe, or to the promotion of charity, morality, piety, benevolence, virtue, and the strengthening of the bonds of union between men of all religious persuasions and creeds."

Here we have a distinct advance on Brahmanism and even on Buddhism, but the religious system indicated in the closing sentence is nevertheless as vague as it is cold; and lacks that vital element which Christianity derives from its recognition of GOD the FATHER and CHRIST the SAVIOUR. However, Rammohun Roy, in his fashion, was a sincere " seeker after GOD ;" and in his vague endeavour to grasp the truth he persevered in the face of an intolerant opposition. He still continued to give a foremost place to the Vedas as channels of religious instruction, but he introduced the Psalms of David; and as time wore on, he separated himself more and more completely from the traditions of orthodox Hinduism. Even his faith in the Vedas came to be much shaken; and finding himself at last in that state of isolation which is the suffering and martyrdom of the man in advance of his age, he quitted India and went to live in England. At Bristol he resided, much esteemed, until his death in 1833.

For awhile the torch which he had lighted flickered ominously near to extinction, until, in 1841, it passed into the hands of Babu Debendronath Tagore. By him it was again lighted up; and as much had happened since Rammohun Roy's departure, as education had gradually weakened the old traditional prejudices, it became the rallying-point of a crowd of earnest inquirers. Debendronath Tagore devoted himself with eager unselfishness, giving unsparingly of his time, his money, and his talents. His work derived no inconsiderable moral support from his unblemished personal character. He provided the Samáj with a printing-press, expended much money in fitting up their place of worship, and collected a valuable library of the Hindu sacred books, besides providing for the support of poor but promising students, sent to Benares to prosecute their studies.

A remarkable change, however, soon came over the faith and teaching of the Samáj. Hitherto, as we have seen, they had been based upon the Vedas, as the authorized rule of Hindu theology; but inquiry and criticism had gradually disclosed their Pantheistic character, and their consequent incompatibility with the creed of the Samáj. Thus it came to pass that about 1850 the Vedas had to go; and the members of the Samáj no longer called themselves Vedantists but Brahmoists, or Brahmists (from *Brahm*, or Brahma, the Supreme Being.) In other words, they openly became Theists.

A religious sect, brought together by a common monotheism and accepting a common covenant, was naturally impelled towards an expansion of their creed. But this expansion in the case of the Brahma Samáj, was probably hastened by the number of branch Samájes that sprang up in the neighbourhood of the metropolis and in some of the larger towns of the Bengal presidency. These branches, constantly increasing in number through the accessions of educated young men from the colleges and zillah schools, naturally looked to the parent Samáj to define and establish their creed; and what must be regarded as an authoritative exposition of it was published in 1868. The following is a summary of it:—

" 1. The book of Nature and Intuition form the basis of the Brahmaic faith.

" 2. Although the Brahmas do not consider any book written by man the basis of their religion, yet do they accept with pleasure and respect any *truth* contained in any book.

" 3. The Brahmas believe that the religious condition of man is progressive, like the other facts of his condition in this world.

" 4. They believe that the fundamental doctrines of their religion are at the basis of every religion followed by man.

" 5. They believe in the existence of One Supreme GOD —a GOD endowed with a distinct personality, and attributes equal to His nature, and intelligence befitting the Governor of the Universe; and worship Him—Him alone. They do not believe in His incarnation.

" 6. They believe in the immortality and progressive state of the soul, and declare that there is a state of conscious existence succeeding life in this world, and supplementary to it as respects the action of the universal moral government.

" 7. They believe that atonement is the only way to salvation. They do not recognise any other mode of reconcilement to the offended but loving Father.

" 8. They pray for *spiritual* welfare, and believe in the *efficacy* of real prayers.

"9. They believe in the Providential care of the Divine Father.

"10. They avow that love towards Him, and performing the works He loveth, constitute His worship.

"11. They recognise the necessity of public worship, but do not believe that they cannot hold communion with the Great Father without resorting to any fixed place at any fixed time. They maintain that we can adore Him at any time and at any place, provided that time and that place are calculated to compose and direct the mind towards Him.

"12. They do not believe in pilgrimages, but declare that holiness can be attained only by elevating and purifying the mind.

"13. They do not perform any rites and ceremonies, or believe in penances, as instrumental in obtaining the grace of GOD. They declare that moral righteousness, the gaining of wisdom, Divine contemplation, charity, and the cultivation of devotional feelings, are their rites and ceremonies. They further say, Govern and regulate your feelings, discharge your duties to GOD and to man, and you will gain everlasting blessedness; purify your hearts, cultivate devotional feelings, and you will see Him who is Unseen.

"14. Theoretically, there is no distinction of caste among the Brahmas. They declare that we are all the children of GOD, and, therefore, must consider ourselves as brothers and sisters."

Briefly speaking, the religious system herein set forth may be described as Christianity without CHRIST; and yet it was unwilling to acknowledge its obligations to Christianity. Its apostles sought to persuade themselves and others that they derived everything from the Vedas and nothing from the Bible; and when they were compelled to abandon the Vedas, they fell back upon Nature as a Divine Revelation. But, as an Anglo-Indian authority contends, it is certain that but for the new life which at this time flowed in with the tide of Western thought, and the study of a literature "saturated at every pore" with Christian sentiment and the high Gospel morality; and but for the strong and ceaseless opposition maintained by Christianity in the person of its missionaries against the Atheism, which was the first, though a short-lived result of the sudden intellectual quickening the young men of Calcutta experienced when Western science was substituted for Oriental myths, neither would the study of the Vedas have been revived, nor would the great lessons of nature have appeared so intelligible as they then became.[1]

We have seen that Brahmanism made one advance under Rammohun Roy; it was led still further forward by Debendronath Tagore; and then he too suddenly halted, as his predecessor had done. The leadership next devolved upon a man of higher courage, not less fitted to lead a great movement by his enthusiasm than by his ability, Babu Keshub Chunda Sen. Keshub was determined that the challenge should be thrown down to orthodox Hinduism: and persuaded Debendronath Tagore, when his daughter was married, to celebrate the occasion without the usual idolatrous ceremony. After this, he purified of their idolatrous element the rites observed at birth and death. Still, Debendronath Tagore supported him; but, at last, when an attempt was made to eliminate not only what was purely idolatrous, but also everything offensive to enlightened feeling and a purer taste, Debendronath and the conservative party opposed, and a schism was the result.

"The time had arrived," says the writer already quoted, "when Brahmism, if it was a power and not mere talk, must do battle with the system of caste distinctions. The first step in this direction taken by Keshub Chunda Sen, was the celebration of a marriage between persons belonging to different castes. That was an innovation such as might well startle the venerable pundits of Nuddea and Benares. There could henceforward be no doubt as to the more than heretical tendency of the theistic doctrine. An electric shock ran through society: all Hindudom was roused from its slumber, and began suspiciously to ponder what Brahmism meant by such daring. But the real test of principle was yet to come. It was comparatively safe to make a few modifications in domestic religious rites: the marriage of people of different castes compromised the principals chiefly: it was necessary that the entire Brahma community should by some act be universally committed to war against

[1] Calcutta Review, lii. 112, 113.

the evils and iniquities of caste. Keshub and his party accepted this necessity, threw off the sacred thread that distinguished them as Brahmans, and insisted that all who desired membership with their Samáj should consent to renounce caste. There could be no greater triumph than this, of principle over traditionalism : it stamped Brahmism as a power in the land, and not an idle theological speculation."

Thenceforward, Keshub Chunda Sen became the recognised leader of "the Brahma Samáj of India," and the new sect adopted an active proselytism. Branch Samájes have been established all over the country; missionaries have been sent as far as Madras and Bombay and the Punjab. Tracts and lectures have been freely circulated. In Calcutta a so-called "church" has been built, and is well attended every Sunday evening, not only by men, but by women, for whom special accommodation is provided. The services are conducted in the vernacular, so as to be intelligible to all worshippers. Brahmist hymns are sung to the accompaniment of the harmonium, and the solemn *mridong* (a kind of drum): passages are read from a book of selections in which the extracts from the Bible greatly outnumber those from any other source; extemporaneous prayers are offered with an intensity of spiritual feeling that could do no disgrace to a Christian congregation; and discourses are delivered which breathe a pure and noble tone of sentiment and feeling. Two weekly periodicals, one Bengali and the other English, the " Dharma Tattwa" and the " Indian Mirror," are the recognised exponents of the views and teaching of the Samáj.

CHAPTER V.

THE HINDU MYTHOLOGY: AND THE VISHNU PURANA.

THE word *Purana* means "old," and the original object of the Puranas would seem to have been the preservation of ancient mythological fictions and historical traditions. But in the form in which they have come down to us they do something more than this. They comprehend, more or less thoroughly, the five following subjects :—1, Primary creation, or cosmogony; 2, Secondary creation, or the destruction and renovation of worlds, including chronology; 3, Genealogy of gods and patriarchs; 4, Reigns of the Manus, or periods called Manwantaras; and 5, History, or such particulars as are extant of the princes of the solar and lunar races, and of their descendants to modern times. According to Professor Wilson, they are evidently derived from the same religious system as the Rámáyana and Mahábhárata, or from what he calls the mytho-heroic stage of Hindu belief. "They present, however, peculiarities which designate their belonging to a later period, and to an important modification in the progress of opinion. They repeat the theoretical cosmogony of the two great poems; they expound and systematise the chronological computations; and they give a more definite and connected representation of the mythological fictions and the historical traditions. But besides these and other particulars, which may be derivable from an old, if not from a primitive era, they offer characteristic peculiarities of a more modern description, in the paramount importance which they assign to individual divinities, in the variety and purport of the rites and observances addressed to them, and in the invention of new legends illustrative of the power and graciousness of those deities, and of the efficacy of implicit devotion to them."

The form of composition adopted in the Puranas is that of a dialogue, in which its contents are related by one imaginary individual in reply to another. Several dialogues are eventually woven together; and they purport to have been held on different occasions between different individuals, in consequence of similar questions having been asked. Usually the immediate narrator is Lomaharshaná or Romaharsháná, the disciple of Vyasa, who, as Plato did for Socrates, communicates to the reader his great master's utterances. The Vyasa or compiler here meant was Krishna Dwaipáyana, the son of Parásara; it is said of him that he taught the Vedas and Puranas to various pupils, but it seems more probable that he was at the head of a school or college, the members of which moulded the sacred literature of the Hindus into its present form.

There appear to have been eighteen Puranas : namely, 1, Brahma; 2, Padma; 3, Vaishnava; 4, Saiva; 5, Bhagavata; 6, Náradíya; 7, Márkándeya; 8, Agneya; 9, Bhavishya; 10, Brahma Vaivarta; 11, Lainga; 12, Váráha; 13, Skánda; 14, Vámana; 15, Kaurma; 16, Mátsya; 17, Gáruda; 18, Bráhmanda.

The Vishnu Purana is described as that in which Parásara, beginning with the events of the Varáha Kalpa, expounds man's moral and religious obligations in about seven thousand stanzas. It is divided into six books :—

The first deals chiefly with the details of creation, primary (Sarga) and secondary (Pratisarga); the first explaining how the universe proceeds from Prakriti or eternal crude matter; the second, in what way "the forms of things are developed from the elementary substances previously evolved, or how they reappear after their temporary destruction." Both these creations are periodical; the first does not end until the life of Brahma ends, when not only the gods and all other forms are annihilated, but the elements are resolved into the primary substance, besides which one only spiritual being exists. The latter occurs at the end of every Kalpa, æon, or day of Brahma, and is wholly limited to the forms of inferior creatures and the lower worlds ; leaving untouched sages and gods and the substance of the heavens. A description of the ages or periods of time on which these events depend is involved in the explanation ; and it is given accordingly in wearisome detail. Their character has been a source of very unnecessary perplexity to European writers; for they belong to a wholly mythological scheme of chronology, which has no reference to any real or supposed history of the Hindus, but prefigures, according to their system, the infinite and eternal revolutions of the universe.

By a singular incongruity the existence of Pradhána, or crude matter, is identified with Vishnu, who is declared to be both spirit and crude matter, and not only crude matter, but all visible substance, and Time. He is Purusha, " spirit ;" Pradhána, " crude matter ;" Vyakta, " visible form ;" and Kála, " time." " This," says Professor Wilson, " cannot but be regarded as a departure from the primitive dogmas of the Hindus, in which the distinctness of the Deity and His works was enunciated ; in which, upon His willing the world to be, it was ; and in which His interposition in creation, held to be inconsistent with the quiescence of perfection, was explained away by the personification of attributes in action, which afterwards came to be considered as real divinities, Brahma, Vishnu, and Siva, charged severally, for a given season, with the creation, preservation, and temporary annihilation of material forms." In the Vishnu Purana, these divinities are declared to be no other than Vishnu.

The earth having been duly prepared for the reception of living creatures, it was peopled by the will-begotten sons of Brahma, the Prajapatis or patriarchs. But it was necessary to provide these " grey forefathers" of the early world with wives. For this purpose, the Manu Swayambhuva and his wife Satarupa, were invented; and their daughters supplied the patriarchs with female partners. Numerous legends were built up on this basis, and the whole story assumed an allegorical form. Swayhambhuva, the son of the self-born or uncreated, and his wife Satarupa, the hundred-formed or multiform, are themselves allegories; and their female descendants, who became the wives of the Rishis, are Faith, Devotion, Content, Intelligence, Tradition, and the like; whilst among their posterity are found the different phases of the moon and the sacrificial fires. There are other legends in explanation of the peopling of the earth. All seem to indicate that the Prajapatis and Rishis were "real personages, the authors of the Hindu system of social, moral, and religious obligations, and the first observers of the heavens, and teachers of astronomical science."

The genealogy is traced of the royal personages of this first race or dynasty, and is continued into the second book; after which comes a detail of the geographical system of the Puranas, with Mount Meru, the seven circular continents, and their surrounding oceans, to the limits of the world. This (except so far as India or Bharata is concerned) is purely mythological. In the early portion of the third book, the arrangement of the Vedas and other sacred writings of the Hindus is described. Then follows an account of the principal Hindu institutions, the duties of castes, the obligations of different stages of life, and the celebration of funeral rites, in a brief but primitive strain, and in harmony with the laws of Manu. "It is a distinguishing feature of the Vishnu Purana, and it is characteristic of its being the work of an earlier period than most of the Puranas, that it enjoins no sectarial or other acts of supererogation; no Vratas, occasional self-imposed observances; no holy days, no birthdays of Krishna, no nights dedicated to Lakshmi; no sacrifices or modes of worship other than those conformable to the ritual of the Vedas. It contains no Máhálinyas or golden legends, even of the temples in which Vishnu is adored."

The fourth book contains a tolerably full list of royal dynasties and individuals, with a dull chronicle of events, the authenticity of which cannot always be accepted. In the fifth book we have the life of Krishna, one of the avatars or manifestations of Vishnu; and in the last an account of the dissolution of the world, "in both its major and minor cataclysms," which, "in the particulars of the end of all things by fire and water, as well as in the principle of their perpetual renovation, presents a faithful exhibition of opinions that were general in the ancient world."

We now proceed to give a few specimens of the contents of this remarkable work.

Origin of Rudra (Bk. i. c. 8.)

In the beginning of the Kalpa, as Brahma proposed to create a son, who should be like himself, a youth of a purple complexion appeared; crying with a low cry, and running about. Brahma, when he beheld him thus afflicted, said to him: "Why dost thou weep?" "Give me a name," replied the boy. "Rudra be thy name," rejoined the great father of all creatures: "be composed; desist from tears." But, though thus addressed, the boy still wept seven times; and Brahma therefore gave to him seven other denominations: and to these eight persons regions and wives and posterity belong. The eight manifestations, then, are named Rudra, Bhava, Sarva, Isana, Pasaputi, Bhima, Ugra, and Mahádeva, which were given to them by their great progenitor. He also assigned to them their respective stations, the sun, water, earth, air, fire, ether, the ministrant Brahman, and the moon; for these are their several forms. The wives of the sun and the other manifestations, termed Rudra and the east, were, respectively: Suvarchalá, Ushá, Vikésí, Sívá, Swáhá, Disas, Dikshá, and Rohini. Now hear an account of their progeny, by whose successive generations this world has been peopled. Their sons were severally: Sawaischara (Saturn,) Sukra (Venus,) the fiery-bodied (Mars,) Mamjava, Skanda, Swarga, Santána, and Budha (Mercury.)

Sacrifice of Daksha.

(This remarkable legend, according to Professor Wilson, is intended to allegorise a struggle between the worshippers of Siva and of Vishnu, in which the former, after a temporary defeat, obtained the victory.)

There was formerly a peak of Meru, named Sávitra, abounding with gems, radiant as the sun, and celebrated throughout the three worlds; of immense extent, difficult of access, and an object of universal adoration. Upon that glorious eminence, rich with mineral treasures, as upon a splendid couch, the deity Siva reclined, accompanied by the daughter of the sovereign of mountains, and attended by the mighty Adityas, the powerful Vasus, and by the heavenly physicians, the sons of Aswini; by Kubera, surrounded by his train of Guhyakas, the lord of the Yakshas, who dwells on Kailása. There also was the great Muni Usanas: there were Rishis of the first order, with Sanatkumará at their head, divine Rishis, preceded by Angiras; Viswavasu, with his bands of heavenly choristers; the sages Nárada and Parvata; and innumerable troops of celestial nymphs.

The breeze blew upon the mountain, bland, pure, and fragrant; and the trees were decorated with flowers that blossomed in every season.

The Vidyadharas and Siddhas, affluent in devotion, waited upon Mahádeva, the lord of living creatures; and many other beings, of various forms, did him homage. Prákshasas of terrific semblance, and Pisáchas of great strength, of different shapes and features, armed with various weapons, and blazing like fire, were delighted to be present, as the followers of the god. There stood the royal Naudin, high in the favour of his lord, armed with a fiery trident, shining with inherent lustre; and there the best of rivers, Ganga, the assemblage of all holy waters, stood adoring the mighty deity. Thus worshipped by all the most excellent of sages and of gods, abode the omnipotent and all-glorious Mahádeva.

In former times Daksha commenced a holy sacrifice on the side of Himavat, at the sacred spot Gangádwara, frequented by the Rishis. The gods, desirous of assisting at this solemn rite, came, with Indra at their head, to Mahadeva, and intimated their purpose, and having received his permission, departed, in their splendid chariots, to Gangádwara, as tradition reports. They found Daksha, the best of the devout, surrounded by the singers and nymphs of heaven, and by numerous sages, beneath the shade of clustering trees and climbing plants; and all of them, whether dwellers on earth, in air, or in the regions above the skies, approached the patriarch with outward gestures of respect. The Adityas, Vasus, Rudras, Maruts, all entitled to partake of the oblations, together with Jishnu, were present.

The (four classes of Pitris) Ushmapas, Somapas, Ajyapas, and Dhúmapas, (or those who feed upon the flame, the acid juice, the butter, or the smoke of offerings,) the

Aswins, and the progenitors, came along with Brahmá. Creatures of every class, born from the womb, the egg, from vapour, or vegetation, came upon their invocation ; as did all the gods, with their brides, who, in their resplendent vehicles, blazed like so many fires.

Beholding them thus assembled, the sage Dadhicha was filled with indignation, and observed : " The man who worships what ought not to be worshipped, or pays not reverence where veneration is due, is guilty, most assuredly, of heinous sin." Then, addressing Daksha, he said to him : " Why do you not offer homage to the god who is the lord of life (Pasubhartri ?)" Daksha spake : " I have already many Rudras present, armed with tridents, wearing braided hair, and existing in eleven forms. I recognise no other Mahádeva." Dadhicha spake : " The invocation that is not addressed to Isa is, for all, but a solitary (and imperfect) summons. Inasmuch as I behold no other divinity who is superior to Sankhara, this sacrifice of Daksha will not be completed." Daksha spake : " I offer in a golden cup, this entire oblation, which has been consecrated by many prayers, as an offering ever due to the unequalled Vishnu, the sovereign lord of all. . . . ."

(After a conversation between the mighty Maheswara and his spouse, whom he addresses in epithets which have quite an Homeric sound :)

The mighty Maheswara created, from his mouth, a being like the fire of fate ; a divine being, with a thousand heads, a thousand eyes, a thousand feet; wielding a thousand clubs, a thousand shafts ; holding the shell, the discus, the mace, and bearing a blazing bow and battle-axe ; fierce and terrific, shining with dreadful splendour, and decorated with the crescent moon ; clothed in a tiger's skin dripping with blood, having a capacious stomach, and a vast mouth armed with formidable tusks. His ears were erect, his lips were pendulous ; his tongue was lightning ; his hand brandished the thunderbolt ; flames streamed from his hair ; a necklace of pearls wound round his neck ; a garland of flame descended on his breast.

Radiant with lustre, he looked like the final fire that consumes the world. Four tremendous tusks projected from a mouth which extended from ear to ear.

He was of vast bulk, vast strength, a mighty male and lord, the destroyer of the universe, and like a large fig tree in circumference; shining like a hundred moons at once; fierce as the fire of love; having four heads, sharp white teeth, and of mighty fierceness, vigour, activity, and courage; glowing with the blaze of a thousand fiery suns at the end of the world; like a thousand undimmed moons; in bulk like Himádri, Kailása, or Sumnu, or Mundara, with all its gleaming herbs; bright as the sun of destruction at end of ages; of irresistible prowess and beautiful aspect; irascible, with lowering eyes, and a countenance burning like fire; clothed in the hide of the elephant and lion, and girt round with snakes; wearing a turban on his head, a moon on his brow: sometimes savage, sometimes mild; having a chaplet of many flowers on his head, anointed with various unguents, adorned with different ornaments and many sorts of jewels, wearing a garland of heavenly Karnikara flowers, and rolling his eyes with rage. Sometimes he danced; sometimes he laughed aloud; sometimes he stood wrapt in meditation; sometimes he trampled upon the earth; sometimes he sang; sometimes he wept repeatedly. And he was endowed with the faculties of wisdom, dispassion, power, penance, truth, endurance, fortitude, dominion, and self-knowledge.

This being then knelt down upon the ground, and raising his hands respectfully to his head, said to Mahádeva: "Sovereign of the gods, command what it is that I must do for thee;" to which Maheswara replied: "Spoil the sacrifice of Daksha." Then the mighty Virabhadra, having heard the pleasure of his lord, bowed down his head to the feet of Prajápati, and starting like a lion loosed from bonds, despoiled the sacrifice of Daksha; knowing that he had been created by the displeasure of Devi. She, too, in her wrath, as the fearful goddess Rudrakáli, accompanied him, with all her train, to witness his deeds. Virabhadra, the fierce, abiding in the region of ghosts, is the minister of the anger of Devi. And he then created, from the pores of his skin, powerful demigods, the mighty attendants upon Rudra, of equal valour and strength, who started by hundreds and by thousands into existence. A loud and confused clamour straightway filled all the expanse of ether, and inspired the denizens of heaven with dread. The mountains tottered, and earth shook; the winds roared, and the depths of the sea were disturbed; the fires lost their radiance, and the sun grew pale; the planets of the firmament shone not, neither did the stars give light; the Rishis ceased their hymns, and gods and demons were mute; and thick darkness eclipsed the chariot of the skies.

Then from the gloom emerged fearful and numerous forms, shouting the cry of battle; who instantly broke or overturned the sacrificial columns, trampled upon the altars, and danced amidst the oblations. Running wildly hither and thither, with the speed of wind, they tossed about the implements and vessels of sacrifice, which looked like stars precipitated from the heavens. The piles of food and beverage for the gods, which had been heaped up like mountains;[1] the rivers of milk; the tanks of curds and butter; the masses of honey, and butter-milk, and sugar; the mounds of condiments and spices of every flavour; the undulating knolls of flesh and other viands; the celestial liquors; pastes and confections which had been prepared; these the spirits of wrath devoured, or defiled, or scattered abroad. And, falling upon the host of the gods, these vast and resistless Rudras beat or terrified them, mocked and insulted the nymphs and goddesses, and quickly put an end to the rite, although defended by all the gods; being the ministers of Rudra's wrath, and similar to himself. Some then made a hideous clamour, whilst others fearfully shouted, when Yajna was decapitated. For the divine Yajna,

[1] We are reminded by this extravagance of great King Arthur's sumptuous feast at Carlisle, as described by Mr. Frere ("Whistlecraft"):—

> "They served up salmon, venison, and wild boars
> By hundreds, and by dozens, and by scores.
>
> "Hogsheads of honey, kilderkins of mustard,
> Muttons, and fatted beeves, and bacon swine;
> Herons and bitterns, peacock, swan and bustard,
> Teal, mallard, pigeons, widgeons, and in fine
> Plum-puddings, pancakes, apple-pies and custard;
> And therewithal they drank good Gascon wine,
> With mead, and ale, and cyder of our own;
> For porter, punch and negus were not known."

the lord of sacrifice, began to fly up to heaven, in the shape of a deer; and Virabhadra, of immeasurable spirit, apprehending his power, cut off his vast head, after he had mounted into the sky.

Daksha, the patriarch, his sacrifice being destroyed, overcome with terror, and utterly broken in spirit, fell prone upon the ground, where his head was spurned by the feet of the cruel Virabhadra. The thirty scores of sacred divinities were all presently bound, with a band of fire, by their lion-like foe; and they all addressed him, crying: "O Rudra, have mercy upon thy servants! O lord, dismiss thine anger!" This spake Brahma, and the other gods, and the patriarch Daksha; and, raising their hands, they said: "Declare, mighty being, who thou art."

Virabhadra said: "I am not a god, nor an Aditya, nor am I come hither for enjoyment, nor curious to behold the chiefs of the divinities. Know that I am come to destroy the sacrifice of Daksha, and that I am called Virabhadra, the issue of the wrath of Rudra. Bhadrakali, also, who has sprung from the anger of Devi, is sent here, by the god of gods, to destroy this rite. Take refuge, king of kings, with him who is the lord of Uma. For better is the anger of Rudra than the blessings of other gods."

Having heard the words of Virabhadra, the righteous Daksha propitiated the mighty god, the holder of the trident, Maheswara. The hearth of sacrifice, deserted by the Brahmans, had been consumed; Yajna had been metamorphosed to an antelope; the fires of Rudra's wrath had been kindled; the attendants, wounded by the tridents of the servants of the god, were groaning with pain; the pieces of the uprooted sacrificial posts were scattered here and there; and the fragments of the meat-offerings were carried off by flights of hungry vultures and herds of howling jackals.

Suppressing his vital airs, and taking up a posture of meditation, the many-sighted victor of his foes, Daksha, fixed his eyes everywhere upon his thoughts. And the god of gods appeared from the altar resplendent as a thousand suns, and smiling upon him, said, "Daksha, thy sacrifice has been destroyed through sacred knowledge, I am well pleased with thee." And he smiled again, and exclaimed, "What shall I do for thee? Declare, together with the preceptor of the gods."

And Daksha, frightened, alarmed, and agitated, his eyes suffused with tears, raised his hands reverently to his brow, and said, "If, lord, thou art pleased; if I have found favour in thy sight; if I am to be the object of thy benevolence; if thou wilt confer upon me a boon, this is the blessing I solicit, that all these provisions for the solemn sacrifice which have been collected with much trouble and during a long time, and have now been eaten, drunk, devoured, burnt, broken, scattered abroad, may not have been prepared in vain." "So let it be," replied Hara, the subduer of Indra. And thereupon Daksha knelt down upon the earth, and praised gratefully the author of righteousness, the three-eyed god Mahádeva, repeating the eight thousand names of the deity whose emblem is a bull.

Public Games. (Bk. v., c. 10.)

As Krishna and Rama proceeded along the high road, they saw coming towards them a young girl, who was crooked, carrying a pot of unguent. Addressing her sportively, Krishna said, "For whom are you carrying that unguent? Tell me, lovely maiden, tell me truly." Spoken to as it were through affection, Kubja,[1] well disposed towards Hari, replied to him also mirthfully, being smitten by his appearance, "Know you not, beloved, that I am the servant of Kamsa, and appointed, crooked as I am, to prepare his perfumes? Of unguent ground by any other he does not approve, and hence I am enriched through his liberal rewards." Then said Krishna, "Fair-faced damsel, give us of this unguent,—fragrant and fit for kings,—as much as we may rub upon our bodies." "Take it," answered Kubja. And she gave them as much of the unguent as was sufficient for their persons. And they rubbed it on various parts of their faces and bodies, till they looked like two clouds, one white and one black, decorated by the many-tinted bow of Indra.

And Krishna, skilled in the curative art, took hold of

---

[1] That is, the crooked. One of the other Puranas calls her Trivakra (or thrice-deformed.)

her under the chin with the thumb and two fingers, and lifted up her head, whilst with his feet he pressed down her feet, and in this way he made her straight.

When she was thus relieved from her deformity, she was a most beautiful woman; and filled with gratitude and affection, she took Govinda by the garment, and invited him to her house. Promising to come at some other time, Krishna smilingly dismissed her, and then laughed aloud on beholding the countenance of Baladeva.

Dressed in blue and yellow garments, and anointed with fragrant unguents, Krishna and Rama proceeded to the hall of arms, which was hung round with garlands. Inquiring of the warders which bow he was to try, and being directed to it, Krishna took it, and bent it. But drawing it with violence, he snapped it in two, and all Mathura resounded with the noise which its fracture occasioned. Abused by the warders for breaking the bow, Krishna and Rama retorted, and defied them, and left the hall.

When Kamsa knew that Akrura had returned, and heard that the bow had been broken, he then said to Chanura and Mushtika, his boxers, "Two youths, cowherd boys, have arrived. You must kill them both, in a trial of strength, in my presence; for they practise against my life. I shall be well pleased if you kill them in the match, and will give you whatever you wish, but not otherwise. These two foes of mine must be killed by you, fairly or unfairly. The kingdom shall be ours in common when they have perished."

Having given them their orders, he sent next for his elephant driver, and desired him to station his great elephant, Kuvalayapida,—who was as vast as a cloud charged with rain,—near the gate of the arena, and drive him upon the two boys when they should attempt to enter. When Kamsa had issued these commands, and ascertained that the platforms were all ready (for the spectators), he awaited the rising of the sun, unconscious of impending death.

In the morning the citizens assembled on the platforms set apart for them; and the princes, with the ministers and courtiers, occupied the royal seats. Near the centre of the circle, judges of the games were stationed by Kamsa, whilst he himself sat apart close by, upon a lofty throne. Separate platforms were erected for the ladies of the palace, for the courtesans, and for the wives of the citizens. Nanda and the cowherds had places appropriated to them, at the end of which sat Akrura and Vasudeva. Amongst the wives of the citizens appeared Devaki, mourning for her son, whose lovely face she longed to behold, even in the hour of his destruction.

When the musical instruments sounded, Chanura sprang forth, and the people cried, " Alas !" and Mushtika slapped his arms in defiance. Covered with blood and mud from the elephant, which, when goaded upon them by its driver, they had slain, and armed with its tusks, Balabhadra and Janardana confidently entered the arena, like two lions amidst a herd of deer. Exclamations of pity arose from all the spectators, along with expressions of astonishment. " This, then," said the people, " is Krishna. This is Balabhadra. This is he by whom the fierce night-walker Putana was slain ; by whom the waggon was overturned, and the two Arjuna trees felled. This is the boy who trampled and danced on the serpent Kaliya ; who upheld the mountain Govardhana for seven nights ; who killed, as if in play, the iniquitous Arishta, Dhenuka, and Kisra. This, whom we see, is Achyuta. This is he who has been foretold by the wise, skilled in the sense of the Puranas, as Gopala, who shall exalt the depressed Yadava race. This is a portion of the all-existing, all-generating Vishnu, descended upon earth, who will, assuredly, lighten her load."

Thus did the citizens describe Rama and Krishna, as soon as they appeared : whilst the breast of Devaki glowed with maternal affection ; and Vasudeva, forgetting his infirmities, felt himself young again, on beholding the countenances of his sons as a season of rejoicing. The women of the palace, and the wives of the citizens, wide opened their eyes, and gazed intently upon Krishna.

" Look, friends," said they to their companions ; "look at the face of Krishna. His eyes are reddened by his conflict with the elephant; and the drops of perspiration stand upon his cheeks, outvying a full-blown lotus in autumn, studded with glittering dew. Avail yourself, now, of the faculty of vision. Observe his breast,—the seat of splendour, marked with the mystic sign,—and his arms, menacing destruction to his foes. Do you not notice Balabhadra, dressed in a blue garment,—his countenance as fair as the jasmine, as the moon, as the fibres of the lotus-stem? See how he gently smiles at the gestures of Mushtika and Chanura, as they spring up.

"And now behold Hari advance to encounter Chanura. What! Are there no elders, judges of the field? How can the delicate form of Hari,—only yet in the dawn of adolescence,—be regarded as a match for the vast and adamantine bulk of the great demon? Two youths, of light and elegant persons, are in the arena, to oppose athletic fiends, headed by the cruel Chanura. This is a great sin in the judges of the games, for the umpires to suffer a contest between boys and strong men."

As thus the women of the city conversed with one another, Hari, having tightened his girdle, danced in the ring, shaking the ground on which he trod. Balabhadra also danced, slapping his arms in defiance. Where the ground was firm, the invincible Krishna contended, foot to foot, with Chanura. The practised demon Mushtika was opposed by Balabhadra. Mutually entwining, and pushing, and pulling, and beating each other with fists, arms, and elbows, pressing each other with their knees, interlacing their arms, kicking with their feet, pressing with their whole weight upon one another, fought Hari and Chanura.

Desperate was the struggle, though without weapons, and one for life and death, to the great gratification of the spectators. In proportion as the contest continued, so Chanura was gradually losing something of his original vigour, and the wreath upon his head trembled from his fury and distress; whilst the world-comprehending Krishna wrestled with him as if but in sport. Beholding Chanura losing, and Krishna gaining strength, Kamsa, furious with rage, commanded the music to cease.

As soon as the drums and trumpets were silenced, a numerous band of heavenly instruments was heard in the sky; and the unseen gods exclaimed: "Victory to Govinda! Kesava, kill the demon Chanura!" Madhusudana, having, for a long time, dallied with his adversary, at last lifted him up, and whirled him round, with the intention of putting an end to him. Having whirled Chanura round a hundred times, until his breath was expended in the air, Krishna dashed him on the ground, with such violence as to smash his body into a hundred fragments, and strew the earth with a hundred pools of gory mire.

Whilst this took place, the mighty Baladeva was engaged, in the same manner, with the demon bruiser, Mushtika. Striking him on the head with his fists, and on the breast with his knees, he stretched him on the ground, and pummelled him there till he was dead. Again, Krishna encountered the royal bruiser Tosaluka, and felled him to the earth with a blow of his left hand. When the other athletes saw Chanura, Mushtika, and Tosaluka killed, they fled from the field; and Krishna and Sankarshana danced, victorious, on the arena, dragging along with them, by force, the cowherds of their own age. Kamsa, his eyes reddening with wrath, called aloud to the surrounding people :—" Drive those two cowboys out of the assembly : seize the villain Nanda, and secure him with chains of iron; put Vasudeva to death with tortures intolerable to his years : and lay hands upon the cattle, and whatever else belongs to those cowherds who are the associates of Krishna."

Upon hearing these orders, the destroyer of Madhu laughed at Kamsa, and, springing up to the place where he was seated, laid hold of him by the hair of his head, and struck his tiara to the ground. Then, casting him down upon the earth, Govinda threw himself upon him. Crushed by the weight of the upholder of the universe, the son of Ugrasena (Kamsa), the king, gave up the ghost. Krishna then dragged the dead body, by the hair of the head, into the centre of the arena; and a deep furrow was made by the vast and heavy carcase of Kamsa, when it was dragged along the ground by Krishna, as if a torrent of water had rushed through it.

Seeing Kamsa thus treated, his brother Sunaman came to his succour: but he was encountered, and easily killed, by Balabhadra. Then arose a general cry of grief from the surrounding circle, as they beheld the King of Mathura thus slain, and treated with such contumely, by Krishna. Krishna, accompanied by Balabhadra, embraced the feet of Vasudeva and of Devaki: but Vasudeva raised him up;

I

and he and Devaki recalling to recollection what he had said to them at his birth, they bowed to Janardana; and the former thus addressed him : " Have compassion upon mortals, O god, benefactor, and lord of deities. It is by thy favour to us two that thou hast become the present upholder of the world. That, for the punishment of the rebellious, thou hast descended upon earth in my house, having been propitiated by my prayers, sanctifies our race. Thou art the heart of all creatures; thou abidest in all creatures; and all that has been, or will be, emanates from thee, O universal spirit. Thou, Achyuta, who comprehendest all the gods, art eternally worshipped with sacrifices : thou art sacrifice itself, and the offerer of sacrifices. The affection that inspires my heart, and the heart of Devaki, towards thee, as if thou wert our child, is, indeed, but an error and a great delusion.

" How shall the tongue of a mortal such as I am call the creator of all things, who is without beginning or end, son? Is it consistent that the lord of the world, from whom the world proceeds, should be born of me, except through illusion? How should he, in whom all fixed and moveable things are contained, be conceived in the womb and born of a mortal being? Have compassion, therefore, indeed, O supreme lord, and, in thy descended portions, protect the universe. Thou art no son of mine. This whole world, from Brahma to a tree, thou art. Wherefore dost thou, who art one with the Supreme, beguile us? Blinded by delusion, I thought thee my son, and for thee, who art beyond all fear, I dreaded the anger of Kamsa; and, therefore, did I take thee, in my turn, to Gokula, where thou hast grown up. But I no longer claim thee as mine own. Thou, Vishnu,—the sovereign lord of all, whose actions Rudra, Maruts, the Aswins, Indra, and the gods cannot equal, although they behold them; thou, who hast come amongst us, for the benefit of the world,—art recognised; and delusion is no more."

We shall furnish but one other specimen :—

Anecdotes of Khandikya and Kesidhwaja.

Maitreya, addressing Parasara, says : " Reverend teacher, I am desirous of being informed what is meant by the term meditation (*yoga*), by understanding which I may behold the Supreme Being, the upholder of the universe."

Parasara, in reply, says that he will repeat the explanation formerly given by Kesidhwaja to the magnanimous Khandikya, also called Janaka.

Whereupon Maitreya replies: "Tell me, first, Brahman, who Kandikya was and who Kesidhwaja; and how it happened that a conversation relating to the practice of Yoga occurred between them."

Thereupon follows Parasara's narrative:

There was Janaka, named Dharmadhwaja, who had two sons, Mitadhwaja and Kritadhwaja; and the latter was a king ever intent upon existent supreme spirit: his son was the celebrated Kesidhwaja. The son of Mitadhwaja was Janaka, called Khandikya. Khandikya was diligent in the way of works, and was renowned, on earth, for religious rites. Kesidhwaja, on the other hand, was endowed with spiritual knowledge. These two were engaged in hostilities; and Khandikya was driven from his principality by Kesidhwaja. Expelled from his dominions, he wandered, with a few followers, his priest, and his counsellors, amidst woods and mountains, where, destitute of true wisdom, he performed many sacrifices, expecting, thereby, to obtain divine truth, and to escape from death by ignorance.

Once, while the best of those who are skilled in devotion (Kesidhwaja) was engaged in devout exercises, a fierce tiger slew his milch-cow, in the lonely forest. When the Raja heard that the cow had been killed, he asked the ministering priests what form of penance would expiate the crime. They replied, that they did not know, and referred him to Kaseru. Kaseru, when the Raja consulted him, told him that he, too, knew not, but that Sunaka would be able to tell him. Accordingly, the Raja went to Sunaka; but he replied: "I am as unable, great king, to answer your question as Kaseru has been; and there is no one now, upon earth, who can give you the information, except your enemy Khandikya, whom you have conquered."

Upon receiving this answer, Kesidhwaja said: "I will go, then, and pay a visit to my foe. If he kill me, no matter; for, then, I shall obtain the reward that attends being killed in a holy cause. If (on the contrary) he tell me what penance to perform, then my sacrifice will be unimpaired in efficacy."

Accordingly, he ascended his car, having clothed himself in the deer skin of the religious student, and went to the forest where the wise Khandikya resided. When Khandikya beheld him approach, his eyes reddened with rage, and he took up his bow and said to him: "You have armed yourself with the deer skin to accomplish my destruction; imagining that, in such an attire, you will be safe from me. But, fool, the deer upon whose backs this skin is seen are slain, by you and me, with sharp arrows. So will I slay you: you shall not go free, whilst I am living. You are an unprincipled felon, who have robbed me of my kingdom, and are deserving of death."

To this Kesidhwaja answered: "I have come hither, Khandikya, to ask you to solve my doubts, and not with any hostile intention. Lay aside, therefore, both your arrow and your anger."

Thus spoken to, Khandikya retired awhile, with his counsellors and his priest, and consulted them what course he should pursue. They strongly urged him to slay Kesidhwaja while he was in his power, since by his death he would again become the monarch of the whole world.

Khandikya replied to them :—"It is, no doubt, true that, by such an act, I should become the monarch of the whole earth. He, however, would thereby conquer the world to come; whilst the earth would be mine. Now, if I do not kill him, I shall subdue the next world, and leave him this earth. It seems to me that this world is not of more value than the next: for the subjugation of the next world endures for ever; the conquest over this is but for a brief season. I will, therefore, not kill him, but tell him what he wishes to know."

Accordingly, Kesidhwaja proceeds to describe the benefits which result from the Yoga or contemplative devotion.

The sage, or Yogin, when first applying himself to contemplative devotion, is called the novice or practitioner (Yoga-yuj); when he has attained spiritual union, he is termed the adept, or he whose meditations are accomplished. Should the thoughts of the former be unvitiated by any obstructing imperfection, he will obtain freedom, after practising devotion through several lives. The latter speedily obtains liberation in that existence in which he reaches perfection, all his acts being consumed by the fire of contemplative devotion. The sage who would bring his mind into a fit state for the performance of devout contemplation must be devoid of desire, and observe invariably continence, compassion, truth, honesty, and disinterestedness : he must fix his mind intently on the supreme Brahma, practising holy study, purification, contentment, penance, and self-control. These virtues, respectively termed the five acts of restraint (Yama) and five of obligation (Niyama), bestow excellent rewards, when practised for the sake of reward, and eternal liberation, when they are not prompted by desire of transient benefits. Endowed with these merits, the sage, self-restrained, should sit in one of the modes termed Bhadrasana,[1] and engage in contemplation.

Bringing his vital airs, called Prana, under subjection, by frequent repetition, is thence called a Pranayama, which is, as it were, a seed with a seed. In this, the breath of expiration and that of inspiration are alternately obstructed, constituting the act twofold ; and the suppression of both modes of breathing produces a third. The exercise of the Yogin, whilst endeavouring to bring before his thoughts the gross form of the Eternal, is denominated Alambana.[2] He is then to perform the Pratyahara, which consists in restraining his organs of sense from susceptibility to outward impressions, and directing them entirely to mental perceptions. By these means the entire subjugation of the unsteady senses is effected; and, if they are not controlled, the sage will not accomplish his devotions. When, by the Pranayama, the vital airs are restrained, and the senses are subjugated by the Pratyahara, then indeed the sage will be able to keep his mind steady in its perfect asylum.

The sage now plunges into transcendentalism which would be barely intelligible, and certainly uninteresting to the

[1] The Yoga philosophy prescribes about eighty-four postures. The one to which allusion is made in the text consisted of sitting with your legs crossed underneath you, and laying hold of your feet, on each side, with your hands.
[2] That is, the silent repetition of prayer.

reader, and we shall therefore decline to follow him, concluding our extract with the description of Vishnu which Kesidhwaja furnishes to his inquiring guest.

Think of him as having a pleased and lovely countenance, with eyes like the leaf of the lotus, marble cheeks, and a broad and brilliant forehead; ears of equal size, the lobes of which are decorated with splendid pendants; a painted neck; and a broad breast, on which shines the Srivatsa mark; a belly falling in graceful folds, with a deep-seated navel; eight long arms, or else four; and firm and well-knit thighs and legs, with well-formed feet and toes. Let him, with well-governed thoughts, contemplate, as long as he can persevere in unremitting attention, Hari, as clad in a yellow robe, wearing a rich diadem on his head, and brilliant armlets and bracelets on his arms, and bearing in his hands the bow, the shell, the mace, the sword, the discus, the rosary, the lotus, and the arrow.

CHAPTER VI.

IN CHINA:—CONFUCIANISM, TAOUISM, AND BUDDHISM.

THE creeds in vogue amongst the Chinese may be regarded as three :—*Confucianism*, the religion of the state; *Taouism*, the religion of the philosophers; and *Buddhism*, the religion of the people.

It has been justly said that a religion which, like Confucianism, has exercised for twenty-four centuries a potent influence over the Chinese mind, though owing its name and origin to a simple citizen, must possess in it something well worthy of consideration. There must be in it a spell which strongly attracts the popular sympathies. This spell is said to be, though possibly we ought to search deeper and farther for it, the purely practical character of its tenets, and the harmony which exists between those tenets and the patriarchal character of the government and the institutions of the country. And in fact it is not so much a religion as an ethical system,—something such as Christianity would be, if we took out of it JESUS CHRIST. Or we may distinguish it as "a system of ceremonies on a moral basis," and, as such, admirably adapted to the tastes and needs of so ceremonial-loving a people as the Chinese. To this day the Ly-pou watch with jealous vigilance the maintenance of all the old traditional rites, and rigidly enforce the observance of the traditional details in the construction of the temples. Moreover such particulars as the six kinds of sceptres, the five kinds of mats, and the five kinds of stools are strictly insisted upon; and it is known that the innumerable prescribed sacrifices offered to the various gods of the heaven and the earth, to a man's forefathers, to the hills and the rivers, the sea and the central mount, the god of the south pole and the god of thunder, are the same now as they have been for upwards of 2,000 years.

The founder of Confucianism, Kong-foo-tse, or Confucius, (as the Jesuits latinised the name,) was born about 550 B.C. in the state Loo, within the district now called Keo-fou Hien, lying to the eastward of the great Imperial canal, in the province of Shang-tung.

Tradition asserts that his father was a descendant of the imperial family of Hoang-ty, of the dynasty of Chang (2,000 B.C.), and the chief minister of his native kingdom. At an early age, as is common with most who are destined to rise to greatness, Confucius gave indisputable proof of no ordinary mental capacity, and these budding powers were carefully developed by the training and tuition of the ablest masters. He was still young when he made himself acquainted with the literature of the period, and especially with the canonical and classical books attributed to the ancient legislators Yam Chun, and others. His amiability of temper is warmly commended, and no shadow of reproach rests upon his moral character; except in so far as he exposed himself to censure by divorcing his wife, after she had borne him a son, in order, it is said, "that he might devote himself the more absolutely to his studies." It is some excuse for him that, at this time, he was only twenty. In the same year he was appointed "superintendent of cattle,"—not exactly the ideal office for a philosophical student. However his assiduity and fidelity soon secured the approbation of his superiors; he was promoted to a more influential position; and there seemed every probability of his attaining to the highest rank, when a sudden revolution in the state for a time obscured his prospects.

The next eight years of his life he spent in travel, assuming the role of a religious reformer, and everywhere gathering round him a crowd of ardent disciples, whom he instructed in the rules and principles of his ethical system. It is said that they numbered as many as 3,000, of whom seventy-two were specially distinguished by their devotion to their master and their rigid observance of his tenets. Returning to Loo, when he was about forty-three years old, he was again called to the service of the state, and from grade to grade rose to the post of Prime Minister, or "governor of the people." Invested with plenary power, he proceeded, with the ardour of an enthusiast, to realise his ideas, and rapidly brought about a vast improvement in both the moral and physical condition of the country. The poor were the particular objects of his care : he provided them with plentiful supplies of cheap and good food, and released them from the thraldom in which the nobles had held them. His energy and wisdom extended to every department of the state ; and with extraordinary fertility of resource, he initiated measures for the extension of commerce, the improvement of the bridges and highways, the impartial administration of justice, and the extirpation of the robber bands which infested the mountains. But the neighbouring sovereigns regarded with alarm the progress of his bold reforms. No doubt they talked about communistic and socialistic doctrines, and the advancing flood of democracy, as timid people do in our own day. At all events they contrived to put such a pressure upon the King of Loo that he was compelled to part with his great minister, who fled from his enemies northward, and found refuge in the kingdom of Tsi, on the Gulf of Petchali. For twelve, or, as some say, fourteen years he wandered from place to place, adding to the number of his proselytes; until spent with fatigue, and bowed down with years, he retired with a few favourite disciples to a quiet valley in his native land, and devoted the remainder of his life to the task of revising and improving the famous writings which for so many centuries have been consecrated by the devout acceptance of the Chinese. He died at the age of seventy-three, in 477 B.C.,[1] "on the eighteenth day of the second moon," after a seven days' illness. Like many other great reformers, though but indifferently treated in his lifetime, he became after death the object of universal admiration, and to this day the Chinese pay homage to the memory of the "Great Master," the "Chief Doctor," the "Wise King of Literature," the "Saint," the "Instructor of Emperors and Kings." His descend-

[1] Others say in 479 B.C., at the age of seventy.

ants have been loaded with honours and privileges, and now constitute the only hereditary nobility in the Chinese empire. Like the princes of the blood, they are exempt from taxation. And in every city of the first, second, and third rank, stands at least one temple dedicated to Confucius, where the emperor himself and the mandarins are bound to worship, with offerings of wine, fruit, and flowers, —with burning of fragrant gums, frankincense, and tapers of sandal wood,—and with singing of appropriate hymns. The eighteenth day of the second moon is kept sacred by the Chinese as the anniversary of his death.

We have already said that the system of Confucius was ethical rather than religious. It is absolutely free from any theological strain, and, indeed, makes no mention of a Creator. "How should I know God," he would say, "when as yet I know not man?" "His system was essentially conservative; he aimed at the correction of new vices which had crept into the body politic by endeavouring to restore the old customs of the country; and hence the high favour in which his system has ever been held by the rulers and magnates of the empire. It inculcated the most perfect subordination, the most servile obedience, and the most scrupulous adherence to ancient usage; every social, civil, and political duty is set forth in it with the greatest precision; but inasmuch as all the parts of the great machine of empire are not absolutely deprived of volition, a rebellious cog-wheel or insignificant pinion will sometimes disarrange and impede the entire machinery."

Confucius held that the universe had been generated by the union of two material principles,—a heavenly and an earthly, Yang and Ya. He represents man as having fallen by his own act from his original purity and happiness, and asserts that by his own act he can recover that condition. For this purpose he must lead a life of obedience to the law, and he must not do unto others that which he would not have others do unto him. He made the supremacy of parental authority the basis of his political teaching, and strongly advocated that the son's submission to the father must be as complete as that of the servant to the master, of the master to the magistrate, of the magistrate to the crown, and of the crown to the law. Of course this implied that the reciprocal obligations must be observed. This rigid application of the family ideal to the administration of the government, and the consequent creation of a pure despotism, has been the cause of all that is most perplexing to Europeans in the Chinese civilisation, and explains why it has never advanced beyond the standard or mark to which it had attained in the era of Confucius.

The Confucian doctrines are set forth in *Gze-Chou,* "The Four Books," and *King,* "The Five Canonical Works," of which the following particulars may interest the reader.

The Ta-heo, or "Great Study."

The *Ta-heo,* or "School of Adults," has been translated by Dr. Marshman, in the "Clavis Sinica." It is a treatise, in two chapters, on politics and morals, rising gradually from the government of oneself to the government of a family, thence to the government of a province, and finally to the control of the affairs of an empire. Its leading principle is self-improvement, self-culture. In one of the sections an eulogium is bestowed upon the beauty of virtue as a means of self-enjoyment. And the book closes with a fine exhortation to be just, and truthful, and honest, to those whom fortune places at the head of the state.

The Chung-Yung, or " The Invariable in the Mean,"

Also translated as "the Safe Middle Course," and "the Infallible Medium," describes the golden mean, the due medium by which a man should regulate his conduct. He is not to be lifted up by prosperity, nor cast down by adversity. Through thirty-three sections, in language sometimes clear and strenuous, sometimes obscure, the subject is pursued, and the whole duty of man inculcated. Here is a passage describing a kingly man which may be compared with one in Seneca :—

"It is only the man supremely holy, who, by the faculty of knowing thoroughly, and comprehending perfectly the primitive laws of living beings, is worthy of possessing supreme authority, and governing men ; who by possessing a soul, grand, firm, constant, and imperturbable, is capable of making justice and equity reign; who by his faculty of being always honest, simple, upright, grave, and just, is able to attract respect and veneration; who by his faculty of being clothed with the ornaments of the mind, and the talents procured by assiduous study, and by the enlightenment that springs from an exact investigation of the most hidden things, and the most subtle principles, can with accuracy discern the true from the false, and the good from the evil."

The Lun-Yu, or "Philosophical Conversation."

This is the Chinese *Phædo*, and contains a record of the conversations held between Confucius and his disciples, but the author lacked the eloquence and imagination of Plato. It is interesting however from its anecdotes of the Great Teacher. In introducing his guests, it seems that he kept his arms extended, like the wings of a bird; that he never ate meat which had not been cut in a straight line; that he never used his fingers to point to anything; and that he would not occupy the mat spread for him as a seat unless it was regularly placed.

The Meng-tze, or "Mencius,"

Is a Commentary upon Confucius, written about a century after his death by his disciple Meng-tze. The subjects treated in it are of various nature. In one part the virtues of individual life and of domestic relations are discussed; in another, the order of affairs. Here are investigated the duties of superiors, from the sovereign to the lowest magistrate, for the attainment of good government. There are expounded the labours of students, peasants, traders, artisans, while, in the course of the work, the laws of the physical world, of the heavens and the earth, the mountains and rivers, of birds, fishes, quadrupeds, insects, plants, and trees, are occasionally described. The great number of affairs which Mencius managed, in the course of his life, in his intercourse with men, his occasional conversations with people of rank, his instructions to his pupils, his expositions of books, ancient and modern,—all these details are incorporated in this publication. It is a collection of historical facts, and of the words of ancient ages, put together for the instruction of mankind.

Mencius died when he was eighty-four years of age; his memory is revered by the Chinese next to that of Confucius, and his descendants are treated with a distinction inferior only to that which is accorded to those of Confucius.

King; or, The Five Canonical Works.

These, which were either written or compiled by Confucius, are the most venerable existing monuments of Chinese literature, and embody the fundamental principles of the earliest creeds and customs of China.

The first is the *Y-King*, or "Sacred Book of Changes," which may be termed a Chinese Cyclopædia, and contains a great variety of subjects, morals, physics, and metaphysics. It is founded on the combinations of sixty-four lines,—some entire, and some broken,—and called *Koua;* the discovery of which has been attributed to Fo-hi, the traditional founder of Chinese civilisation. He found them, it is said, on the shell of a tortoise, and asserted that they were capable of explaining all things. It does not seem easy, however, to explain *them*, and the commentaries upon them are more numerous than even the commentaries upon Shakespeare. The Imperial Library at Peking contains no fewer than 1450.

Second in order comes the *Shu-King*, or "Book of History," which, despite its imperfect and fragmentary condition, is full of interest. It contains a concise narrative of Early Chinese history, down to the eighth century before our era; including the speeches addressed by several emperors to their high officers, and numerous valuable documents of great antiquity. Reference is made in its pages to a great deluge, which some suppose to be the Flood recorded in the book of Genesis, but others, with more probability, identify with one of the early and extensive inundations of the Hoang-Ho.

The third is the *Shi-King*, or "Book of Sacred Songs," a collection of 311 poems, ancient, national, and official, the best of which every well-educated Chinaman commits to memory. They range from the eighteenth to the third century before our era, and are divided into four parts: first, the Ku-fung, or songs of "the manners of different states;" second and third, songs for state occasions; and fourth, Soong, a collection of eulogies on the various emperors of the Chow dynasty. This book is described as replete with very interesting and probably authentic information on the ancient manners of China, and is frequently quoted by both Confucius and Mencius, and by them recommended to the study of their disciples.

Fourth comes the *Li-King*, or " Book of Rites and Ceremonies," in which we find a mass of fragments dating from the time of Confucius downwards, and throwing a vivid light on the permanent characteristics of the Chinese civilisation, and on the causes which made it what it is in all its iron immutability. The ceremonial usages of China, as prescribed in this ritual, number about 3000; and one of the six tribunals, the Ly-pou, is specially charged with their custody and interpretation.

Fifth and last is the *Chun-tsien*, or *Tchuntsiou*, or " Book of Spring and Autumn," so called from the seasons in which it was respectively begun and ended by Confucius. Here the Great Teacher has simply written down the earlier history of his native land of Loo; with the view of recalling the princes of his age to a conservative spirit of reverence for the customs of the past by indicating the misfortunes that took place after they fell into neglect.

Strictly speaking, Confucianism has no priests, no distinct sacerdotal order; the emperor himself is the patriarch or head, and every magistrate, within the sphere of his jurisdiction is a religious official or hierophant. " Generally, all literary persons, and those who propose to become such, in attaching themselves to it do not necessarily renounce practices borrowed from other religions. But, in fact, faith does not seem to have anything to do with the matter; and habit alone induces them to conform to ceremonies which they themselves turn into ridicule—such as divinations, horoscopes, and calculating lucky and unlucky days, all of which superstitions are in great vogue throughout the empire."

China possesses an enormous number of pagodas, or idol-temples; Peking boasts of 10,000; every village has several, and they are distributed all along the roads and all over the fields. Some are remarkable for their splendour; but the majority do not differ in appearance, or very slightly, from other buildings. Often they are nothing more than small chapels, in which are niches containing idols and vases filled with burning perfumes, or the ashes of gilt paper on which prayers have been printed, these papers having been burnt, as a religious rite, by devotees. The worshippers, if such they may be called, display the utmost indifference of behaviour in these temples : they enter them to enjoy a rest or a sleep ; or they walk about with their hats on, whistling, smoking, laughing, chattering. Round the sides are seated the vendors of the aforesaid gilt paper prayers and pastiles ; ever and anon they demand attention to their wares by striking a gong ; while the people incessantly burn paper models of clothing, shoes, money, junks, and the like, to assist their deceased friends on their long journey. For though the Chinese have no distinct recognition of a future state, the worship of the dead is a prominent element of their religion. Noble and peasant alike bring offerings, or send them by proxy, and kneel before the shades of their ancestors : this duty at least is always remembered, whatever other may be forgotten.

The following may be given as an example of the prayers used upon such occasions :—

" I, Lea Kwang, second son of the third generation, presume to come before the grave of my ancestors. Revolving years have brought again the season of Spring : I sweep your tomb with reverence, and, prostrate, beg you to be spiritually present, and grant that your posterity may be illustrious. At this season I desire to recompense the root of my existence, and reverently, therefore, before your holy spirit present the five-fold offering of pork, fowl, duck, goose, and fish ; with five fruits and the drink *samshu* ;[1] entreating that you will condescend to inspect them. This announcement is presented on high."

Such offerings as are not accepted by the priests are generally taken home again to furnish full the worshipper's own table.

The Ritual State Worship, which concerns the Emperor

[1] A strong spirituous liquor, distilled from wine.

and his court, but affects not the great body of the people, we must glance at very briefly. It may be defined as the ceremonial of a philosophical pantheism, unconnected with any theological doctrine. Three classes of natural objects are distinguished, to which the " Great," the " Medium," and the " Lesser" Sacrifices are offered. The first class, the *Ta-sze*, includes the Heaven and the Earth, and along with and equal to these, the great Temple of Imperial Ancestors. Among the *Chung-sze*, or " Medium Sacrifices," are the Genii, the Great Light and the Evening Light (that is, the Sun and the Moon), the Gods of Land and Grain, the God of Letters, and the Inventors of Agriculture, Manufactures, and the Useful Arts. To the " Lesser Sacrifices," or *Scaou-sze*, belong the Founder of the Art of Healing, as well as the spirits of statesmen, scholars, and persons of eminent virtue. They are offered also to various natural phenomena, such as the clouds, the rain, the wind, the thunder. The God of War, and Lung Wang, the dragon-king, who represents the rivers and streams, have their worshippers; nor is Tien-How, the Queen of Heaven, forgotten. There are, besides, a host of household deities, like the Lares and Penates of the ancients, who are propitiated by domestic sacrifices at the new year, when they are supposed to pay a brief visit to the Other World, and report, as it were, the doings and misdoings of the families over which they preside.

The chief sacrificial seasons are these: the winter solstice for all offered to heaven, the summer season for all offered to earth. The others have their appointed dates. Then, in the course of the year, numerous festivals of a more or less religious character are held. First among them is the Imperial Ploughing of the Sacred Field, which takes place towards the end of March. The Emperor, attended by some of the princes of the blood and his chief ministers, then proceeds to a field on one side of the central street in Peking, where fitting preparations have, of course, been made. After certain sacrifices, consisting chiefly of grain preserved from the produce of the same field, the Emperor takes the plough, and drives a few furrows. His example is followed by the princes and ministers in succession : a red tablet indicating the space allotted to each distinguished amateur. The "five sorts of grain" are then sown; and when the Emperor has seen the work completed by the attendant husbandmen, the field is committed to the charge of an officer whose business it is to collect and store the produce with a view to future sacrifices to the Gods of the Harvest.

Of the *Shae-tung*, or Feast of Lanterns, every traveller has spoken. There are also the *Too-te-tan*, or birthdays of the familiar gods of the city; the *Tsing-ming-tsee*, or Feast of Tombs; the festivals of all and sundry deities; and the birthdays of the living Emperor and Empress, as well as the anniversaries of the deaths of their predecessors, which, however, are observed only by the mandarins. So numerous are the festivals that were they celebrated everywhere by everybody there would be neither "time" nor "hands" for the works of agriculture or commerce, trade, science, or the arts.

We pass on to a brief account of

TAOUISM.

The founder of Taouism, the doctrine of Tao, or Reason, was a celebrated philosopher named Lao-tsze, who was born in the third year of the Emperor Ting-wang, of the Chow dynasty (B.C. 604) in the state of Tseu, now known as Hoo-pih and Hoo-nan. He preceded Confucius by half a century. His family name was *Le*, or Plum, and his youthful name, *Urh*, or Ear, in allusion to the exceptional size of his "auricular appendages." The events of his career are so obscured in an atmosphere of legend and fable, created by admiring disciples, that it is difficult to get at any authentic particulars; but he seems to have been an assiduous student, and the historian or chronologist of a king of the Chow dynasty. Visiting, about B.C. 600, the western parts of China, he gained there a knowledge of the system of Fo, or Buddha, and soon afterwards began to develope his own religious teaching. So great was his fame that Confucius went to see him; but the interview was hardly of the character that might have been expected when two religious philosophers met. Lao-tsze reproached the younger sage with pride and ostentation and vanity, affirming that philosophers loved retirement and seclusion, and made no boast of virtue and knowledge. It speaks well for the good nature of Confucius that he replied to this tirade by highly commending Lao-tsze to his followers, and describing him as a dragon soaring to the clouds of Heaven, unsurpassed and unsurpassable.

Lao-tsze inquired of Confucius if he had discovered the *Taou*, the "path" or "reason" by which Heaven acts, and was informed that the philosopher had searched for it unsuccessfully. Lao-tsze replied that the wealthy dismissed their friends with presents, and sages theirs with good counsel; and that for himself, he humbly claimed to be thought a sage—an indirect way of advising Confucius to continue his quest of the *Taou*. Retiring to Han-kwan, he wrote there his *Taou-tih-king*, or Book of Reason and Virtue. He died, or as his followers say, ascended to Heaven on a black buffalo, in the twenty-first year of the reign of King-wang of the Chow or Cheu dynasty, or B.C. 523, having attained the age of 119 years.[1]

The contrast between the system of Lao-tsze and that of Confucius may be indicated in a word: the former was *speculative*, the latter *practical*, and it is no wonder, therefore, that the latter, addressing itself to man's actual necessities and daily duties, prevailed over the former. But, in an abstract sense, Lao's, as originally defined by himself, was the purer and more elevated; for it aimed at securing the immortality of man through the contemplation of GOD, the subjugation of the passions, and the absolute tranquillity of the soul. He taught that Silence and the Void generated the Taou, the "Logos" or reason by which movement was

---

[1] In Rashiduddin's "History of Cathay" we read: "In the reign of Din-Wang, the twentieth King of the eleventh dynasty, *Tai Shang Lao Kun* was born. This person is stated to have been accounted a prophet by the people of Khita; his father's name was Han; like Shak-muni (Buddha) he is said to have been conceived by light, and it is related that his mother bore him in her womb no less a period than eighty years. The people who embraced his doctrine were called شين شن *Shan-shan*, or *Shin-shin*." The title used by Rashiduddin signifies "the Great Supreme Venerable Ruler."

produced ; and that all beings containing in themselves the duality of male and female sprang from them.

Man, he said, was composed of two principles, the material and the spiritual : from the latter he emanated, and to it he ought to return, by throwing off the fetters and snares of the world, crushing out the material passions, the desires of the soul, and the pleasures of the body, and abandoning riches, honours, and the ties of life.

Before Lao-tsze's time, the Chinese seem to have worshipped the *Shang-te*, or Supreme Ruler, and the *Tien*, or Heaven : but Lao-tsze preached in their place the *Taou*, or "reason" of the Kosmos. Of a Supreme Creative and Eternal Power he had no conception. There was as little theology in his system as in that of Confucius ; but its morality was not less admirable ; it insisted on the practice of those virtues which form the moral code of all the higher religions,—charity, benevolence, chastity, and the free-will, moral agency, and responsibility of man. But there was an obscurity about Lao-tsze's teaching, which enabled his followers successfully to pervert it, and it gradually assumed a form which the Teacher himself would undoubtedly have been the first to repudiate. The Taossi, as they were called, professed to have discovered the drink of immortality, and practised divination, alchemy, the invocation of spirits, and other superstitious rites. These follies were gravely ridiculed by the Joo-Keaou, or sect of Confucius, and gradually were abandoned by all but the most illiterate.

Among the host of deities worshipped by this sect we may instance the *San-tsing*, or "Three Pure Ones," the three-fold ruler of the assembled gods in heaven, the sun, the moon, and the stars, who delivers his name and benevolent commands to be promulgated amongst mankind, that all who see and recite that name may be delivered from all evil, and obtain infinite happiness. " It is impossible to doubt," says a writer, " that we see here traces of a Divine revelation, corrupted though it has now become. China has her Trinity in Taouism as well as in Buddhism ; as other Pagan nations have had theirs in the Orphic mythology, where there were 'counsel, and light, and life ;' in the Platonic theology, which had its 'good, and mind, and the soul of the world,' as in the Egyptian mysteries there were 'On, and Isis, and Neith;' and in that of Fo, 'Brahma, Vishnu, and Seeva.'"

The Taossi, Tien-sze, or "Celestial Doctors,"—the priests of Taouism,—are outwardly distinguished amongst the Chinese by the manner in which they dress their hair. They shave the sides of the head, and coil the remaining hair in a tuft on the crown. Moreover, they wear slate-coloured robes. There are two orders; one, the keepers of the temples, vowed to celibacy; the others, who are free to marry, live in their own houses, or wander about the country selling charms and medical nostrums. In the feast of one of their deities, the "High Emperor of all the Sombre Heavens," they assemble before his temple, and having kindled a huge fire, about fifteen or twenty feet in diameter, go over it barefoot, carrying the gods in their arms. "They firmly assert," says Williams, "that if they possess a sincere mind they will not be injured by the fire; but both priests and people get miserably burnt on these occasions." Escayrac de Lauture says that they leap, dance, and whirl round the fire, striking at the devils with a straight Roman-like sword, and sometimes wounding themselves as the priests of Baal and Moloch were wont to do.

Some interesting particulars of the Buddhist temples of China are supplied by Mr. Fortune. He speaks of the temple of Tien-tung as a congeries of temples, a collection of spacious structures, which occupy the site of former buildings. All of these are crowded with idols, or images of the favourite gods, such as the "Three precious Buddhas," "the Queen of Heaven," represented as sitting on the celebrated lotus or nelumbium—"the God of War," and many other deified kings and great men of former days. Many of these images are from thirty to forty feet in height, and have a striking appearance as they stand arranged in the spacious lofty halls. The priests themselves reside in a range of low buildings, erected at right angles with the different temples and courts that divide them. Each has a little temple under his own roof; a family altar crowded with petty images, where he is often engaged in private devotion.

Mr. Fortune, after inspecting the various temples and the belfry, which contains a noble bronze bell of large dimensions, was conducted to the house of the principal priest, where dinner was already spread upon the table. The Buddhist priests are not permitted to eat animal food at any of their meals. The dinner, therefore, consisted entirely of vegetables, served à la Chinoise, in numerous small round basins, the contents of each—soups excepted—being cut up into small square bits, to be eaten with chopsticks. The Buddhist priests contrive to procure a quantity of vegetables of different kinds, which, by a peculiar mode of preparation, are rendered very savoury. "In fact," says Mr. Fortune,[1] "so nearly do they resemble animal food in taste and in appearance, that at first we were deceived, imagining that the little bits we were able to get hold of with our chopsticks were really pieces of fowl or beef. Such, however, was not the case, as our good host was consistent on this day at least, and had nothing but vegetable productions at his table. Several other priests sat with us at table, and a large number of others of inferior rank with servants, crowded around the doors and windows outside."

During dinner, Mr. Fortune learned that about a hundred priests were connected with the monastery, but that many were always about on missions to various parts of the country. A considerable portion of land in the vicinity belonged to the temple, and supplied its revenue: large sums were raised every year from the sale of bamboos, which are here very excellent, and of the branches of trees and brushwood, which are made up in bundles for firewood. Many rice and tea farms also belong to the priests and are cultivated by them. In addition to the sums thus raised, a considerable revenue must accrue from the contributions of the devotees who frequent the temple, as well as from the alms and donations collected by the mendicant priests of the order, who are sent out on begging excursions at stated periods of the year. There are, of course, all grades of priests; some being merely the servants of the others, both domestic and agricultural.

The temple forms the centre of a fine landscape. It

[1] Robert Fortune, "Three Years' Wanderings in the Northern Provinces of China," p. 170, et sqq.

stands at the head of a fertile valley, with green hills all around it; this valley echoes with the music of several bright mountain streams, and yields abundant crops of rice. On the lower slopes of the more fertile hills grow masses of tea shrubs, with dark green leaves, lending a fine background to the picture. A long avenue of Chinese pine trees leads up to the temple. At first it is straight, but near the temple it winds picturesquely round the edges of the artificial lakes, to end at a flight of stone steps. Behind, and on each side, the mountains rise in irregular ridges, from 1,000 to 2,000 feet above the sea level; not bare and desolate like the mountains of the south, but clothed to their tops with a dense tropical-looking growth of brushwood, shrubs, and trees. Some of the finest bamboos of China flourish in the ravines, and the sombre-coloured pine attains to a large size on the acclivities.

A quaint account of the origin of the monastery was given by one of the head priests:—

"Many hundred years ago a pious old man retired from the world, and came to dwell in these mountains, giving himself up entirely to the performance of religious duties. So earnest was he in his devotions that he neglected everything relating to his temporal wants, even to his daily food. Providence, however, would not suffer so good a man to starve. Some boys were sent in a miraculous manner, who daily supplied him with food. In the course of time the fame of the sage extended all over the adjacent country, and disciples flocked to him from all quarters. A small range of temples was built, and thus commenced the extensive buildings which now bear the name of 'Tien-tung,' or the 'Temple of the Heavenly Boys;' *Tien* signifying heaven, and *tung*, a boy. At last the old man died, but his disciples supplied his place. The fame of the temple spread far and wide, and votaries came from the most distant parts of the empire—one of the Chinese kings being amongst the number—to worship and leave their offerings at its altars. Larger temples were built in front of the original ones, and these again in their turn gave way to those spacious buildings which form the principal part of the structure of the present day."

Mr. Fortune remarks that a large number of Buddhist

temples are scattered over all this part of the country. Their architects have shown as keen a sympathy with nature as the Cistercian founders in Europe, always building them in the most lovely and picturesque situations, amongst the green hills, and in the shelter of spreading woods—the leafy enclosures that in England indicate the presence of an old manor house, or "ancestral hall." *Poo-to*, or the Worshipping Island, as foreigners call it, is one of the eastern islands in the Chusan Archipelago, and seems to be one of the great Buddhist centres. The principal group of temples is situated in a fine romantic glen, and from the high ground above it, seems like a town of considerable size. As the traveller approaches nearer, he finds the view of great interest. In front extends a large artificial pond, filled with the broad green leaves and noble red and white flowers of the nelumbium speciosum,—a plant in high favour with the Chinese. Access to the monastery is obtained by a very ornamental bridge thrown across this piece of water.

The temples or halls containing the idols are extremely spacious; many of the idols are thirty or forty feet high, generally made of wood or clay, and then richly gilt. In a temple of far less pretentious character than any of the others Mr. Fortune met with some exquisite bronze statues, of undoubted value.

Having examined these temples, our traveller made his way towards another group of them, about two miles to the eastward, and close on the sea shore. Entering the courts through a kind of triumphal arch, which looked out upon the sapphire sea, he found that these temples were constructed on the same plan.

On the following day he inspected various parts of the island. In addition to the larger temples just noticed, about sixty or seventy smaller ones are built on all the hill sides, each containing three or four priests, who are all under the abbot, or superior, residing near one of the large temples. "Even on the top of the highest hill," he says, "probably 1,500 or 1,800 feet above the level of the sea, we found a temple of considerable size and in excellent repair. There are winding stone steps from the sea-beach all the way up to this temple, and a small resting-place about half-way up the hill, where the weary devotee may rest and drink of the refreshing stream which flows down the sides of the mountain, and in the little temple close at hand, which is also crowded with idols, he can supplicate Buddha for strength to enable him to reach the end of his journey. We were surprised to find a Buddhist temple in such excellent order as the one on the summit of the hill proved to be in. It is a striking fact, that almost all these places are crumbling fast into ruins. There are a few exceptions, in cases where they happen to get a good name amongst the people from the supposed kindness of the gods; but the great mass are in a state of decay."

The island of Poo-to is nothing but a residence for Buddhist priests, and no other persons are allowed to live there but their servants and attendants. No women are admitted, as the principles of Buddhism insist upon sacerdotal celibacy. There are about 2,000 priests, many of whom are constantly absent on begging expeditions for the maintenance of their religion. On certain high days, at different periods of the year, many thousands of both sexes, but more particularly females, visit these temples, clothed in their gayest attire, to pay their vows and engage in the other practices of heathen worship. In the temples or at the doorways stand little stalls, for the sale of incense, candles, paper made up to resemble ingots of Sycee-silver, and other holy things, which are regarded as acceptable offerings to the gods, and are either consumed in the temples or carried home to bring, it is supposed, a blessing upon the homes and families of their purchasers. The profits of these sales go, of course, to the maintenance of the establishment. Whatever we may think of the superstitious character of Buddhism, it is impossible to doubt the sincerity of its disciples, when we find them sometimes travelling a distance of several hundred miles to worship in their temples.

"I was once staying," says Fortune,[1] "in the temple of Tien-tung when it was visited for three days by devotees from all parts of the country. As they lined the roads on their way to the temple, clad in the graceful and flowing

[1] " Three Years' Wanderings," p. 185.

costumes of the East, the mind was naturally led back to those days of Scripture History when Jerusalem was in its glory, and the Jews, the chosen people of GOD, came from afar to worship in its temple."

Mr. Gutzlaff, the missionary, is of opinion that the priests and devotees of Buddhism entertain no sincere conviction of the truth of their creed. Describing a visit to Poo-to, he says: "We were present at the vespers of the priests, which they chanted in the Pali language, not unlike the Latin service of the Romish Church. They held rosaries in their hands, which rested folded upon their breasts. One of them had a small bell, by the tinkling of which their service was regulated; and they occasionally beat the drum and large bell to rouse Buddha's attention to their prayers. The same words were a hundred times repeated. None of the officiating persons showed any interest in the ceremony, for some were looking round laughing and joking, while others muttered their prayers. The few people who were present, not to attend the worship, but to gaze at us, did not seem, in the least degree, to feel the solemnity of the service." But to condemn the whole Buddhist sect from this solitary instance would be as reasonable as to pronounce all Protestants insincere because a West-end congregation in London may have shown signs of frivolity and indifference! Mr. Fortune, on the contrary, declares that he was much impressed by the solemnity with which the devotional exercises of the Buddhists were generally conducted. "I have often walked," he says, "into Chinese temples when the priests were engaged in prayer, and although there would have been some apology for them had their attention been diverted, they went on in the most solemn manner until the conclusion of the service, as if no foreigner were present. They then came politely up to me, examining my dress and everything about me with the most earnest curiosity. Nor does this apply to priests only; the laity, and particularly the female sex, seem equally sincere when they engage in their public devotions. Whether they are what they appear to be, or how often they are in this pious frame of mind, are questions which I cannot answer. Before judging harshly of the Chinese, let the reader consider what effect would be produced upon the members of a Christian church by the unexpected entrance of a small-footed Chinese lady, or a Mandarin, with the gold button and peacock feather mounted on his hat, and his long tail dangling over his shoulders. I am far from being an admirer of the Buddhist priesthood; they are generally an imbecile race, and shamefully ignorant of everything but the simple forms of their religion, but nevertheless there are many traits in their character not unworthy of imitation."

The superstitious credulity of the Chinese is demonstrated by the nature of their various religious ceremonies. In all the southern towns every house has its temple or altar, both within and without. In the interior the altar generally occupies the end of the principal hall or shop, as the case may be; is raised a few feet from the ground, and adorned with an effigy of the household god, enveloped in gaudy tinsel paper. By the way, of what we call "taste," the Chinese do not seem to know even the rudiments; nor do they appear to have any feeling for harmony of colour or proportion. On the first day of the Chinese month, and other festivals, candles and incense flare and smoke on the table in front of it. The altar outside the door is like to a small furnace, and here the same ceremonies are regularly performed.

The traveller, as he passes in the neighbourhood of small villages, or in even more sequestered localities, comes upon little joss-houses or temples, all glaringly decorated in the same style with paintings and tinsel paper, and stuck round about with bits of candles and sticks of incense. Shops for the sale of idols of all kinds and sizes, but of unvarying ugliness, at prices varying from a few pence to many pounds, are found in all the large towns. Some are evidently very ancient, and have passed through the hands of a long succession of proprietors. It is a capital custom—is it not?—when you are tired of your god, because he does not fulfil your wishes, to purchase another and a more powerful at a slight increase of price! A deity who would really gratify *all* our petitions would be worth—so far as this world is concerned—a heavy sum!

Nothing in China is more remarkable than the periodical

offerings of a Chinese family to its gods. The traveller already cited witnessed such a ceremony in a house at Shanghai. The principal hall was duly set out at an early hour in the morning; a large table was placed in the centre; and shortly afterwards covered with small dishes filled with the various articles commonly used as food by the Chinese. All these were of the very best description which could be procured. After a certain time had elapsed numerous candles were lighted, and from the burning incense rose columns of fragrant smoke. The inmates of the house and their friends were all clothed in their best attire, and came in turn to *ko-too*, or bow lowly and repeatedly in front of the table and the altar. "The scene," says our authority, "although it was an idolatrous one, seemed to me to have something very impressive about it, and whilst I pitied the delusion of our host and his friends, I could not but admire their devotion. In a short time after this ceremony was completed a large quantity of tinsel paper, made up in the form and shape of the ingots of Sycee silver common in China, was heaped on the floor in front of the tables, the burning incense was then taken from the table and placed in the midst of it, and the whole consumed together. By-and-by, when the gods were supposed to have finished their repast, all the articles of food were removed from the tables, cut up, and consumed by people connected with the family."

On another occasion, Mr. Fortune, when at Ning-po, having been abroad all day, did not return to the city until nightfall. The city gates were closed, but, on knocking, he was admitted by the warder. Passing into the widest and finest street in the city, he observed a blaze of light and a general liveliness very unusual in any Chinese town after dark. The sounds of music fell upon his ear, the monotonous beat of the drum and gong, and the more pleasing and varied tones of several wind instruments. On approaching nearer he discovered that a public offering was being made to the gods, and it proved to be a more striking scene than he could have anticipated. The table was spread in the open street, and all the preparations were on a large and expensive scale. Instead of small dishes, whole animals were sacrificed. On one side of the table was placed a pig, on the other a sheep ; the former, scraped clean in the usual fashion, the latter skinned ; of both the entrails had been removed, and on both were placed flowers, an onion, and a knife. The other parts of the table "groaned" with the delicacies in vogue among the more respectable Chinese, such as fowls, ducks, numerous compound dishes, fruits, vegetables, and rice. At one end of the table, when the gods were supposed to sit during the meal, chairs were set ; and chopsticks were laid in order by the side of every dish. The whole place glared with light, and wreaths of incense filled the air with sweet odours. At intervals, bands of musicians struck up the favourite national airs, which are all of a plaintive cast, and altogether the scene was a strange and curious revelation of human superstition.[1]

Processions in honour of the gods are of frequent occurrence. Mr. Fortune speaks of one which he saw at Shanghai as at least a mile in length. The gods, or josses, arrayed in the finest silks, were carried about in splendid sedan-chairs, in the centre of a long train of devotees, all superbly dressed for the occasion, and all bearing their different insignia of office. The dresses of the officials exactly resembled those of some of the attendants who figure in the suite of the higher mandarins. Some wore on the sides of their hats a broad fan, composed of peacock-feathers ; others strutted in gaudy theatrical costumes, with two long black feathers stuck, like horns, in their low caps. The scowling executioners carried long conical black hats on their heads, and whips in their hands, for the prompt chastisement of the refractory. Bands of music, in different parts of the procession, played at intervals as it marched along.

On arriving at a temple in the suburbs, it came to a halt. The gods were taken out of the sedan-chairs, and with a great exhibition of reverence, replaced in the temple, from which they had been removed in the morning. Then their worshippers bent low before their altars, burning incense, and depositing their gifts. Numerous groups of well-dressed ladies and their children were scattered over the ground in

[1] Fortune, pp. 190, 191.

the neighbourhood of the temple; all were kneeling, and apparently they conducted their devotions with great earnestness. A large quantity of paper, in the shape of the Sycee silver ingots, was piled up on the grass by the different devotees, and when the ceremonies of the day were being brought to a conclusion, the whole was burned in honour of, or as an offering to, the gods.

CHAPTER VII.

*AMONG THE MALAYS: THE SLAMATAN BROMOK;
THE DYAKS; THE PAPUAN TRIBES;
THE AHETAS.*

THE SLAMATAN BROMOK.

A RELIGIOUS ceremony exists in Java which has an obvious affinity to the old Nature-Worship, and finds its excuse in the dread with which the uncivilised races regarded the mysterious forces of Nature, unseen in themselves, but palpable in their results. About three miles from the town of Tosari, rises the barren cone of the Bromok, a still active volcano, which is strangely situated in the bosom of green wooded hills and mountains,— a significant blur upon the landscape. The traveller who desires to accomplish its ascent climbs up the rough and almost precipitous slope by a path winding through immense breadths of a tall yellow grass called the alang-alang. When he has attained to the brink of the Monegal, an enormous extinct crater, reputed to be the largest in the world, he will do well to pause, and survey the landscape before him. Of the knot of mountains on which his eye rests, the foremost is called the Batok, or Butak, that is, the Bald; in allusion, probably, to its barren summit, for its sides are well clothed with herbage. It is shaped like a cone, with deep grooves down its declivities, indicating the course taken by the lava-streams formerly ejected from its interior. To its right, a little in the rear, stretches the sharp pointed chain of the Dedari and Widadarea, or "abode of fairies;" while, on the left, shrouded in smoke clouds, which partially conceal its bulk, is situated the mass of the dreary Bromok.

Descending into the crater, we cross its sandy floor, the Dasar,—or, as it is appropriately called, the Sandy Sea,— where grows not tree nor shrub, and the only signs of vegetation are a few scattered patches of dried and scrubby grass. The surface is strangely corrugated or ridged, like the sea-sand at ebb of tide; and the whole landscape is as full of gloom as the waste of the African Sahara.

Like many other volcanoes, the Bromok is a truncated cone. From one of its sides project numerous irregular masses, or mounds of mud and sand, incrusted in a baked clay like red lava. Some of these have been largely reduced in size by the heavy tropical rains, which have ploughed deep broad fissures in the Sandy Sea; while others, still supplied with liquid matter from the volcano, are encroaching on the Dasar, and covering so much of it as lies within the more immediate neighbourhood of the crater. Large blocks of lime and limestone lie embedded in these mounds; also huge black stones veined like marble and glittering like granite. These, as well as the scoriæ which abound in every direction, were products, it is supposed, of the last eruption of the Bromok.

Climbing to the summit of the ridge, and looking down into the abyss of the crater, the traveller at first is tempted to suppose that before him lies one of the "circles" of Dante's mediæval Inferno. A yawning pit in the centre belches dense volumes of sulphureous smoke, accompanied by terrific sounds, like groans and shrieks and yells. The inner crater forms a large basin, about 350 feet in diameter, with irregular broken sides, descending to a depth of fully 250 feet. The sides, as well as the bottom, are encrusted with deposits of yellow sulphureous matter.

The ceremony of the benediction of this dread volcano takes place two or three times a year; it is not without its picturesque details. Groups of pilgrims are scattered about the Sandy Sea; some eating, others praying; some singing, others laughing, talking, chaffering. Men are selling, and finding a ready market for, amulets, charms, and volcanic stones, which, in language as extravagant as that of the European proprietor of a patent pill, they declare to be sovereign remedies for every human malady. Provisions of all kinds are on sale, and lie exposed upon roughly constructed stands, resembling those which are seen at English fairs; a plank or two, supported on a couple of stone trestles. "Wodonos and Mantries"—the Javanese nobles—parade up and down in gay attire, their burnished krisses glittering amidst the folds of their sarong. Old men and old women, who have come to pay their last homage to the shrine, totter along feebly; watching with delight, however, the frolics of their grandchildren as they scamper about in unchecked glee.

At one part of the Sandy Sea twenty mats are ranged in a row, and upon each a young priest kneels, having before him a box of myrrh, frankincense, aloes, and other spices, which are sold for offerings. At right angles runs another row, with the same number of priests, all kneeling in the Arab fashion, their bodies partly resting on the calves of their legs. These are older than the former group, and may be regarded as the patriarchs of their respective villages. Behind each stands a payong-bearer, shading his master from the sun with a large umbrella. Their dress consists of a white gown worn over the sarong, which is tied to the waist by a broad red belt. Over the shoulders hang two bands of yellow silk, bound with scarlet, and their ends ornamented with tassels and gold coins. The head-dress consists of a large turban, adorned with gay silken scarfs. In front of each priest are spread small packets made of plantain leaves, containing incense, sandal-wood chips, and other preparations; wooden censers, throwing forth jets of fragrant smoke; and a vessel, made of plaited ratan, for holding water.

At a short distance from the priests a motley crowd is assembled, waiting for the various offerings they have deposited upon specially prepared bamboo stands, to be consecrated. These offerings consist of cocoa-nuts, plantains, pine-apples, mangoes, and other fruits; of baskets of young chickens; of trays loaded with all kinds of cakes; of strips of silk and calico; of gold, silver, and copper coins.

After spending a few minutes in prayer, the priest dips his goupillon or cup into the vessel of water before him, mutters a few unintelligible words, and sprinkles the oblations as they are successively presented. Then all the holy men bow their heads, and repeat loudly and distinctly a ritual prayer.

The oldest rises up, followed in succession by his sacerdotal companions, uttering a phrase which sounds like "Ayo, ayo, Bromok!" and probably means, "Forward, forward to the Bromok!" At this signal all the crowd rush to the Bromok, impressed with a belief that he who first gains the ridge will be the favourite of fortune, and presently meet with some exceptional stroke of good luck. At intervals some of the older priests come to a halt, spread their mats, and prostrate themselves in prayer for five or ten minutes, thus securing an interval of rest at the same time that they win a reputation for special devoutness.

On reaching the summit of the volcano, the various families and individuals again present their offerings to the priests, who mumble over them a few additional words: they are then thrown into the crater, each person eagerly repeating some prayer or wish. And thus concludes the strange ceremony by which the spirits of the Bromok are supposed to be propitiated. The crowd descend from the volcano to join in various games and pastimes; towards evening they begin to disperse, and as the night spreads its cloud of darkness over the scene, the Sea of Sand resumes its ordinary aspect of loneliness and desolation.

THE DYAKS OF BORNEO.

It is not certain that the Dyaks possess any religion. Temminck asserts that they *have*, and that it bears a close resemblance to "fetichism." The god Djath, he says, rules the sublunar world, and the god Sangjang presides over hell. These gods wear the human form, but are invisible; the Dyaks invoke them by sprinkling rice on the ground, and offering various sacrifices. In the houses of the Dyaks, adds Temminck, wooden idols are frequently met with.

Other travellers are of opinion that they profess a kind of Pantheism, and represent them as believing, like the ancient Greeks, in a multitude of gods, gods above and gods below the world, as well as innumerable good and evil spirits, of whom Budjang-Brani is undoubtedly the most wicked. All diseases are caused by the agency of evil demons, and all misfortunes; and therefore the Dyaks make vigorous efforts to drive them away by shouts, and shrieks, and the discordant gong. So in some of the West Indian islands the natives, during an eclipse, would seek, by a horrible clamour, to frighten away the monster they supposed to be devouring the moon.

Some authorities go so far as to represent the Dyaks as cherishing vague ideas of the Unity of the Godhead and the immortality of the soul.

Madame Ida Pfeiffer was by no means a philosophical traveller, but she was an honest observer; and as the result of her explorations in Borneo, she positively affirms that among the tribes she visited are neither temples nor idols, priests nor sacrifices. On the occasions of their births, marriages and funerals they perform certain ceremonies, but these appear to be devoid of all religious character. Usually on such occasions they kill fowls as well as hogs. When concluding treaties of peace they always slaughter swine, but they do not eat them, and in this custom we may trace perhaps the propitiatory idea. A few tribes burn their dead, and preserve the ashes in hollow trees; others inter them in the least accessible localities, such as the summits of lofty mountains; others bind the corpse to the trunk of a tree in the position in which S. Peter was crucified, that is, with the feet upwards and the head downwards.

In Bouru.

The inhabitants of Bouru, one of the islands of the Malay Archipelago, profess a creed which was taught them by one called Nabiata. From some of its articles he would seem to have been a Mohammedan, or acquainted with Mohammedanism; but whence he came, or how, or when he made his way to Bouru, it is impossible to ascertain. The natives say that there is one Supreme Being, Who created all things, and is the source of both good and evil. He permits the existence of evil spirits. Those who pray to Him He rewards with prosperity; those who neglect this duty He never fails to punish. It was owing to His infinite love for man that He sent him this inspired teacher Nabiata, who resided among the mountains, and delivered his Master's will in seven commandments :—

1. Thou shalt not kill nor wound.
2. Thou shalt not steal.
3. Thou shalt not commit adultery.
4. Thou shalt not set thyself up against thy *fenna* (priest.)
5. A man shall not set himself up against the chief of his tribe.
6. A chief shall not set himself up against him who is over his or other tribes.
7. The chief over more than one tribe shall not set himself up against him who is placed over all the tribes.

Nabiata also taught that though the body perishes, the soul will live for ever; that those who keep the foregoing commandments, (and all the acts of men are duly recorded by the Supreme Being,) shall dwell in His presence far above the firmament; while those who have lived wickedly shall never rise to the abode of the happy, nor shall they remain upon earth, but for ever and ever, lonely and in sorrow, wander among the clouds, yearning with a desire that can never be fulfilled, to join their brethren in the heaven above or on the earth beneath.

Nabiata also introduced the rite of circumcision, and ordained that it should be performed on children of both sexes when they attained the age of eight or ten years.

THE PAPUAN TRIBES.

Among the Dorians, or the inhabitants of the north coast of New Guinea, near Port Dory, an almost childish superstition prevails. Always and everywhere they carry about with them a variety of charms and talismans, such as bits of bone, or quartz, or carved wood, to which, for some reason or other, an artificial value has come to be attached. Those among them who have acquired a slight knowledge of Mohammedanism use verses of the Koran written upon narrow strips of paper by the Mohammedan priests of Ceram and Tidore. But most of the Dorians are pagans, and worship an idol called "Karwar," a clumsy figure of which, carved in wood, holding a shield, and distinguished by an exceptionally large head, with a sharp nose and a wide mouth, is kept in every house, and plays the part of a dumb oracle. Its owner, when involved in any difficulty or danger, hastens to crouch before it, bowing or salaaming repeatedly, with his hands clasped upon his forehead. If while thus engaged he experiences an emotion of doubt or despondency, it is considered an evil sign, and he proceeds to abandon whatever may have been his wish or object. It will thus be seen that everything depends upon the votary's temperament or natural disposition,—if he be a sanguine and resolute man, it is not likely that he will be conscious of any untoward sensation; and, in such a case, he of course concludes that he has the sanction of his "Karwar." In other words, his will fortifies him to carry out his wishes. But even among civilised nations a similar method of "consulting the oracle,"—of soliciting the advice of another with the intention of following it only if it coincides with one's own desires,—is sometimes heard of!

The Dorians appear to maintain a priestly caste; but its functions are confined to the interpretation of dreams and omens; besides which its members act as "medicine men." There are no religious rites, no sacrifices. The two notable events of marriage and death pass with little show. In the former, the intending bride and bridegroom sit down before the Karwar, the woman offers the man homage in the shape of tobacco and betel-leaf; then they join hands, rise up, and are recognised as man and wife. When a death occurs, the corpse is wrapped in a white calico shroud, and interred in a pit about five feet deep. There it lies upon its side in the midst of its weapons and ornaments, and a porcelain dish under its ear. The grave is afterwards filled up with earth, roofed over with dried grass, and crowned with the Karwar of the departed.

The Aruans, like the Papuans, belong to the Australo-Malay division of the Archipelago, and their religious system is but a little more developed. And here we may note that as we recede from Asia and advance through the great chain of the Eastern islands to Australia, we observe a gradual religious decadence, until the depth of barbarism is reached in the wretched aboriginal tribes of the great "island continent." The Aruans have no idea of a heaven or a hell; no sense of any "world beyond the grave," but their funeral rites are conducted on an extensive scale.

When an Aruan dies, his kinsmen at once assemble and destroy all the goods and chattels he has accumulated during his lifetime; breaking even the gongs in pieces, which are carefully thrown away. The body is next laid out on a small mat, and propped up against a ladder for three or four days; after which the relatives again assemble, and apparently to prevent further decay, cover the exposed parts with lime. Meanwhile the hut is filled with the fumes of burning dammar or resin, and the guests sit in the perfumed atmosphere drinking large draughts of arrack, and of a spirit which they contrive to distil from the juice of some indigenous fruit. The stimulant soon does its work; they give vent to their feelings in violent shouts, which mingle with the howls and wails of the women and the hoarse discord of the gongs. Food is offered to the deceased, and the mouth crammed with various kinds of edibles, rice, and arrack.

By this time all the friends and relatives of the departed have assembled—as at a Scotch funeral; the body is placed on a kind of bier, which is strewn with numerous pieces of cloth according to the wealth of the deceased; while large dishes of China porcelain are set beneath to catch any moisture that may fall from it. A high value is afterwards set upon these dishes. Being taken out of the house, the body is supported against a post, and another effort made to induce it to eat. The hollow jaws are again stuffed with lighted cigars, rice, fruit, and arrack; and the mourners join in a loud chant, inquiring whether the sleeper will not awake at the sight of so many friends and fellow-villagers. Alas, the long slumber continues! The body is again placed upon its bier, which is carried into the forest, and it is hoisted upon the summit of four posts. A tree, usually the *Pavetta Indica*, is then planted near it; and at this final ceremony none, it is said, but naked women are allowed to be present. This is called the *sudah buang*, and signifies that the body is thenceforth abandoned to the silence of the wilderness as unable any longer to see, hear, think, or feel.

The religion of savage or uncivilised men is, necessarily, coloured and determined by the natural influences that surround them, and according as they live in the African desert or the American forest, among the snows of Siberia or on the table-land of Tibet, will bear its distinctive and appropriate character. We do not doubt, therefore, but that Sherard Osborn is right in the explanation he offers of the superstitious credulity of the Malays, that the wonderful phenomena peculiar to the seas and islands of the great Eastern Archipelago could never be intelligible to an uneducated and highly imaginative race except on the supposition of supernatural agency. Of course, this superstitious temperament is not confined to the Malayan race. It is found, as we have said, in all savage peoples, and springs from that profound though often vague and undefinable sense of an overruling and mysterious Power which the influence of Nature impresses on the heart of man.

There were proofs by the thousand among the Malays with whom Admiral Sherard Osborn came in contact, of that connection with the Unseen World which men in every stage of civilisation seem to accept and to be desirous of developing. And he relates a striking instance of their great credulity, which we may quote here as not wholly without illustrative value.

Sherard Osborn's gunboat was lying one night close to the southern point of the Quedah river, where it flows into the Strait of Malacca. The air was chill and damp, and the sky obscured with clouds, through which a young moon sped occasional shafts of silver light.

About eleven o'clock his attention was directed to his look-out man, a Malay, who, seated upon the fore-deck gun, was spitting violently, and giving rapid utterance to expressions apparently of reproof or defiance. Another Malay quickly joined him; pointed towards the jungle-loaded shore; and then he too began the spitting and ejaculatory process. After awhile, with an evident air of relief, the second Malay went down below. Unable any longer to restrain his curiosity, Sherard Osborn walked forward. The look-out man had turned his back to the jungle, but ever and anon threw a furtive glance over his shoulder, and uttered sentences in which the name of "Allah" frequently occurred. He seemed delighted at the coming of his captain, and, springing to his feet, saluted him.

"Anything new?" said Osborn; "any prahus in sight?"
"Teda, Touhan—no, sir," was the reply; and then observing that his officer was looking in the direction of the jungle, he made signs that it was better to look anywhere but there.

Calling Jamboo, his interpreter, Osborn desired him to ask the Malay what he saw in the jungle. Judge his astonishment at the reply:

"He says he saw a spirit, sir."

"Nonsense. Ask him how or where? It may be some Malay scouts."

Again came the answer: that the man had distinctly seen an *untoo*, or spirit, moving about among the trees close to the margin of the water; and that he had been assiduously praying and expectorating, in order to prevent it from approaching the gunboat, as it was evidently a very bad spirit, very dangerous, and clothed in a long dress.

Sherard Osborn reprimanded his interpreter for repeating so ridiculous a fancy, and ordered him to explain to the man that there were no such things as "spirits," and that if he had seen anything, it must have been an animal or a man. But he was earnestly assured by Jamboo, the interpreter, that Malays frequently saw untoos; that some were dangerous, and some harmless; and that as for the untoo he had just seen, the captain would see it too, if he looked carefully.

Accordingly, the English captain sat down by the side of the Malay sailor, and looked in the same direction. The gunboat lay at anchor about one hundred and fifty yards from the jungle; the water flowed up to its very margin; among the spreading roots of the mangrove trees lay small ridges of white shingle and broken shells, which receded into darkness or shone out into distinct relief as the moonlight fell upon them. When these white gleams became visible, Osborn immediately pointed to them, and hinted that these were the Malay's "spirit."

"No, no!" he answered vehemently, and Jamboo added, "He says he will warn you immediately he sees *it*."

Suddenly he touched his officer, and pointing earnestly, exclaimed, "Look, look!"

Sherard Osborn *did* look, and for a moment yielded to the

delusion as he caught sight of what appeared to be, and probably was, the figure of a female with drapery thrown around her. Gliding out of the dark forest shadows, it halted at a hillock of white sand not more than three hundred yards distant. Osborn rubbed his eyes; the interpreter called vigorously on a Romish saint, and the Malay spat energetically, as if some unclean animal had crossed his path. Again the captain looked, and again he saw the form, which had passed a dense clump of trees, and was slowly crossing another avenue in the forest.

"Feeling the folly," says Sherard Osborn, "of yielding to the impression of reality which the illusion was certainly creating in my mind, I walked away, and kept the Malay employed in different ways until midnight; he, however, every now and then spat vehemently, and cursed all evil spirits with true Mohammedan fervour."

THE ORANG-LAUTS.

Of this singular race of Malays, the Orang-Lauts, "Men of the Seas," or "Sea-Gipsies," it is said that they do not seem to know anything of a Creator. "A fact so difficult to believe," says Mr. Thomson, "when we find that the most degraded of the human race, in other quarters of the globe, have an intuitive idea of this unerring and primary truth imprinted on their minds, that I took the greatest care to find a slight image of the Deity within the chaos of their thoughts, however degraded such might be, but was disappointed. They knew neither the God nor the Devil of the Christians or Mohammedans, although they confessed they had been told of such; nor any of the demi-gods of Hindu mythology, many of whom were recounted to them."

The three great epochs of individual life, birth, marriage, death, pass unnoticed by them. At birth, the mother's joy is the only welcome to a world it is not likely to find very bright or happy. At marriage, the sole solemnity is the exchange between the male and the female of a mouthful of tobacco and a cheepah, or gallon, of water. At death, the body of the deceased is wrapped in his rags and tatters, and with, perhaps, a few tears from the attendant women, committed to the earth. They have none of that exquisite enjoyment of life which is felt by a cultured race; and neither the entrance upon it nor the passage from it seems to them an event calculated to awaken any emotion of interest. And as they are absolutely without religion, so are they wholly free from superstition; the solemn influences of Nature seem to produce no effect upon their stolid dispositions. Of the pârus, and dewas, and nambangs, and other phantom forms which, in the quick imagination of the Malay, haunt each mountain, rock, and tree, they nothing know; and knowing nothing, they do not fear. Terror is as often the result of knowledge as of ignorance. The mind that has no conception of an unseen world or a supernatural force, must necessarily be free from all apprehension of it.

Passing on to the Philippine Islands, we meet there with the Ahetas, who, like the Orang-Lauts, have no religious system, but, unlike the Orang-Lauts, cherish at least a religious sentiment. It appears that they have learned from— or have taught—the Tanguianes, a brave race dwelling in the vicinity, the practice of worshipping—for a day—the trunk of a distorted tree, or a fragment of rock, in which they trace some fancied resemblance to an animal. Then they turn away from it, and think no more about gods until they encounter another strange and fantastical form, for the existence of which they are unable to account: this, in turn, they make the object of a fugitive devotion. For the dead their reverence is pathetic. Year after year they visit their graves, with as much fidelity as a Christian mourner, though without the Christian's faith in a future reunion, and place there a modest offering of tobacco and betel. The bows and arrows of the departed are suspended above his grave on the day of interment, and the Ahetas fondly believe that every night he rises from his resting-place to pursue the shadowy hunt in the haunted glades of the forest.

In the case of an aged person afflicted with a mortal illness, they adopt too often a summary procedure, not waiting for him to die before they bury him. But no sooner has the body been deposited in the grave, than it becomes imperative, according to their traditions, that his death should be avenged; and, accordingly, the warriors of the tribe sally forth, with lance and arrow, to slay the first living creature they encounter,—whether man, or stag, or wild hog, or buffalo. When thus in quest of an expiatory victim, they take the precaution of breaking off the young shoots of the shrubs as they pass by, and leave the broken ends hanging in the direction of their roots, as a warning to travellers or neighbours to shun the path they are taking; for were one of their own people to be the first to come across the avengers, they dare not suffer him to escape any more than Agamemnon could spare his daughter Iphigenia. As she suffered for her father's vow, so must the ill-fated Aheta suffer for the custom of his tribe.

Their superiority to many savage races is attested by their faithfulness in marriage; they practise monogamy. When a young man has chosen his future partner, his friends or relatives ask the consent of their parents, which is never refused. The marriage day is fixed, and in the morning, before sunrise, the maiden is despatched into the forest, where she conceals herself or not, according to her inclinations towards her suitor. An hour's grace is allowed, and the young man then goes in search of her: if he succeed in finding her, and bringing her back to her friends before sunset, she becomes his wife; but if he fail, he is required to abandon all further claim to the damsel. A strange custom! But there is this much at least to be said for it, that it allows the maiden more liberty of choice than she always enjoys in civilised society!

Whether the Ahetas (or Negritos) sprang from a mixture of Malay and Papuan blood, or are of purely Papuan origin, our ethnologists do not seem to have determined. But in their present development they are certainly superior to the Papuan races.[1]

[1] M. de la Gironiere, cit. in "The Eastern Archipelago," pp. 522, 526, 527.

CHAPTER VIII.

*THE SAVAGE RACES OF ASIA: THE SAMOJEDES;
THE MONGOLS; THE OSTIAKS; IN TIBET.*

THE SAMOJEDES.

THE Samojedes are a people of Arctic Asia, where they inhabit the forests and stony tundras of Northern Russia and Western Siberia; driving their herds of reindeer from the banks of the Chatanga to the ice-bound shores of the White Sea, or hunting the wild beasts in the thick forests which extend between the Obi and the Yenisei.

Their superstition is of a very coarse and degrading character. It is true that they recognise the existence of a Supreme Deity, named Jilibeambaertje, or Num, who resides in the air, and, like the Greek Zeus, sends down rain and snow, thunder and lightning; and they afford a proof of that latent capacity for poetical feeling, which some of even the most barbarous tribes possess, in their description of the rainbow as "the hem of his garment." To them, however, he seems so elevated above the things of earth, so indifferent to the woes or joys of humanity, that they regard it as useless to seek to propitiate him either by prayer or sacrifice; and accordingly they appeal to the inferior gods who have, as they believe, the control of human affairs, and can be affected by incantations, vows, or special homage.

The bleak and lonely island of Waigatz is still, as in the days of the Dutch adventurer, Barentz, supposed to be the residence of the chief of these minor divinities. There a block of stone, pointed at the summit, bears a certain resemblance to a human head, having been wrought into this likeness by a freak of Nature. The Samojede image-makers have taken it for their model, and multiplied it in wood and stone; and the idols thus easily manufactured they call *sjadæi*, because they wear a human (or semi-human) countenance (*sja*.) They attire them in reindeer skins, and embellish them with innumerable coloured rags. In addition to the *sjadæi*, they adopt as idols any curiously contorted tree or irregularly shapen stone; and the household idol (*Hahe*) they carry about with them, carefully wrapped up, in a sledge reserved for the purpose, the *hahengan*. One of the said Penates is supposed to be the guardian of wedded happiness, another of the fishery, a third of the health of his worshippers, a fourth of their herds of reindeer. When his services are needed, the Hahe is removed from its resting-place, and erected in the tent or on the pasture-ground, in the wood, or on the river's bank. Then his mouth is smeared with oil or blood, and before him is set a dish of fish or flesh, in return for which repast it is expected that he will use his power on behalf of his entertainers. When his aid is no longer needed, he is returned to the hahengan.

Besides these obliging deities, the Samojede believes in the existence of an order of invisible spirits which he calls *Tadebtsois*. These are ever and everywhere around him, and bent rather upon his injury than his welfare. It becomes important, therefore, to propitiate them; but this can be done only through the intervention of a *Tadibe*, or sorcerer; who, on occasion, stimulates himself into a wildly excited condition, like the frenzy of the Pythean or Delphic priestess. When the credulous Samojede invokes his assistance, he attires himself in full necromantic costume: a kind of shirt, made of reindeer leather; and trimmed with red cloth. Its seams are similarly trimmed; and the shoulders are decorated with red cloth tags, or epaulettes. A visor of red cloth conceals his face, and upon his breast gleams a plate of polished metal.

Thus imposingly arrayed, the Tadibe takes his drum of reindeer skin, ornamented with brass rings, and, attended by a neophyte, walks round and round with singular stateliness, while invoking the presence of the spirits by a discordant rattle. This gradually increases in violence, and is accompanied by the droning incantation of the words of enchantment. In due time the spirits are supposed to appear, and the Tadibe proceeds to consult them : beating his drum more gently, and occasionally pausing in his lugubrious chant,—which, however, the novice is careful not to interrupt,—to listen, as he pretends, to the answers of the deities. At length the interrogations cease; the chant breaks into a fierce howl; more and more loudly rattles the drum : the Tadibe appears possessed by a supernatural influence; his body writhes; the foam-drops gather on his lips. All at once the wild intoxication ceases; and the Tadibe delivers the supposed will of the Tadebtsois : advises how a stray reindeer may be recovered, or the disease of the Samojede worshipper relieved, or the fisherman's labour may secure a plenteous " harvest of the sea."

The Tadibe's office is usually hereditary; but occasionally some outsider, predisposed by nature to hysteric manifestations, and gifted with a warm, irregular imagination, is initiated into its mysteries. His morbid fancy is intensified by long solitary self-communings and protracted fasts and vigils; and his frame debilitated by the use of pernicious narcotics and stimulants, until he comes to believe that he has been visited by the spirits. He is then received as a Tadibe, with numerous ceremonies, which take place at midnight, and is invested with the magic drum. It is evident, therefore, that the Tadibe, if he deceive others, is the victim to some extent of self-deception. But, in order to impose upon his ignorant countrymen, he does not disdain to resort to the commonest cheats of the conjuror. Among these is the notorious rope-trick, introduced into England by the performers known as the " Davenport Brothers," and since repeated by so many " professional artists." With hands and feet to all appearance securely fastened, he sits down on a carpet of reindeer skin, and, the lights being put out, summons the spirits to his assistance. Their presence is speedily made known by singular noises; squirrels seem to rustle, snakes to hiss, bears to growl. At length the disturbance ceases; the lights are rekindled; and the Tadibe steps forward unbound; the spectators of course believing that he has been assisted by the Tadebtsois.

Not less barbarous than the poor creatures who submit

to his guidance, the Tadibe is incapable, and probably not desirous, of improving their moral condition. Similar impostors, claiming and exercising a similar spiritual dictatorship,—*Schamans*, as the Tungusi call them, *Angekoks* among the Eskimos, *Medicine-men* among the Crees and Chepewyans,—we find among all the Arctic tribes of the Old and New World, where their authority has not been overthrown by Christianity or Buddhism; and this dreary superstition still prevails over at least half a million of souls, from the White Sea to the extremity of Asia, and from the Pacific to Hudson's Bay.

Like the peoples of Siberia, the Samojedes offer up sacrifices to the dead, and perform various ceremonies in their honour. Like the North American Indians, they believe that the desires and pursuits of the departed continue exactly the same as if they were still living; and hence, that they may not be in want of weapons or implements, they deposit in or about the graves a sledge, a spear, a knife, an axe, a cooking-pot.

At the funeral, and for several years afterwards, the kinsmen sacrifice reindeer over the grave.

When a chief or Starochina dies,—the owner, it may be, of several herds of reindeer,—his nearest relatives fashion an image, which is kept in the tent of the deceased, and receives the same measure of respect that was paid to the man himself in his lifetime. At every meal it occupies his accustomed seat; every evening it is solemnly undressed, and duly laid down in his bed. For three years these honours are regularly paid; after which the image is buried, in a belief that the body must by that time have decayed, and lost all recollection of the past. Only the souls of the Tadibes, and of those who have died a violent death, are in the enjoyment of immortality, and hover about the air as disembodied spirits.

THE OSTIAKS.

Further to the east, and occupying the northernmost part of Siberia from the Oural Mountains to Kamtschatka, are the Ostiaks.

The Russians have imposed upon this people the Chris-

THE SAVAGE RACES OF ASIA. 159

tian religion, as taught by the Greek Church; but it seems probable that the majority adhere in secret to their heathen creed. Madame Felinska, a Polish lady, who for some years lived in exile in Siberia, relates that, one day, when she was seeking a pathway through a wood, she came upon a couple of Ostiaks, on the point of performing their devotions. These are certainly of a much simpler kind than the rites enjoined by the Greek Church : the worshipper simply places himself before a tree—he appears to prefer the larch —in some sequestered forest-nook, and performs in rapid succession the most extravagant contortions and gestures. As the practice is prohibited by the Russian Government, it is necessarily made a matter of secresy.

An Ostiak generally carries about him a rude image of one of the deities or demons which he adores under the name of Schaïtan; but he conforms to Russian customs by wearing a small crucifix of copper on his breast. The Schaïtan is a rude imitation of the human figure, carved in wood. It is of different sizes, according to the uses for which it is intended; if for wearing on the person, it is a miniature doll; but as part of the furniture of an Ostiak's hut it is made on a large scale. It is always attired in seven pearl-broidered chemises, and suspended to the neck by a string of silver coins. In every hut it fills the place of honour,—sometimes in company with an image of the Virgin Mary or some Russian saint; and when they sit down to their meals, the Ostiaks are careful to offer it the daintiest morsels, smearing its lips with fish or raw game; this sacred duty fulfilled, they attack with eagerness the viands set before them.

The Ostiak priests are called *Schamans.* Their influence is very great, but is wholly employed in the promotion of their own selfish interests, through the encouragement of the basest superstitions.

WEATHER-CONJURING AMONG THE MONGOLS.

There are many allusions in Mongol history to the practice of weather-conjuring. The operation was performed by means of a stone supposed to be endowed with magical virtues, called *Yadah* or *Jadah Tásh:* this was suspended over or hung in a basin of water with sundry ceremonies.

Ibn Mohalhal, an early Arab traveller, asserts that the *Kimák*, a great tribe of the Turks, possessed such a stone. In the war waged against Chinghiz and Aung Khan by a powerful tribal confederation in 1202, it is recorded that Sengun, the son of Aung Khan, who had been despatched to arrest the enemy's advance, caused them to be enchanted, so that all the movements they attempted against him were defeated by dense mists and blinding snow-storms. So thick was the mist, so intense was the darkness, that men and horses stumbled over precipices, and many also perished with cold.

The celebrated conqueror, Timur, in his *Memoirs*, records that the Jets resorted to incantations to produce heavy rains which hindered his cavalry from acting against them. A *Yadachi*, or weather-conjuror, was taken prisoner, and after he had been beheaded the storm ceased.

Babu refers to one of his early friends, Khwaja ka Mulai, as conspicuous for his skill in falconry and his knowledge of *Yadageri*, or the science of inducing rain and snow by means of enchantment. The Russians were much distressed by heavy rains in 1552, when besieging Kazan, and universally ascribed the unfavourable weather to the arts of the Tartar queen, who was an enchantress.

Early in the 18th century, the Emperor Shi-tsung issued a proclamation against rain-conjuring, addressed to the Eight Banners of Mongolia. "If," indignantly observes the Emperor, "if I, offering prayers in sincerity, have yet cause to fear that it may please heaven to leave MY prayer unanswered, it is truly intolerable that mere common people wishing for rain should of their own fancy set up altars of earth; and bring together a rabble of Hoshang (Buddhist Bonzes) and Taossi to conjure the spirits to gratify their wishes."

The belief in the efficacy of weather-conjuring prevailed all over Europe. In the *Cento Novelle Antiche*, certain necromancers gave specimens of their skill before the Emperor Frederic Barbarossa; and the weather began to be overcast; and lo, of a sudden rain fell with continued thunders and lightnings, as if the world were come to an end, and hailstones of the size and appearance of steel caps.

In Tibet.

Marco Polo, describing his visit to the Kaan's Palace at Chandu, once known as Kaipingfu, speaks of the immense stud of pure white mares which the Kaan kept there, and adds :—" When the Kaan sets out from the Park on the 28th of August, the milk of all those mares is taken and sprinkled on the ground. And this is done on the injunction of the Idolaters and Idol-priests, who affirm that it is an excellent thing to sprinkle that milk on the ground every 28th of August, so that the Earth and the Air and the False Gods shall have their share of it, and likewise the spirits that inhabit the Air and the Earth. And then those beings will protect and bless the Kaan and his children and his wives and his folk and his gear, and his cattle and his horses, his corn and all that is his."

Marco Polo proceeds :—" But I must now tell you a strange thing which hitherto I have forgotten to mention. During the three months of every year that the Emperor resides at that place, if it should happen to be bad weather, there are enchanters and astrologers in his train, who are such adepts in necromancy and diabolic arts, that they are able to prevent any cloud or storm from passing over the spot on which the Emperor's Palace stands. The sorcerers who do this are called Tebet and Kesimar, which are the names of two nations of idolaters. Whatever they do in this way is by the help of the Devil, but they make those people believe that it is compassed by dint of their own sanctity and the help of GOD. . .

" There is another marvel performed by those Bacsi of whom I have been speaking as knowing so many enchantments. For when the great Kaan is at his capital and in his great palace, seated at his table, which stands on a platform some eight cubits above the ground, his cups are set before him on a great buffet in the middle of the hall pavement, at a distance of some ten paces from the table, and filled with wine, or other good spiced liquor such as they use. Now when the Kaan desires to drink, these enchanters by the power of their enchantments cause the cups to move from their place without being touched by anybody, and to present themselves to the Emperor !

This every one present may witness, and there are oftentimes more than ten thousand persons thus present. 'Tis a truth and no lie ! and so will tell you the sages of our own country who understand necromancy, for they also can perform it."

On the occasion of one of these Idol Festivals, the Bacsi would go to the Prince and say :—"Sire, the feast of such a god is come." And he would continue :—" My Lord, you know that this god, when he gets no offering, always sends bad weather and spoils our seasons. So we pray you to give us such and such a number of black-faced sheep," (naming any number they please). "And we beg also, good my Lord, that we may have such a quantity of incense, and such a quantity of lign-aloes, and—so much of this or so much of that, according to the measure of their cupidity or the probability of their expectations being gratified—"that we may perform a solemn service and a great sacrifice to our Idols, and that so they may be induced to protect us and all our property."

When the Bacsi have obtained from the Kaan the fulfilment of their desires, they make a great feast in honour of their god, and hold great ceremonies of worship with grand illuminations and quantities of incense of a variety of odours, which they make up from different aromatic spices. And when the viands are cooked, they set them before the idols, and sprinkle the bush about, affirming that in this way the idols obtain a sufficiency. Thus it is that they keep their festivals. Each idol, we must add, has a name of his own, and a feast-day, just as the Saints of the Christian Church have their anniversaries.

Large minsters and abbeys are theirs, some of them of the size of a small town, with upwards of 2,000 monks in a single abbey. These monks dress more decorously than the rest of the people, and have the head and the beard shaven. Among them a limited number are, by their rule, allowed to marry.

Another kind of devotees were called the Seusin, men of extraordinary abstemiousness, who led a life of extreme endurance. Their sole food was bran mixed with hot water, so that one might call their lives a prolonged fast. They had numerous idols, and idols of a monstrous size, but they also worshipped fire. Idolaters not belonging to this sect naturally called them "heretics," on the old principle that "my doxy" is "orthodoxy," and "your doxy" "heterodoxy." Their dresses were made of hempen stuff, black and blue, and they slept upon mats. In fact, says Marco Polo, "their asceticism is something remarkable."

Chandu, or Xanadu, and its palace, suggested to Coleridge one of his most exquisite passages of description :—

> " In Xanadu did Kubla Kaan
>   A stately pleasure dome decree :
> Where Alph, the sacred river, ran,
> By caverns measureless to man,
>   Down to a sunless sea.
> So twice five miles of fertile ground,
> With walls and towers were girdled round :
> And there were gardens bright with sinuous rills,
>   Where blossomed many an incense-bearing tree ;
> And here were forests, ancient as the hills,
>   Enfolding sunny spots of greenery."

Xanadu has disappeared, and so has its palace, but the superstitions practised in it are still in vogue among the Mongolian peoples. The word "Bakhshi," however, has come to have a different meaning in different districts; among the Kirghiz Kazzaks it is applied, as Marco Polo applied it, to a conjuror or medicine-man ; among the modern Mongols it signifies "a teacher," and is bestowed on the oldest and most learned priest of a community ; in Western Turkestan it means "a bard ;" in our Indian army it is "a paymaster."

The jugglery of the goblets, to which Marco Polo refers, was not uncommon in Mediæval Europe. Colonel Yule cites[1] the Jesuit Delrio as lamenting the credulity of certain princes, otherwise of pious repute, who allowed diabolic tricks to be played in their presence; as for instance that things of iron, and silver goblets, or other heavy articles, should be moved by bounds from one end of a table to the other, without the use of a magnet or of any attachment. The pious prince appears to have been Charles IX., and the conjuror a certain Cesare Maltesio. In old legends

---

[1] Col. Yule, "Book of Sir Marco Polo," Vol. I. pp. 306, 307.

this trick is one of the sorceries ascribed to Simon Magus. "He made statues to walk; leapt into the fire without being burnt; flew in the air; made bread of stones; changed his shape; assumed two faces at once,"—an accomplishment not confined to conjurors,—"converted himself into a pillar; caused closed doors to fly open of their own will; and made the vessels in a house seem to move of themselves."

Colonel Yule asserts that the profession and practice of exorcism and magic in general is much more prominent in Lamaism, or Tibetan Buddhism, than in any other known form of that religion. "Indeed," he says, "the old form of Lamaism, as it existed in Marco Polo's day, and till the reforms of Tsongkhapa (1357-1419), and as it is still professed by the *Red* sect in Tibet, seems to be a kind of compromise between Indian Buddhism and the old indigenous Shamanism. Even the reformed doctrine of the Yellow sect recognises an orthodox kind of magic, which is due in great measure to the combination of Sivaism with the Buddhist doctrines, and of which the institutes are contained in the vast collection of the *Jud* or Tantras, recognised among the holy books. The magic arts of this code open even a short road to the Buddhahood itself. To attain that perfection of power and wisdom culminating in the cessation of sensible existence, requires, according to the ordinary paths, a period of three *asankhyas* (or say Unaccountable Time × 3), whereas by means of the magic arts of the *Tantras*, it may be reached in the course of three *rebriths* only, nay, of one! But from the Tantras also can be learned how to acquire miraculous powers for objects entirely selfish and secular, and how to exercise these by means of *Dhárani*, or mystic Indian charms."

The commonplace and vulgar exhibition of such exploits as blowing fire, cutting off heads, and swallowing knives, is formally repudiated by the orthodox Yellow Lamas; but as the crowd cannot be satisfied without them, each of the great Yellow Lama monasteries in Tibet maintains a conjuror, as of old each European sovereign kept his jester. This conjuror is not a member of the monastic fraternity, and lives in a particular part of the convent, out of the atmosphere of their sanctity. He is called *Choicong*, or protector of religion, and is free to marry. The Choicong hand down their magic lore from generation to generation orally, and by their cries and howls, and their frenzied gestures, and their fantastic dress, are connected with the Shamanist devil dancers.

Magic seems to have always borne the same character in every country. The marvels accomplished by the Indian mystic charms, or *Dhárani*, are exactly those which the Mediæval magicians of Europe professed to achieve. To make water flow backwards, to resuscitate the dead, to fly through the air, to read a man's inmost thoughts, these were the wonders done by Simon Magus in his day, and by Albertus Magnus and his followers in their day; and form what may be called the ordinary stock-in-trade of the old necromancers. The Bakhshis included them in their series of performances. "There are certain men," says Ricold, "whom the Tartars honour above all in the world, viz., the *Baxitæ* (or *Bakhshis*), who are a kind of idol priests. These are men from India, persons of deep wisdom, well conducted, and of the gravest morals. They are usually acquainted with magic arts, and depend on the counsel and aid of demons; they exhibit many illusions, and predict some future events. For instance, one of eminence among them was said to fly; the truth however was (as it proved) that he did not fly, but did walk close to the surface of the ground without touching it; and would seem to sit down without having any substance to support him." Ibn Batuta describes a performance of this kind as witnessed by him at Delhi, in the presence of Sultan Mahomed Tughlak. Francis Valentyn, at a later date, speaks of it as common in India. He was told, he says, that a man would first go and sit upon three sticks which had been so put together as to form a tripod, after which, first one stick, then a second, then a third would be removed from under him, and yet the man would not fall, but would remain suspended in the air. He could not bring himself to believe it, so manifestly contrary was it to reason, yet he had spoken with two friends who had both seen it done on the same occasion, and one of them mistrusting his own eyes, had felt about with a long stick to ascertain if there were not something on which the body rested, but could discover nought.

Superstition, like history, repeats itself,—some of the marvels with which the Lama conjurors and the Tartar Bakhshis deluded their people are repeated by the spiritualistic "mediums," of the present day and put forward by them as the credentials of their pretended mission.

They fall short, however, of the extraordinary feats performed by the professional jugglers who laid no claim to a religious character, if we may credit the accounts of the early travellers. Ibn Batuta, for instance, gravely describes what he saw, or thought he saw, at a great entertainment given by the Viceroy of Khansa:—

A juggler, he says, one of the Kaan's slaves, made his appearance, and at the Amir's bidding, began to display his surprising accomplishments. Taking a wooden ball, with several holes in it, through which long thongs were passed, he laid hold of one of these, and slung the ball into the air. It went so high, that the spectators wholly lost sight of it. Observe, that the scene was the palace-court, *sub Jove*. There remained only a little of the end of the thong in the juggler's hand, and of this he desired a juvenile assistant to lay hold, and mount. He did so, climbing by the thong, and was speedily lost to sight also. The conjuror called him thrice, but receiving no answer, snatched up a knife, as if in a great rage, laid hold of the thong, and in *his* turn disappeared. By-and-by he threw down one of the boy's hands, then a foot, then the other hand, the other foot, the trunk, and lastly, the head! Finally, he himself came down, all puffing and panting, and with blood-besmeared clothes kissed the ground before the Amir, addressing him in Chinese. The Amir made some reply; and straightway the juggler took the boy's *disjecta membra*, laid them in their places, gave a kick, and lo and behold, the boy arose and stood erect, "clothed and in his right mind." "All this," says Ibn Batuta, "astonished me beyond measure,"—and no wonder!— "and I had an attack of palpitation like that which overcame me once before in the presence of the Sultan of India, when he showed me something of the same kind. They gave me a cordial, however, which cured the attack. The Kazi Afkharuddin was next to me, and quoth he,

'Wallah ! 'tis my opinion there has been neither going up nor coming down, neither maiming nor mending; 'tis all hocus pocus !'"

Impartial scientific observers have passed a similar verdict on the proceedings of the "mediums," who, however, have never achieved anything so surprising as the feat here recorded. Before we incredulously reject the Arab traveller's narrative, let us compare it with an account furnished by Edward Melton, an Anglo-Dutch traveller, of the performances of some Chinese conjurors, which he saw at Batavia. Passing over the basket-murder trick, which Houdin and others have made familiar to the English public, we come to "a thing which surpasses all belief;" which, indeed, Mr. Melton would scarcely have ventured to relate had not thousands witnessed it at the same time as himself.

One of the gang took a ball of cord, and grasping one end in his hand hurled the other up into the air with such force that it was entirely lost to sight. He then climbed up the cord as rapidly as a sailor up his ship's rigging, and to such a height that he became invisible. Melton stood full of astonishment, and at a loss to know what next would happen ; when, behold, a leg tumbled out of the air ! A conjuror who was on the watch for it immediately snatched it up, and threw it into a basket. Down came a hand, and then another leg, and, in short, all the members of the body successively fell from the air, to find shelter in the basket. The last of the ghastly shower was the head; and no sooner had it touched the ground than the man who had gathered the limbs and stowed them in the basket, turned them all out again topsy-turvy. Straightway they began to creep together, until they composed a whole man, who stood up and walked about just as before, having sustained apparently no damage ! "Never in my life," says Melton, "was I so astonished as when I beheld this wonderful performance, and I doubted now no longer that those misguided men did it by the help of the Devil. For it seems to me totally impossible that such things should be accomplished by natural means."[1]

[1] Edward Melton, "Engelsch Edelmans Zeldzaame en Gedenkwaardige Zee en Land Reizen," &c., 1660, 1677, p. 468.

The Emperor Jahángir in his "Memoirs" (cited by Yule) describes the exploits of some Bengali jugglers, who exhibited before him. Two of them bear a close resemblance to the foregoing. Thus: they produced a man whom they divided limb from limb, actually severing his head from the body. These mutilated members they scattered along the ground, where they remained for some time. A sheet or curtain was extended over the spot, and one of the men placing himself under it, in a few minutes reappeared, in company with the individual supposed to have been so roughly dissected, in such perfect health and condition, that one might have safely sworn he had never received the slightest wound or injury.

Again: they produced a chain, fifty cubits long, and one end of it threw towards the sky, when it remained as if fastened to something in the air. A dog was then brought forward, and being placed at the lower end of the chain, ran up it to the other end, and immediately vanished. In the same manner a boy, a panther, a lion, and a tiger were successively sent up the chain to disappear, in their turn, at the other end of it. And, lastly, the chain was taken down and put away in a bag, without any of the spectators discovering in what manner the different animals had been spirited into space!

The surprising dexterity of these jugglers is emulated by their descendants, and many of the Indian conjurors produce illusions scarcely less wonderful than any we have described.

Take the pretty mango-trick. The juggler who exhibits has no other drapery than half a yard of cotton, and no other apparatus than a handful of common toys. He has none of those elaborate mechanical contrivances, on which the European professors of legerdemain mostly rely for their effects.

He takes a mango-stone, buries it in a little mud, and covers it with a jar.

A few minutes later, the jar is lifted up; and lo, a tender green seed-leaf has delicately sprouted. Another peep into the magic hotbed, and we see that the tiny leaf has withered, and that a flourishing young tree has sprung into sudden existence.

Or we have the egg-trick, which an eye-witness thus describes :—[1]
"One of the party, a very handsome woman, fixed on her head a fillet of strong texture, to which were fastened, at equal distances, twenty pieces of string of equal length, with a common noose at the end of each. Under her arm she carried a basket, in which were carefully deposited twenty eggs. Her basket, the fillet, and the nooses were carefully examined by us. There was evidently no deception.

"The woman advanced alone, and stood before us. She then began to move rapidly round on one spot, whence she never for one instant moved, spinning round and round like a top.

"When her pace was at its height, she drew down one of the strings, which now flew horizontally round her head, and, securing an egg in the noose, she jerked it back to its original position, still twirling round with undiminished velocity, and repeating the process until she had secured the whole twenty eggs in the nooses previously prepared for them. She projected them rapidly from her hand the moment she had secured them, until at length the whole twenty were flying round her in an unbroken circle. Thus she continued spinning at undiminished speed for fully five minutes ; after which, taking the eggs one by one from their nooses, she replaced them in her basket ; and then in one instant stopped, without the movement of a limb, or even the vibration of a muscle, as if she had been suddenly transformed into marble. The countenance was perfectly calm, nor did she exhibit the slightest distress from her extraordinary exertions."

The basket-murder trick, to which we have already referred, is as follows :—

The juggler stepping forward, invites your examination of a light wicker basket, and when you profess yourself satisfied, he places it over a child, about eight years old, who is perfectly naked. He then asks the child some indifferent question, and you hear her reply to it from the basket. Question and answer are repeated frequently, each time in a louder and more impassioned manner, until the juggler,

[1] Miss Gordon Cumming. "From the Hebrides to the Himalayas," ii. 68, 69.

in a seeming fit of rage, threatens to kill the girl, who vainly supplicates for mercy.

The dramatic character of the scene is as perfect in its realism as it is horrible. The man plants his foot furiously on the frail basket, and plunges his sword into it again and again, while the ears of the spectators are rent and their hearts touched by the child's cries of agony. For a moment it is impossible to believe that you are witnessing a deception, as you listen to the passionate shrieks and watch the man's furious face. Blood flows in a stream from the basket, and by degrees the groans of the victim grow fainter and fainter, until all is hushed in a silence so intense that you hear your heart beat. You are about to rush on the murderer, and inflict summary punishment, when he mutters a few cabalistic words, takes up the basket, and shows you—only a little blood-stained earth; while the child, you know not how or whence, has come to mingle with the crowd, and ask for baksheesh.

Two simpler exploits may be recorded :—

Taking a large, wide-mouthed, earthen vessel, filled with water, the conjuror turns it upside down, and, of course, the contents run out.

He then reverses the jar, which to your amazement is seen to be perfectly full, while all the earth round about is —dry! The jar is again emptied, and submitted to the inspection of the spectators. He asks you to fill it to the brim ; after which he reverses it : not a drop of water flows, and yet when you look into it, it is perfectly empty. At last the conjuror breaks the jar by way of a practical demonstration of the fact that it is made of common earthenware.

A large basket is produced : the conjuror raises it, and a Pariah dog appears crouching on the ground. The basket-cover is replaced; and a second examination shows you a bitch with a litter of seven puppies. A goat, a pig, and various other animals, come forth in due time from this inexhaustible cornucopia.

All these exploits are performed by a single exhibitor, who stands quite alone, and at a distance of several feet from the crowd, so that collusion with confederates would seem to be impossible.

CHAPTER IX.

SOME AFRICAN SUPERSTITIONS.

AFRICA is the land of superstition,—dark, cruel, ghastly superstition. It accompanies its victim from the cradle to the grave; throws its fell shadow over every scene and incident of life. We cannot attempt, nor do we desire, to paint it in all its horrors. For our purpose it will be sufficient to glance at some of the ceremonies, hideous or grotesque, which are practised by the Equatorial Savage.

In his childhood he has to be initiated into certain mysteries. What those are Mr. Winwood Reade learned from a negro steward, who informed him that he was taken into a fetich, or idol house, severely flogged, and plastered with goat-dung: this ceremony, like the rites of masonry, being conducted to the sound of music. Afterwards from behind a kind of screen or shrine issued uncouth and terrible sounds such as he had never before heard. These, he was told, emanated from the spirit called Ukuk. He afterwards brought to Mr. Winwood Reade the instrument with which the fetich-man produces the noise. It may be described as a whistle made of hollowed mangrove wood, about two inches long, and covered at one end with a scrap of bat's wing. For a period of five days after initiation the novice wears an apron of dry palm leaves.

He is next instructed in the science of fetich; and afterwards he learns what kinds of food are forbidden to his tribe, for one tribe may not eat crocodile, another hippopotamus, nor a third buffalo. He learns to reverence and dread the spirit *Ukuk*, which dwells, it is said, in the bowels of the earth, and visits the upper world only when he has some business to perform. On the occasion of his visits, he abides in the fetich-house, which is built in a peculiar form, roofed with dry plantain leaves, and always kept in darkness. Thence strange dread sounds, like the growling of a tiger, are heard to proceed, so that the women and children shudder as they listen. When the mangrove-tube is thus at work, the initiated hasten to the house, and a "lodge" or "council" is held.

"The natives of Equatorial Africa worship also the spirits of their ancestors; a worship for which their minds are prepared by the veneration which they pay to old age. Young men never enter the presence of an aged person without curtseying (a genuine curtsey like that of a charity-school girl), and passing in a stooping attitude, as if they were going under a low door. When seated in his presence, it is always at a humble distance. If they hand him a lighted pipe, or a mug of water, they fall on one knee. If an old man, they address him as *rora*—father; if an old woman as *ngwe*—mother. It is customary for only the old people to communicate bad news to one another; and it is not to be wondered at that we find the negroes such perfect courtiers, since it is the etiquette of the country that the aged should only be addressed in terms of flattery and adulation.

"When they die their relics are honoured. In the Congo country their bodies are dried into mummies. Here, their bones are sometimes stored up and visited at set periods. Or, when a person noted for his wisdom has died, his head, when partially decomposed, is often cut off and suspended, so as to drip upon a mass of chalk placed underneath. This matter is supposed to be the wisdom which formerly animated the brain, and which, rubbed upon the foreheads of others, will communicate its virtue."

It can easily be understood how this reverence paid to the relics of one's ancestors would develope into the worship of their spirits. The Equatorial Savage believes that the manes of his forefathers influence his life and fortunes entirely to his advantage, and by a dying friend or relative will often send messages to them. Mr. Reade adds that a son has been known to kill his aged mother from a conviction that her spirit would be of more service to him than her substance; a reason for matricide which would hardly be accepted as conclusive in civilised countries! The savage lives, however, in constant communion and sympathy with the spirit-world. The visions which come to him in his dreams, and the sounds which he fancies himself to hear, are those of the Unseen. And as he is always brooding upon his dreams and relating them to his friends, he necessarily dreams the more, until it becomes difficult for him to draw a line between the dream and the reality.

When any calamity befalls the tribe, or at the approach of any imminent danger, they gather together on the brink of some lofty bluff, or on the forest's haunted threshold, and stretching their arms towards the sky, while the women wail and the children weep, they call upon the spirits of the departed to come and help them.

They have a remarkable ceremony which illustrates the force and vividness of their belief in spirits:

When the dead are weary of staying in the bush, they come for one of their people whom they most affect. And the spirit will say to the man: "I am tired of dwelling in the bush; please to build for me in the town a little house as close as possible to your own." And he tells him to dance and sing too; and accordingly the man assembles the women at night to join in dance and song.

Then, next day, the people repair to the grave of the *Obambo*, or ghost, and make a rude idol; after which the bamboo bier on which the body is conveyed to the grave, and some of the dust of the ground, are carried into a little hut erected near the house of the visited, and a white cloth is draped over the door.

It is a curious fact, which seems to show that they have a legend something like the old Greek myth of Charon and the Styx, that in one of the songs chanted during this ceremony occurs the following line: "You are well dressed, but you have no canoe to carry you across to the other side."

According to Mr. Reade, these savages have their Naiads and Dryads; their spirits of the mountains and the forests, the lakes and the streams, and the high places. They have also their Typhon and their Osiris, their Good and Evil

Genius; thus recognising, in common with almost every other race, the enduring antagonism between the Principles and Powers of Good and Evil. The Evil Spirit, *Mbwiri*, they worship with a special homage; his might is to be dreaded, and his anger, if possible, averted. He is the lord of earth; and before him, as before a tyrant whose hand can grasp their lives and fortunes, they bend in humble adoration. But as the Good Spirit will do them no injury, they conceive it unnecessary to address to it any regular or formal prayer. "The word by which they express this Supreme Being answers exactly to our word of God. Like the Jehovah of the Hebrews, like that word in masonry which is only known to masters, and never pronounced but in a whisper and in full lodge, this word they seldom dare to speak; and they display uneasiness if it is uttered before them. Twice only," says Mr. Reade, "I remember having heard it. Once when we were in a dangerous storm, the men threw their clenched hands upwards and cried it twice. And again, when I was at Ngambi, taking down words from an Ashira slave, I asked him what was the word for God in the language of his country. He raised his eyes, and pointing to heaven, said in a soft voice, *Njambi*."

Epileptic diseases, in almost all uncivilised countries, are assumed to be the result of demoniac possession. In Africa the sufferer is supposed to be possessed by Mbwiri, and he can be relieved only by the intervention of the medicine-man or fetich. In the middle of the street a hut is built for his accommodation, and there he resides until cured, or maddened, along with the priest and his disciples. There for ten days or a fortnight a continuous revel is held; much eating and drinking at the expense of the patient's relatives, and unending dances to the sound of flute and drum. For obvious reasons the fetich gives out that Mbwiri regards good living with aversion. The patient dances, usually shamming madness, until the epileptic attack comes on, with all its dreadful concomitants—the frenzied stare, the convulsed limbs, the gnashing teeth, and the foam-flecked lips. The man's actions at this period are not ascribed to himself, but to the demon which has control of him. When a cure has been effected, real or pretended, the patient builds a little fetich-house, avoids certain kinds of food, and performs certain duties. Sometimes the process terminates in the patient's insanity; he has been known to run away to the bush, hide from all human beings, and live on the roots and berries of the forest.

"These fetich-men are priest doctors, like those of the ancient Germans. They have a profound knowledge of herbs, and also of human nature, for they always monopolize the real power in the state. But it is very doubtful whether they possess any secrets save that of extracting virtue and poison from plants. During the first trip which I made into the bush I sent for one of these doctors. At that time I was staying among the Shekani, who are celebrated for their fetich. He came attended by half-a-dozen disciples. He was a tall man, dressed in white, with a girdle of leopard's skin, from which hung an iron bell, of the same shape as our sheep bells. He had two chalk marks over his eyes. I took some of my own hair, frizzled it with a burning glass, and gave it to him. He popped it with alacrity into his little grass bag; for white man's hair is fetich of the first order. Then I poured out some raspberry vinegar into a glass, drank a little of it first, country fashion, and offered it to him, telling him that it was blood from the brains of great doctors. Upon this he received it with great reverence, and dipping his fingers into it as if it was snap-dragon, sprinkled with it his forehead, both feet between the two first toes, and the ground behind his back. He then handed his glass to a disciple, who emptied it, and smacked his lips afterwards in a very secular manner. I then desired to see a little of his fetich. He drew on the ground with red chalk some hieroglyphics, among which I distinguished the circle, the cross, and the crescent. He said that if I would give him a fine 'dush,' he would tell me all about it. But as he would not take anything in reason, and as I knew that he would tell me nothing of very great importance in public, negotiations were suspended."

The fetich-man seldom finds a native disposed to question his claim to supernatural powers. He is not only a doctor and a priest,—two capacities in which his influence is necessarily very powerful; he is also a witch-finder, and this is an office which invests him with a truly formidable authority. When a man of worth dies, his death is invariably ascribed to witchcraft, and the aid of the fetich-man is invoked to discover the witch.

"When a man is sick a long time," said Mongilombas, "they call *Ngembi*, and if she cannot make him well, the fetich-man. He comes at night, in a white dress, with cock's feathers on his head, and having his bell and little glass. He calls two or three relations together into a room. He does not speak, but always looks in his glass. Then he tells them that the sickness is not of Mbwiri, nor of Obambo, nor of God, but that it comes from a witch. They say to him, 'What shall we do?' He goes out and says, 'I have told you: I have no more to say.' They give him a dollar's worth of cloth; and every night they gather together in the street, and they cry, 'I know that man who witch my brother. It is good for you to make him well.' Then the witch makes him well. But if the man do *not* recover, they call the bush doctor from the Shekani country. He sings in the language of the bush. At night he goes into the street; all the people flock about him. With a tiger-cat skin in his hand, he walks to and fro, until, singing all the while, he lays the tiger skin at the feet of the witch. At the conclusion of his song the people seize the witch, and put him, or her, in chains, saying, 'If you don't restore our brother to health, we will kill you.'"

One evening, as Mr. Reade was sitting in a mission house at Corisco, with the windows open, he heard a wild and piteous cry rising from a village at a short distance. A sudden silence fell upon his friends. The school was in the next room, and two girls who belonged to that village lifted up their voices and wept. It was the death-knell, and the knell of more lives than one. A chieftain for some time had been lying in a hopeless condition, and a woman had been denounced for having bewitched him. She had a son of about seven years of age, and fearing lest when he reached manhood, he should become her avenger, the accusers included him also in their denunciation. Both had been made prisoners, and on the death of the chief would be killed.

The following day was Sunday, and Mr. Reade accompanied Mr. Mackay, the missionary, to the village. The man was not dead; but he had suddenly become speechless, and his attendants had concluded that the spirit had departed. Entering the house, Mr. Reade found him lying on the bamboo bedstead in a state of stupor. The house was thronged with women, who had stripped off their garments and shaved the heads in token of mourning, and were "raining tears" in their purchased and admirably acted grief. Sometimes one of them would sit by his side, and flinging her arms around him, would shriek—almost in the very words of the Irish death-wail,—" Why did ye die, darling? why did ye die?" For they regarded him as really dead, when he could neither look at them nor speak to them.

In contrast to their loud sorrow was the silent mourning of the men who, hushed and fasting, sat in the chief house of the town. In their midst crouched the seven years old boy, the marks of a severe wound visible on his arm, and his wrists securely bound together. The dogged expression of the child's face was something wonderful. It wore that look of stolid endurance which seems natural to the negro. One of the men with horrible pleasantry held an axe below his eyes; but the boy contemplated it without emotion—he displayed all the cold indifference of the ancient Stoicism. When his name was first mentioned, his eyes flashed; but this indication of passion was only momentary. He showed the same indifference when a plea was put in for his life, as when, just before, he had been threatened and taunted with death.

Mr. Reade did not see the unfortunate mother, but was afterwards told that she had been flogged into confessing that she and she only had bewitched the man. Her son had acknowledged the crime as soon as he was charged with it. It is well known that such confessions amount to nothing. During the witch epidemic in Mediæval Europe, scores of unhappy creatures confessed to the practice of witchcraft, though by so doing they doomed themselves to death. The imagination in some way or other is powerfully excited, and completely overcomes the judgment; or it may be from a fear of torture or a thirst for notoriety that such confessions are made.

Mr. Mackey, the missionary, said that he had come to

speak to Okota, the nearest kinsman of the dying chief, upon whom, in all such cases, the responsibility rests. Okota came out from the throng, placed his stool near the feet of the missionary, and listened to him attentively.

"Death," said the missionary, "must come to all. It is foolish to think that because a man dies he has been bewitched."

"Yes," replied Okota, "death must come to all, but not always from GOD. Sometimes it comes from the hand of man."

"But how do you know that in this instance it comes from the hand of man?"

"The woman has been given *quai* (the drink of ordeal) to drink, and the *quai* says that she bewitched him."

"But the *quai* is not always right. When Cabinda went to the Muni, he was a long time lost. All people said that he was dead. A man you declared was the witch, you gave him *quai;* *quai* said that the man had killed Cabinda, but Cabinda came back alive, and *quai* was wrong."

A roar of laughter acknowledged the force of this pertinent reply.

"It is not only *quai*," said Okota, "the woman confesses that she has used the arts of witchcraft. Will any man come to you and say, 'I have stolen your fowl,' if he has not stolen it? This woman is killing my brother, when my brother is dead I will kill her."

After so decisive a declaration, further argument was useless, and Mr. Mackey was compelled to retire, unsuccessful.

The ordeal drink of Equatorial Africa is not identical with the "red-water" of Northern Guinea. It is prepared from the root of a small shrub called *Nkazya,* or *Quai.* Half a pint of the decoction is given to the accused, and small sticks being laid down on the ground at a distance of two feet apart, he is compelled to step over them five times. If the potion act upon him as a diuretic, he is pronounced innocent; but in some persons it produces vertigo. The sticks before his dizzy eyes rise like great logs, and in his awkward efforts to stride across them, he reels, falls to the ground, and is immediately assumed to be guilty.

Ultimately the chief died, and the woman and boy both

suffered death. The woman was taken out to sea in a boat, killed with an axe, and thrown overboard. The boy was burnt alive, bags of gunpowder being tied to his legs to shorten his sufferings.

Apart from these superstitions, Mr. Reade asserts that the negroes possess the remnants of a noble and sublime religion, though they have forgotten its precepts, and debased its ceremonies. They still retain their belief in GOD, the One, the Supreme, the Creator. He has made mankind and the world; He thunders in the air, He destroys the wicked with His bolts. He rewards the good with long life; He gives them the rain, the fruits of the earth, and all things that are good. He is far above all the other gods.

In some parts of Guinea the daily prayer is, "O GOD, I know Thee not, but Thou knowest me, Thy aid is necessary to me." At meals they say, "O GOD, Thou hast given me this, Thou hast made it grow." And when they work, "O GOD, Thou hast caused that I should have strength to do this." And another of their prayers runs, "O GOD, help us, we do not know whether we shall live to-morrow; we are in Thy hand."[1]

[1] This chapter is adapted from Mr. Winwood Reade's "Savage Africa," (Edit. 1863.)

CHAPTER X.

THE ZULU WITCH-FINDERS.

ENGLISH Law now reigns in Zululand, and the occupation of the Witch-finders is almost gone; but in times past they were potent personages, whom an enslaving superstition had armed with despotic influence. The Zulu witch-finders are regular Amazons—perfectly fearless, with a martial gait, and grave composure of mien. It is their pride, according to Lady Barker, to be looked upon as men when once they embrace their dread profession, which the men sometimes share with them. They are permitted to bear shield and spear as warriors, and they hunt and kill with their own hands the wild beasts and reptiles whose skins they wear. " It is not difficult to understand," says Lady Barker,[1] " bearing in mind the superstition and cruelty which existed in remote parts of England not so very long ago— how powerful such women become among a savage people, or how tempting an opportunity they could furnish of getting rid of an enemy. Of course they are exceptional individuals ; more observant, more shrewd, and more dauntless, than the average fat, hard-working Kafir women ; besides possessing the contradictory mixture of great physical powers and strong hysterical tendencies. They work themselves up to a pitch of frenzy, and get to believe as firmly in their own supernatural discernment as any individual among the trembling circle of Zulus to whom a touch from the whisk they carry is a sentence of instant death."

The magician, like the melodramatist, must have his ac-

[1] "A Year's Housekeeping in South Africa," p. 173.

companiment of music, and the Zulu witch-finders are attended by a circle of black girls and women, who, like a Greek chorus, clap their hands together, and drone through a low monotonous chant, the measure and rhythm of which change at times with a stamp and a swing. Not less necessary is a ceremonial dress; for such things appeal directly to the imagination of the crowd, and prepare them to be readily influenced by the necromancer's devices. The "Isinyanga," "Abangoma," or "witch-finders," whom Lady Barker describes for us, were attired with an eye for effect which would have done credit to a London theatre. It will suffice to depict one of them, by name Nozinyanga. Her fierce face, spotted with gouts of red paint on cheek and brow, was partly overshadowed by a helmet-like plume of the tall feathers of the sakabula bird. In her right hand she carried a light sheaf of assegais or lances, and on her left arm was slung a small and pretty shield of dappled ox-hide. Her petticoat, made of a couple of large gay handkerchiefs, was worn kilt-wise. But if there were little decoration in her skirts, the deficiency was more than compensated by the bravery of the bead-necklaces, the goat's-hair fringes, and the scarlet tassels which covered her from throat to waist. Her ample chest rose and fell beneath a baldric of leopard skin, fastened across it with huge brazen knobs; while down her back hung a beautifully dried and flattened skin of an enormous boa-constrictor.

The interest attaching to these women is derived from the fact that it was of old the custom, among the Zulu and other South African tribes, to attribute all mishaps or catastrophes, political or social, to the agency of witches. It is not for Englishmen to look down with contempt upon this manifestation of barbarism and ignorance, considering that a similar belief prevailed very generally among us up to the reign of Charles I., and, in truth, is not wholly extinct even now: while the extent to which the science of witch-finding was developed in New England will be known to every reader of Cotton Mather.

When the community had resolved that a certain misfortune was due to the witches, the next step obviously would be to detect and punish them. For this purpose the king would summon a great meeting, and cause his subjects to sit on the ground in a ring or circle, for four or five days. The witch-finders took their places in the centre, and as they gradually worked themselves up to a frantic state of frenzy, resembling demoniacal possession, they lightly switched with their quagga-tail one or other of the trembling spectators, who was immediately dragged away and butchered on the spot. And not only he, but all the living things in his hut—wives and children, dogs and cats—not one was left alive, nor was a stick left standing. Sometimes a whole kraal would be exterminated in this way; and the reader will perceive how terribly the cruel custom could be made to gratify private revenge or to work out the king's tyrannical inclinations.

A terrible little sorceress is described under the name of Nozilwane,[1] whose weird wistful glance had in it something uncanny and uncomfortable. She was really dressed beautifully for her part, in lynx skins folded over and over from waist to knee, the upper part of her body being covered by strings of wild beasts' teeth and fangs, beads, skeins of gaily-coloured yarn, strips of snake's skin, and fringes of Angora-goat fleece. This, as a decoration, was both graceful and effective; it was worn round the body and above each elbow, and fell in soft white flakes among the brilliant colouring and against the dusky skin. Lynx-tails depended like lappets on each side of her face, which was overshadowed and almost hidden by a profusion of sakabula feathers. "This bird," says Lady Barker, "has a very beautiful plumage, and is sufficiently rare for the natives to attach a peculiar value and charm to the tail-feathers; they are like those of a young cock, curved and slender, and of a dark chestnut colour, with a white eye at the extreme tip of each feather." Among all this thick, floating plumage were interspersed small bladders, and skewers or pins wrought out of tusks. Each witch-finder wore her own hair, or rather wool; highly greased, and twisted up with twine until it ceases to wear the appearance of hair, and hangs around the face like a thick fringe, dyed deep red.

Bent double, and with a creeping, cat-like gait, as if seeking a trail, out stepped Nozilwane. Every movement of her undulating body kept time to the beat of the girls'

---

[1] Lady Barker, "A Year's Housekeeping in South Africa," p. 179.

hands and their low crooning chant. Presently she pretended to find the thing she sought, and with a series of wild pirouettes leaped into the air, shaking her spears and brandishing her little shield like a Bacchante. Nowamso, another of the party, was determined that her companion should not carry off all the applause, and she too, with a yell and a leap, sprang into the dance to the sound of louder grunts and harder hand-claps. Nowamso showed much anxiety to display her back, where a magnificent snake skin, studded in a regular pattern with brass-headed nails, floated like a stream. She was attired also in a splendid kilt of leopard skins, decorated with red rosettes, and her toilette was considered more careful and artistic than any of the others. Brighter her bangles, whiter her goat-fringes, and more elaborately painted her face. Nozilwane, however, had youth and a wonderful self-reliance on her side. The others, though they all joined in and hunted out an imaginary enemy, and in turn exulted over his discovery, soon became breathless and spent, and were glad when their attendants led them away to be anointed and to drink water.

"As for another of the 'witch-finders,' the great, big Nozinyanga, she danced like Queen Elizabeth, 'high and disposedly,' and no wonder, for I should think she weighed at least fifteen stone. Ungiteni, in a petticoat of white Angora-goat skin, and a corsage of bladders and teeth, beads and viper skins, was nothing remarkable; neither was Um-à-noujozzla, a melancholy-looking personage, with an enormous wig-like coiffure of red woollen ringlets and white skewers. The physiognomy, too, was a trifle more stolid and commonplace than that of her comrades, and altogether she gave me the impression of being a sensible, respectable woman, who was very much ashamed of herself for playing such antics. However, she brandished her divining brush with the rest, and cut in now and then to 'keep the fleer' with the untiring Nozilwane."

Lady Barker and her friends grew tired of this imaginary " witch-finding," and to end the affair it was proposed to test the professed power of the "weird women" to discover lost property. A silver pipe stem had recently "gone a-missing," and they were requested to find what had been lost, and where. They set to work in a curious and interesting way. In front, squatted on heels and haunches, a semicircle of about a dozen men, who were supposed to have invited the assistance of the sisterhood. They had no idea of what was asked for, and were told to go on with their part until a signal was given that the article had been named.

"What is it the Inkos has lost?" they cried; "discover, reveal, make plain to us."

The witch-finders, by their singing and dancing, had wrought themselves up to a highly-excited and enthusiastic condition, so that they unhesitatingly accepted the challenge, Nowamso crying, "Sing for me : make a cadence for me." Then, after a moment's pause, she went on rapidly, in her own language.

"Is this real? is it a test? is it but a show? Do the white chiefs want to laugh at our pretensions? Has the white lady called us only to show other white people that we can do nothing? Is anything really lost? is it not hidden? No, it *is* lost. Is it lost by a black person? No, a white person has lost it. Is it lost by the great white chief? No, it is lost by an ordinary white man. Let me see what it is that is lost. Is it money? No. Is it a weighty thing? No, it can be always carried about—it is not heavy. All people like to carry it, especially the white Inkosi : it is made of the same metal as money. I could tell you more, but there is no earnestness in all this,—it is only a spectacle."

Between each of these ejaculations she made a pause, looking eagerly into the faces of the men before her, who, for sole answer, gave a loud, simultaneous snap of finger and thumb, pointing towards the ground as they did so, and shouting the one word, "Yiz-ora," (the first syllable strongly accented and much prolonged;) "discover, reveal !" They can say nothing more to urge her on, because they themselves are ignorant : but the weird women watch their countenances eagerly, to detect, if they can, some unconscious sign or token that their guesses are near the truth. Suspecting a trick, Nowamso lapses into silence; but Nozilwane rushes about like one possessed, sobbing and quivering with excitement, "It is this—it is that !" The tall Nozinyanga strikes her lance firmly into the ground, and cries haughtily, in her own tongue, " It is his watch !" throwing around a haughty glance, as if daring any one to contradict her. The others then join hands, and gallop round and round, making a suggestion here and a suggestion there, all alike improbable; the "inquirers," as the kneeling men are called, affording them no assistance. At last Nozilwane strikes home : " His pipe !" she exclaims ; " Yoziva, yoziva, a thing which has come off his pipe."

And so it is. Nozilwane's pluck, and perseverance, and cunning scrutiny of our faces at each hit she made, have brought her off victoriously.

A murmur, or rather grunt, of admiration goes around. The " inquirers" jump up, and " subside into ebony images of impassive respectability." The weary chorus disperses in small groups, and the exhausted sisterhood drop, as if by one consent, on their knees, sitting back on their heels, and raise their right hands in salutation.[1]

[1] Abridged from Lady Barker, "A Year's Housekeeping in South Africa," pp. 181—184.

CHAPTER XI.

ZABIANISM AND SERPENT-WORSHIP.

THERE can be no question as to the antiquity or universality of Serpent-Worship, whatever may be the difference of opinion as to its origin. According to Bryant it began in Chaldea, and was "the first variation from the purer Zabaism." But this statement requires from us a brief preliminary explanation of that ancient form of worship.

Zabaism, or Zabism, has had its two sects,—first the Chaldean Zabians of the Kuran,—the " Parsified" Chaldee heathen, or non-Christian Gnostics,—the ancestors of the present Mendaites, or so-called Joannes Christians, who reside in the neighbourhood of the Persian Gulf, and speak a corrupt form of Chaldee-Aramaic. And second, the Pseudo-Zabians, or Syrian Zabians, in Harran, Edessa, Rakkah, and Bagdad. It is the latter who now chiefly represent Zabism.

The first named, or Chaldean Zabians, who transferred the name to the Harranic, and greatly influenced the development of the peculiar system of the latter, are the people so designated in the Kuran, and by the Mohammedans of to-day. The Harranians, who rose about A.D. 830, profess to derive their denomination from one Zâbi, who is variously called a son of Seth, son of Adam, or a son of Enoch or Idris, or a son of Methuselah, or of some fictitious Badi or Mari, a supposed companion of Abraham; while Mohammedan writers trace it to the word *ssaba*, " to turn, to move," because its professors turned from the path of true religion, that is, Islam, or, as the Zabians say, because they have turned *to* the proper faith.

The Zabian creed, as professed by the Harranic Zabians, would appear to resolve itself into the following elements :—

It teaches that the Creator is, in His essence, primitivity, originality, and eternity, One; but in His numerous manifestations in bodily figures, manifold. Chiefly He is personified by the seven principal planets, and by the good, knowing, excellent earthly bodies. This, however, is without any disturbance of His unity. It is, say the Zabians, as if the seven planets were His seven limbs, and as if our seven limbs were His seven spheres in which He manifests Himself,—so that He speaks with our tongues, sees with our eyes, hears with our ears, touches with our hands, comes and goes with our feet, and acts through our members.

It teaches further, that GOD is too great and too sublime to occupy Himself directly with the affairs of this world; that its government He has therefore entrusted to other gods, and that it is only to the highest things of destiny He Himself devotes His attention,—an attribution of cold superiority and intellectual indifference in striking contrast to the idea of GOD *the Father* developed by Christianity, that all-loving, as well as all-powerful GOD, Who watches over the fall of a sparrow, and listens with tender ear to the prayer of even the meanest of His creatures. Moreover, Zabism inculcates the chilling doctrine that man is too feeble to offer his homage directly to the Supreme, and must therefore address the inferior deities to whom the regimen of the world has been handed. In this way we see that the veneration shown to the planets and the worship of idols are only a symbolism resulting from the humiliating doctrines just defined.

Zabism is a polytheistic system,—it absolutely revels in gods and goddesses. There are the spirits that direct and guide the planets, the spirits that originate or represent every action in this world,—not a natural effect, great or little, which does not emanate from a deity. Whatever appears in the air, whatever is formed near the sky or springs from the earth, must be traced to certain gods that govern these manifestations, so that every flake of snow, every drop of rain has its presiding spirit.

These spirits also "mould and shape everything bodily from one form into the other, and gradually bring all created things to the state of their highest possible perfection, and communicate their powers to all substances, beings, and things. By the movement and guidance of these spiritual beings, the different elements and natural compositions are influenced in such a way that the tenderest plant may pierce the hardest cliff. He who guides this world is called the first spirit. These gods know our most secret thoughts, and all our future is open to them. The female deities seem to have been conceived as the feeling or passive principle. These gods or intelligences emanate directly from GOD without His will, as rays do from the sun. They are, further, of abstract forms, free of all matter, and neither made of any substance or material. They consist chiefly of a light in which there is no darkness, which the senses cannot conceive by reason of its immense clearness, which the understanding cannot comprehend by reason of its extreme delicacy, and which fancy and imagination cannot fathom."

Free from all animal desires, these spirits are created wholly for love and harmony, for friendship and unity. They are unaffected by local and temporal changes, and control the planetary spheres, without finding the motion of the heaviest too heavy, or of the lightest too light. Their never-ending existence is a prolonged happiness, owing to their nearness to the Supreme GOD; whom they praise day and night, like the Angels, with no sense of fatigue or satiety, and whose will they ever obey with the keenest joy. Free agents, they are never inclined towards the evil. They turn towards the good as readily as the flower towards the light.

Passing on to the cosmogonical part of the Zabian system, we find that it is based on the existence of five primæval principles,—the Creator, Reason, the Soul, Space, and the Void. These are the constituents of all creation. But apart from these, or comprehending these, the Zabians seem to have regarded two principles, GOD and the Soul, as specially active and ever-living. Some writers represent them as believing also in a passive principle, Matter; and in two principles which are neither living nor passive, Time and Space. They appear to have regarded Matter as primeval and everlasting, and to have ascribed to it the origin and duration of Evil. GOD Himself created only the spheres, and the heavenly bodies which they contain. These spheres (fathers) convey the types or ideas to the elementary substances (mothers), and out of the combination, conjunction, and motion of these spheres and elements are produced the various earthly things (children). According to the Zabians, the world is renewed with every "world-year," or cycle, that is once every 36,425 ordinary years. And at the close of each cycle, the life, vegetable, animal, and human that had flourished within it cease to multiply, and new forms or types spring into existence.

The vacillating and contending nature of man is due to the contradictory elements of which he is composed. The desires and passions which sway him to and fro, depress him to the low standard of the brute creation, and his fall would be complete but for such religious rites as purifications, sacrifices, and other means of grace. Through these he is able again to draw near to the great gods, and to attain a resemblance unto them. The human soul is dual, that is, it consists partly of the nature of the animal soul and partly of that of the angelic soul. It is immortal, and subject to future recompense and punishment, but not for ever, nor in any world but this, though at different epochs of existence. Hence, our present happiness is a reward for the good deeds done by us in an earlier stage of existence; and our present suffering the just chastisement for evil actions committed in the past. In its nature they hold that the soul is primitive, because otherwise it must be material, and a material soul is an impossibility.

"The soul," says Kathibi, one of the Zabian teachers, "is thus immaterial, and exists from eternity; is the involuntary reason of the first types, as GOD is the First Cause of the Intelligences. Once on a time the soul beheld matter and loved it. Glowing with the desire of assuming a bodily shape, it would not again separate itself from that matter of which the world was created. Since that time, the soul forgot itself, its everlasting existence, its original abode, and knew nothing more of what it had formerly known. But GOD, who converts all things to the best, united it to matter, which it loved, and out of this union the heavens, the elements, and other composite things arose. In order that the soul might not wholly perish within matter, He endowed it with intelligence, whereby it conceived its high origin, the spiritual world, and itself. It further conceived through it that it was but a stranger in this world, in which it was subject to many sufferings, and that even the joys of this world are but the sources of new sufferings. As soon as the soul had perceived all this, it began to yearn again for its spiritual home, as a man who is away from his birthplace pines for his homestead. It then also learned, that, in order to return to its primitive state, it had to shake off the fetters of sensuous desires, and liberate itself from all materialistic tendencies. Far from them all, it would once more regain its heavenly sphere, and enjoy the bliss of the spiritual world."[1]

Such is an outline of the religious system which flourished from the middle of the ninth to the middle of the eleventh century, under the name of Zabism.

Evidently, out of *this* Zabaism Serpent-worship could not spring, because it is of much greater antiquity. What then is the Zabism to which Bryant alludes? A purely imaginary creed, which the mediæval, Jewish, Arabic, and Persian writers identified with star-worship. The Mohammedan and other writers of the twelfth century bestowed the name of Zabians indifferently upon the ancient Chaldeans, the Buddhists, even the ante-Zoroastrian Persians; and Bryant has followed their mistaken example. As a matter of fact, Serpent-worship is a relic of nature-worship, —more particularly of the old solar worship,—and the Serpent at first was unquestionably an emblem of the Sun.

In Babylon large serpents of silver supported the image of the goddess Rhea, in the temple of Bel, or Belus; and the name Bel itself is thought by some writers to be an abbreviation of Ob-el, "the Serpent-God." In the Apo-

[1] Quoted from Chwolson ("Die Ssabier und der Ssabismus," 1856,) by Chambers.

cryphal book of Bel and the Dragon, we read: "In that same place there was a great Dragon, which they of Babylon worshipped. And the king said unto Daniel: Wilt thou say that this is of brass? lo, he eateth and drinketh: thou canst not say he is no living god: therefore worship him."

Speaking of the earlier stage of the Persian religion, Eusebius remarks that all the Persians worshipped the First Principles under the form of Serpents, having dedicated to them temples in which they performed sacrifices, and held festivals and orgies, esteeming them the greatest of Gods, and governors of the Universe.

These first principles were the principles of Good and Evil, or Ormuzd and Ahriman, whose terrible struggle for the supremacy of the universe was symbolised in Persian mythology by two serpents contending for the mundane egg. They are represented as standing upon their tails, and each of them has fastened its teeth upon the disputed prize. But, more generally, the Evil Principle alone was represented by the serpent, and a fable in the Zendavesta recalls to our recollection the opening of the Book of Genesis; for it says that Ahriman assumed a serpent's form in order to destroy the first of the human race, whom he accordingly poisoned.

In the Saddu, or Suddu, it is said: "When you kill serpents, you shall repeat the Zendavesta, whereby you will obtain great merit; for it is the same as if you had killed so many devils."

Mithras, the Persian sun-god, was represented encircled by a serpent; and in his rites a custom was observed similar to that practised in the mysteries of Sebazius: a serpent was cast into the bosom of the neophyte, and taken out at the lower part of his garments.[1]

The hierogram of the winged circle and serpent is a remarkable and significant emblem of Ophiolatreia, and is found in almost every country where Serpent-worship prevailed. It is to be traced in the Egyptian, the Persian, and even the Aztec hieroglyphics; and on the monuments of China, Greece, Italy, Asia Minor, and India. Enthusiasts allege that it has been discovered in Britain. It seems to

[1] Deane, p. 49.

have been a general symbol of *consecration*, and as such mention is made of it by the poet Persius :

> " Pinge duos angues ; pueri sacer est locus."
> *Satir.* i. 113.

Reference is here made to *two* snakes, which, as we have seen, is the hierogram of the worshippers of the Two Principles, each being represented by a serpent. Generally, however, it is one serpent only that issues from the winged circle, and sometimes the circle is without wings. As a consecrating symbol, the ophite hierogram was inscribed upon the massive portals of the Egyptian temples. Mr. Deane contends that the Druids " with the consistent magnificence which characterised their religion," transferred the symbol from the portal to the temple ; and instead of placing the circle and serpent over the entrance into their sanctuaries, erected the whole building in the form of the ophite hierogram, as at Abury in Wiltshire, and Stanton Drew in Somersetshire. The former represents the ophite hierogram with one serpent, the latter is double ; in both cases the circle has no wings.

In Argyllshire, near Oban, exists a huge serpent-shaped mound, discovered by Mr. Phené in 1871, which must be mentioned in this connection. Looking down upon it from the high ground to the westward, you see it rising conspicuously from the flat grassy plain, which extends for some distance on either side, with scarcely an undulation, save two artificial circular mounds, in one of which lie several large stones forming a cromlech. A recent visitor writes :

" Finding ourselves in the very presence of the Great Dragon, we hastened to improve our acquaintance, and in a couple of minutes had scrambled on to the ridge which forms his backbone, and thence perceived that we were standing on an artificial mound three hundred feet in length, forming a double curve like a huge letter S, and wonderfully perfect in anatomical outline. This we perceived the more perfectly on reaching the head, which lies at the western end, whence diverge small ridges, which may have represented the paws of the reptile. On the head rests a circle of stones, supposed to be emblematic of the solar disc, and exactly corresponding with the solar circle as represented on the head of the mystic serpents of Egypt and Phœnicia, and in the great American Serpent Mound. At the time of Mr. Phené's first visit to this spot there still remained in the centre of this circle some traces of an altar, which, thanks to the depredations of cattle and herd-boys, have since wholly disappeared. . . .

"The circle was excavated on the 12th of October, 1871, and within it were found three large stones, forming a chamber, which contained burnt human bones, charcoal, and charred hazel-nuts. Surely the spirits of our Pagan ancestors must rejoice to see how faithfully we, their descendants, continue to burn our hazel-nuts on Hallow-e'en, their old autumnal Fire Festival, though our modern divination is practised only with reference to such a trivial matter as the faith of sweethearts! A flint was also found, beautifully and minutely serrated at the edge; nevertheless, it was at once evident, on opening the cairn, that the place had already been ransacked, probably in secret, by treasure-seekers, as there is no tradition of any excavation for scientific purposes having ever been made here.

"On the removal of the peat-moss and heather from the ridge of the serpent's back, it was found that the whole length of the spine was carefully constructed with regularly and symmetrically placed stones, at such an angle as to throw off rain; an adjustment to which we doubtless owe the preservation, or at least the perfection, of this most remarkable relic. To those who know how slow is the growth of peat-moss, even in damp and undrained places, the depth to which it has here attained, though in a dry and thoroughly exposed situation and raised from seventeen to twenty feet above the level of the surrounding moss, tells of many a long century of silent undisturbed growth, since the days when the serpent's spine was the well-worn path daily trodden by reverent feet. The spine is, in fact, a long narrow causeway, made of large stones, set like the vertebræ of some huge animal. They form a ridge sloping off in an angle at each side, which is continued downwards with an arrangement of smaller stones, suggestive of ribs."

This strange memorial of a departed age and a vanished faith, lying in the silence and solitude of the lonely shore of Loch Nell, recalls to mind the eloquent lines of an American poet :[1]

> " All desolate their ruins rest,
> Like bark that in mid-ocean rolls,
> Her name effaced, her masts o'erthrown,
> And none remaining of the souls
> That once sailed in her, to relate
> From what far distant port she came;
> Whither she sailed and what her fate,
> And what her nation and her name.
> But only may conjecture guess
> The fancied story of this place,
> And from these crumbling ruins gain
> Some knowledge of the vanished race."

It must be noticed that the serpent-mound has been so disposed that the worshipper standing at the altar would naturally look eastward, directly along the whole length of the great reptile, and across the dark lake, to the threefold peaks of Ben Cruachan. That this position was intentionally selected is evident from the fact that the three peaks are visible from no other point.

And hence arises the not wholly fanciful conjecture that the people who erected the great mound had some dim idea of the Triune character of GOD. The serpent was the emblem of His wisdom, as the solar circle was of His Eternal Unity; and this marked reverence for the triple-peaked mountain seems to indicate that with a knowledge of His unity was combined a recognition of His threefold manifestation.

The writer whom we have already quoted remarks that, whatever doubts may arise on speculative points, the clearly defined outlines of the great Serpent-mound of Oban are beyond dispute; though it may long prove a fertile subject for discussion, whether its serpentine, or rather, Saurian form is to be accepted as direct evidence of ophiolatry in this land, or whether we should regard it as simply the representative of some tribe,—as, in short, a Totem of some extinct British race answering to the Nagas, or snake-tribes of the East. The former supposition seems the more reasonable, when we remember that the serpent and the serpent's egg were held sacred by the Druids. Serpent-worship

[1] Isaac McLellan.

prevailed in every nation of antiquity. It flourished in Greece and Rome, in Egypt and Chaldea, in Arabia and Central Asia; it extended throughout the Indian peninsula from Cape Comorin to Kashmir; it was practised in Ceylon and the islands of the eastern seas; in Mexico and Peru; throughout the whole of Africa. Passing northward, we find that it existed in Scythia and Scandinavia, as also among vast tribes near the Oural mountains and throughout Northern Europe, and particularly among the tribes on the Ob or Obi river, which owes its name, it is said, to the veneration paid to the reptile. Until the end of the fourteenth century, when Christianity was introduced, the people of Poland worshipped domestic serpents, which were allowed to run free in every house, and carefully tended, every mishap that occurred being attributed to some negligence in their service. The Lapps, the Finns, the Norwegians, the Swedes, the Danes, all fostered these strange household gods, and shared with them the children's milk. The Vandals also kept them; some lived in hollow trees, and thither repaired the women, with their offerings of milk, as is common at the present day in Ceylon and many parts of India. Long after they had accepted the faith of CHRIST, the Lombards continued a form of serpent-worship, adoring, or paying homage to, a golden viper and a tree. In 663, Barbatus, Bishop of Benevento, finding the custom still observed, made a successful appeal to the worshippers to cut down the tree, and allow him to melt the golden viper into a sacramental chalice.

One of the most interesting of the supposed Serpent-temples, or *dracontia*, is that of Karnak. It is situated half a mile from the village of that name, in the department of the Morbihan in Brittany, and about nine miles from the picturesque town of Auray. It is also within a mile of the Bay of Quiberon.

The whole length of "the Stones of Karnak," as the temple is called, measures, if we include its sinuosities, eight miles. The width varies from 250 to 350 feet. The highest stones are as much as seventeen feet high, and from thirty to forty feet in circumference. Vacant spaces have unfortunately been cleared by ruthless spoliators for the erection of the adjacent villages of Ploermel and Karnak, and the boundary walls of the neighbouring fields. But what toil and time must have been originally expended on its construction, we may infer from the fact that it consisted of eleven rows of stones, about ten thousand in number, of which upwards of three hundred averaged from fifteen to seventeen feet in height, and from sixteen to twenty or thirty feet in girth; one stone even measuring the huge circumference of forty-two feet.

A glance at any engraving of this famous antiquity will show that the course of the avenues is distinctly sinuous, and that it defines the figure of an enormous serpent undulating over the ground. Necessarily, however, the resemblance is more striking to one who views the original *in situ*. To such, the alternations of the high and low stones, regularly disposed, may seem to mark with sufficient accuracy "the swelling of the serpent's muscles as he moves along," though this seems rather a flight of imagination. But at all events the spectator will acknowledge the evidence of design which clearly appears in the construction of the avenues.

The Dracontium contains ten regularly defined areas; one near the village of Karnak, which is shaped like a bell or horse-shoe; the other, towards the eastern extremity, which approaches the figure of a rude circle, and is in reality a parallelogram with rounded corners.

The circle and the horse-shoe were both sacred figures in the Druidical religion, as may be seen in Stonehenge, where they are united, the outer circles enclosing inner horse-shoes. The connection between the latter symbol and the Celtic faith is not very clear, unless it be intended as a representation of the moon. It has been conjectured that from this symbol, whatever may have been its signification, arose the superstition—even not now wholly defunct—of nailing a horse-shoe over a door as a protection against evil spirits.

It is curious that at Erdeven, where the temple begins, an annual dance, descriptive of the Ophite hierogram of the circle and serpent, is still celebrated by the peasants at the Carnival. But the only tradition which survives respecting the stones is one which lingers in various parts of England where similar memorials are found, that they were originally endowed with life, and were petrified as they stand. Some of the Bretons believe they were the Roman army who pursued the centurion Cornelius on account of his conversion to Christianity, and were stricken into stone through his prayers. Others imagine that certain supernatural dwarfs erected them in a single night, and that each still inhabits the stone he reared.

Mr. Deane tells us that near the Karnak side of the dracontium rises a singular mound of great elevation, which has once been conical, and the upper portion of which is evidently artificial.[1] He regards it as analogous to the remarkable hill of Silbury, which occupies much the same position towards the Albury dracontium. Probably these mounds served as altars, on which, in conformity with the practices of the Solar worship, was kept burning the perpetual fire kindled by the sun. They are of common occurrence in Persia, and seem to be identical with "the high places" of Scripture where the priests of Baal celebrated their sacrifices. The conical mound near Karnak—which may be seen for miles around—has been consecrated by the Christians to the Archangel Michael, who is the patron saint of every height, hill, or cone, natural or artificial, in Brittany. The reason of this dedication has been conjectured to be that S. Michael is the assailant and conqueror of the spiritual Dragon of the Apocalypse. The mutilated image of that great serpent lies prostrate below the mound; and when its worshippers were converted to the religion of CHRIST, they naturally erected on the Solar mount a chapel consecrated to its archangelic slayer. This consecration indicates, therefore, the triumph of Christianity over Ophiolatry; and it is but consistent, says Deane, that the people who allegorised the conversion of the Ophites by the metaphor of a victory over *serpents*, should, in token of the victory, erect upon the high places of idolatry chapels to the great Archangel.

It is possible that the mound gave name to the adjacent village: that is, Karn-ak, or Carnac, from "*cairn*," a hill, and "*hac*," a snake. The "serpent's hill" would be no unsuitable title for Mont S. Michel. In the same manner

[1] Deane, pp. 370—373.

the group of pillars called *Lemaenac*, may have been named from *maen*, stones, and *hac*.

It is curious to find proofs of the existence of Serpent-worship in the New World as in the Old; to meet with its traces in Mexico as well as in Egypt or Chaldea. But certain it is that the religion of Mexico had many features which were common to the Egyptian and Chaldean creeds; the same Solar Worship, the same pyramidal monuments, and the same Ophiolatrous symbols.

For instance, we learn that the temple of Huitziliputli, in Mexico, was built of great stones, in the fashion of snakes tied one to another, and that the circuit was called "the circuit of snakes," because the walls of the enclosure were covered with the figures of snakes. This truculent-looking deity held in his right hand a staff cut in the fashion of a serpent; and the four corners of the ark or tabernacle, in which he was seated, terminated each with a carved effigy of a serpent's head.

The Mexican astronomers represented a century by a circle, with a sun in the centre, surrounded by the symbols of the years. The circumference was a serpent twisted into four knots at the cardinal points.

The Mexican month was divided into twenty days, two of which were symbolised by the serpent and dragon. Further, the doorway of the temple, dedicated to "the god of the air," was so wrought as to resemble a serpent's mouth.

The Mexicans, however, went beyond the *symbolical* worship of the sacred serpent, and like many other branches of the Ophite family, they fostered living serpents in their dwellings as household gods. Mr. Bullock asserts that they make the rattlesnake an object of their worship and veneration; and that representations of this reptile, and of others of its species, are very commonly met with among the remains of their ancient idolatry. He says that the finest known to be in existence may be seen in a deserted part of the cloister of the Dominican convent, opposite to the Palace of the Inquisition. It is curled up in an irritated, erect position, with the jaws extended, and is represented in the act of gorging a woman, richly dressed, who lies between its fangs, crushed and lacerated.

The Conquistadors, or Spanish followers of Cortez, all assert that the Aztecs, or inhabitants of Mexico, worshipped an idol wrought into the shape of a serpent. Bonal Dias del Castello, one of the Spanish invader's veteran captains, and the chronicler of the expedition, describes the interior of the principal temple, to which he and his leader were conducted by the Emperor Montezuma : " When we had ascended to the summit of the temple, we observed on the platform as we passed, the large stones on which were placed the victims intended for sacrifice. Here was a great figure representing a Dragon, and much blood lay spilled. Cortez, addressing Montezuma, requested him to do him the favour to show his gods. After consulting the priests, Montezuma led them into a tower where was a kind of hall. Here were two altars, highly adorned with richly-wrought timbers on the roof; above the roof, spread gigantic figures like unto men. The one on the right hand was Huitzilopochtli, their war god, with a great face and terrible eyes. This figure was entirely covered with gold and jewels, and his body wreathed about with golden serpents. Before the idol smoked a pan of incense, in which the hearts of three human victims were burning, mixed with copal. The other great figure, on the left, with a face like a bear's, was the god of the infernal regions. His body was everywhere covered with figures of devils, having serpents' tails. In this place was kept a drum of most enormous dimensions, the head of which was made of the skins of large serpents. At a short distance from the temple stood a tower, and at the door grinned frightful idols, like serpents and devils : in front of these were tables and knives for sacrifice."

Mr. Bullock, who made a valuable collection of Mexican antiquities, describes an idol, " the goddess of war," on which Cortez and his followers may possibly have looked :

"This monstrous idol," he says, "is, with its pedestal, twelve feet high, and four feet wide. Its form is partly human and partly composed of rattlesnakes and the tiger. The head, enormously wide, seems that of two rattlesnakes united ; the fangs hanging out of the mouth, on which the still-palpitating hearts of the unfortunate victims were rubbed as an act of the most acceptable oblation. The body is that of a deformed man, the place of arms being supplied by the heads of rattlesnakes, placed on square plinths, and united by fringed ornaments. Round the waist is a girdle, which was originally encrusted with gold; and beneath this, reaching nearly to the ground, and partly covering its deformed cloven feet, a drapery entirely composed of wreathed rattlesnakes, which the natives call "a garment of serpents. . . . . . . Between the feet, descending from the body, another wreathed serpent rests his head upon the ground."

"The only worship," says Mr. Deane,[1] "which can vie with that of the Serpent in antiquity or universality, is the adoration of the SUN. But uniformly with the progress of the Solar superstitions has advanced the sacred serpent from Babylon to Peru. If the worship of the Sun, therefore, was the first deviation from the truth, the worship of the Serpent was one of the first innovations of idolatry. Whatever doubt may exist as to which was the first error, little doubt can arise as to the primitive and antediluvian character of both. For in the earliest heathen records we find them inexplicably interwoven as the first of superstitions. Thus Egyptian mythology informs us, that Helios (the Sun) was the first of the Egyptian gods; for in early history, kings and gods are generally confounded. But Helios married Ops, the serpent deity, and became father of Osiris, Isis, Typhœus, Apollo, and Venus: a tradition which would make the superstitions coeval. This fable being reduced to more simple laws, informs us, that the Sun, having married the Serpent, became, by this union, the father of Adam and Eve, the Evil Spirit, the Serpent-solar deity, and Lust; which appears to be a confusion of Scriptural truths, in which chronological order is sacrificed from the simplification of a fable. But—*ex pede Herculem*—from the small fragments of the truth which are here combined, we may judge of the original dimensions of the knowledge whose ruins are thus heaped together. We may conclude that, since idolatry, lust, the serpent, and the evil spirit, are here said to have been synchronous with the First Man and Woman, the whole fable is little more than a mythological version of the events in Paradise.

Mr. Deane, who lived before the days of Comparative

[1] Deane, pp. 446, 447.

Mythology, read into the old fables a meaning which they are hardly capable of bearing. It is clear enough that Serpent-worship had an astronomical origin; but we may agree with him that it was as ancient and universal as the worship of the Sun, with which, indeed, it was closely connected.

We shall now borrow a few illustrations of the character, extent, and significance of Serpent-worship from Mr. Fergusson's elaborate work,[1] in which he deals particularly with the Topes at Sanchi and Amravati. But, first, a word or two in explanation of the origin and purpose of the Topes will be desirable.

The era of stone architecture in India seems to have begun with the reign of Asoka about 250 B.C. It is contemporaneous with the rise of Buddhism, whose followers gradually usurped the place formerly occupied by the Aryans. The Buddhist buildings then erected may be divided into three principal classes :

1st. *Topes* or *Stupas*, with their surrounding rails and lats :

2nd. *Chaityas*, which, in form and purpose, closely resemble the early Churches of the Christians, though several of those cut in the rock were, in all probability, excavated before the Christian era : and,

3rd. *Viharas*, or Monasteries, forming in the earliest times the dwellings of the monks or priests who ministered in the Topes or Chaityas, but afterwards becoming the independent abode of monastic communities, who had chapels or oratories appropriated to their use within the walls of their monasteries.

We are here concerned only with the Tope or Stupa.

In its origin we suspect that it simply took the place of the mound or tumulus which the Turanian and other races had from earliest ages been accustomed to raise over the last resting-place of their dead. No such tumuli now exist in India, having probably been washed away by the tropical rains or river-floods ; but some are still found in Afghanistan. The Indian type is distinguished from the tumulus of other

[1] "Tree and Serpent-worship," by James Fergusson, (edit. 1868.)

countries by its material and its shape. It is built of brick or stone, in a rounded or conical form. It is distinguished also by the circumstance that instead of being the place of interment of a corpse, it is the depository of relics.

Besides being used as a relic-shrine, the Tope was frequently employed as a memorial tower to indicate a sacred spot. Of the 84,000 Stupas which, according to tradition, Asoka erected, fully one half would seem to have been raised to mark the scenes where Buddha or some Bôdhisatwa had performed a miracle or done something worthy of being remembered by the faithful.

The " rails," or stone-circles, surrounding the Indian Topes are often of as much importance as the Topes themselves; and in the case of Sanchi and Amravati, are even *more* important. As with the Topes, they are sepulchral in origin. "The circles of rude stones found all over Europe certainly are so in most cases. They may sometimes enclose holy spots, and may possibly have in some instances places of assembly, though this is improbable. Their application to the purposes of ancestral worship is, however, not only probable, but appropriate. Sometimes a circle of stones encloses a sepulchral mound, as at New Grange in Ireland, and very frequently in Scandinavia and Algeria. In India rude stone circles are of frequent occurrence." Some hundreds are found in the neighbourhood of Amravati alone, and all are sepulchral; but like the Topes when adopted by the Buddhists, they were "sublimated into a symbol instead of a reality."

Reference must briefly be made to another group of early Buddhist monuments, the lats or stembhas, of which very few are now extant in India, the British engineer having used them for his roads, and the native zemindar for his rice or sugar mills. Those erected by Asoka are uniform in character: circular stone shafts, monoliths, thirty or forty feet high, and surmounted by a capital of a bell-shaped or falling leaf form, imitated from the later Grecian architecture. They were erected in order that certain edicts might be engraved upon them, which Asoka desired to keep constantly in the remembrance and before the eyes of his subjects. But in the fifth century, those raised by the Guptas had no other object than to perpetuate the name and fame of their royal founders.

The Topes at Sanchi form part of a large group of Topes situated between the towns of Bhilsa and Bhopul in Central India. They range over an area about seventeen miles from east to west, and about ten miles from north to south, in five or six different clusters, and number in all between forty and fifty of various dimensions. It is believed that the smallest are merely the places of interment of local chiefs; others are strictly Dagobas, or relic-shrines; while the largest is a chaitya or stupa, designed apparently to consecrate some sacred spot, or perpetuate the memory of some remarkable event in Buddhist history.

Architecturally speaking, it consists, first, of a basement 121 feet in diameter and 14 feet in height. This is surmounted by a platform or procession path, within which the dome or tumulus itself rises in the shape of a truncated hemisphere to a height of 39 feet. The summit is a level area, measuring 34 feet across, and surrounded by a circular railing or barrier of stones, which enclosed a square Tu or reliquary, $11\frac{1}{2}$ feet square, and this in its turn enclosed a circular support for the sacred and symbolic umbrella that always crowned these edifices.

At a distance of $9\frac{1}{2}$ feet from the base, the tope is encircled by a rail, eleven feet high, and consisting apparently of one hundred pillars, exclusive of the gateways. Each pillar seems to have been the gift of an individual, and even the rails between them have apparently been contributed by different persons. The rail or circle is devoid of sculpture; but four gateways which were added to it about the Christian era are covered with sculptured work of the most elaborate kind.

The human figures represented in these sculptures belong in the main to two great races. One of them is easily recognised as " Hindus,"—" meaning by that term the civilized race who formerly occupied the valley of the Ganges, and who, from their capitals of Ayodhyâ and Indraprastha or Pâtaliputra (Palibothra), had been the dominant class in India for at least two thousand years before the time to which we are now referring." It may be taken as proved that these people were originally pure immigrant Aryans, but by intermixture with other races their blood took, as it were, a new colouring, though they did not lose the civilisation and pre-eminence which they owed to their intellectual superiority.

We know them in the sculptures by their costume; by the dhoti, wrapped round the loins exactly as it is worn now-a-days; the chadder over their shoulders; and the turban on their heads. So much for the dress of the men; of the undress of the women it is more difficult to speak. They are always decorated with enormous bangles about the wrists and ankles, and strings of beads round the neck; but with the exception of a bead belt round the body below the waist they wear little body clothing. From this belt slips of cloth are sometimes suspended, more generally at the sides or behind than in front,—and sometimes also a cloth not unlike a dhoti, invariably of transparent texture. This scantiness of attire can hardly be regarded as finding compensation in the dimensions and amplitude of the head-dress, which, consisting of two long plaits of hair mixed with beads, and a thick roll of cloth, forms almost a kind of tippet, covering the whole of the woman's back.

Mr. Fergusson remarks :[1]

"It is, however, not only in the Topes that this absence of dress is so conspicuous. In all the sculptures at Karli, or Ellora, or Mahavellipore, or in the paintings in Ajanta, the same peculiarity is observable. Everywhere, indeed, before the Mahometan conquest, nudity in India conveyed no sense of indecency. The wife and mother of Buddha are at times represented in this manner. The queen on her throne, the female disciples of Buddha, listening to his exhortations, and on every public occasion on which women take part in what is going on, the costume is the same. It is equally remarkable that in those days those unveiled females seem to have taken part in every public transaction and show, and to have mixed with the men as freely as women do in Europe at the present day.

"All this is the more remarkable, as in Buddhist books modesty of dress in women is frequently insisted upon. In the Dulva, for instance, a story is told of the King of Ka-

[1] "Asiatic Researches," Vol. XX. p. 85.

linga presenting to the King of Kosála (probably Padh), a piece of muslin, which afterwards fell into the hands of a lewd priestess. She, it is said, wore it in public, while it was so thin that she, notwithstanding this, appeared naked to the great scandal of all who witnessed the exhibition.[1] The probability is, that the story and the book that contains it are of very much more modern date than our sculptures. It certainly is in direct conflict with their evidence."

The want of shame in women, to which this exposure of the person bears witness, is always the mark and sign of inferior civilisation.

The other race depicted in the sculptures has its distinctive characteristics. The male costume consists of a kilt,—not a cloth wrapped round the loins, but a kilt, shaped, sewn, and fastened by buckle or string;—and also of a cloak or tippet, which seems to be similarly shaped and sewn. As for the hair, it is twisted into a long rope or plait like a Chinaman's, and then folded round the head in a conical form, or a piece of cloth or rope was treated in this way. The beard is worn, whereas no single individual of the Hindu race, either at Sanchi or Amravati, has any trace of beard or moustache; a circumstance the more remarkable, because, according to Nearchus, the Hindus dyed their beards with various colours, so that some were red, some white, some black, others purple, some green. The female dress differs from that of the Hindus even more than the male. A striped petticoat is gathered in at the knees so as to form a neat and modest garb, and a cloak or tippet like that of the men is thrown generally over one shoulder so as to leave one breast bare, but sometimes both are covered. The head-dress is a neat and elegant turban.

Who then are these people? From the peculiarities of their costume, and their living in the woods, some authorities are inclined to regard them as priests or ascetics, though, it is to be noted, they are nowhere represented as worshipping Topes, hero-wheels, or the disc and crescent symbols (the sun and moon.) In one compartment, however, they are evidently worshipping the serpent in a fire-temple. Fergusson concludes that they were the aboriginal inhabitants of Malwa, to whom came the Hindus as con-

[1] Fergusson, "Tree and Serpent-worship," p. 93.

querors or missionaries (or both ?) The Topes were erected and the sculpture wrought by the conquering race, and the others are always represented as inferior and engaged in servile employments, but not as converts to Buddhism. The only act of adoration in which we see them concerned is the adoration of the five-headed Naga. Mr. Fergusson proposes to call them Dasyus, not because such a name has any local or traditional authority, but because in the Vedas and the heroic poems it seems to be applied to the aboriginal people of India as opposed to the Aryans.

Proceeding now to a consideration of the sculptures, we find that one half of those at Sanchi represent religious acts, such as the worship of the Dagoba or of Trees. Once or twice the Wheel is the object of adoration, and once the Serpent. Other bas-reliefs represent events in history, and some again are devoted to the ordinary incidents of every man's life. Their general execution is vigorous though rude. Those at Amravati "are perhaps as near in scale of excellence to the contemporary art of the Roman empire under Constantine, as to any other that could be named; or, rather, they should be compared with the sculptures of the early Italian Renaissance, as it culminated in the hands of Ghiberti, and before the true limits between the provinces of painting and sculpture were understood."

Let us describe an upper bas-relief which has been found on the eastern gateway.

Here the people whom Mr. Fergusson calls Dasyus are represented worshipping the five-headed Naga, or Serpent, which appears in a small hexagonal temple, raising its head over something very like an altar. In front stands a pot of fire,—probably a fire-altar,—and in spite of Mr. Fergusson's doubts, we think both the Serpent and the Fire are connected with the old Sun-worship.[1]

In the foreground an old man is seated in a circular leaf-

[1] "We know," says Mr. Fergusson, "that two of the principal Vedic gods—Indra (the firmament) and Agni (fire)—were adopted into their pantheon by the early Buddhists, and it seems more reasonable to connect this appearance of fire with the pre-existing worship of Agni than with any far-fetched allusion to solar worship." But what was Agni but a type of the sun?

thatched hut, with, according to a frequent Indian custom, a scarf bound round his knees and loins. Behind him in the hut is suspended his upper garment, and in front a bearded senior, of his own tribe, is, to all appearance, addressing him. Near this individual stands another pot of fire, with three pairs of tongs or ladles, and a bundle of sticks to feed the flame. Close beside him we see one elephant, two buffaloes, sheep, and deer. The scene takes place in a forest. Above are trees and cocks, with monkeys and peacocks; below, a reedy marsh opens into a lake blooming with lotus-flowers and occupied by geese.

A lower bas-relief in the same gateway puts before us a very different scene :

In the centre of the upper part blooms the sacred Buddhist Tree, behind its altar, with its Chattee and garlands, occupying a position similar to that of the serpent in the other bas-relief. Two Garudas or Devas, or flying figures, present garlands, and two females, instead of griffins, approach it on either side.

In the lower part of the picture, the Inja, or chief male personage, sits enthroned upon the Naga, and is sheltered by its five-headed hood. On his right crouch three women on stools, eating and drinking, and each with her tutelary or snake behind her; and above them are a female Chaori bearer and a woman with a bottle—there are snakes behind both. On the other side are two women playing on drums, two on harps, one on a flute, and a fifth dancing, but all likewise with snakes, and all in the costume which Mr. Fergusson defines as that of the Hindus.

The worship of the Naga by the bearded Dasyus as represented in the upper bas-relief, does not occur again at Sanchi, and occurs only once at Amravati. There, however, the five-headed snake is seen very frequently in front of the dagoba, and in a position which is designed to command the worship, not only of the Dasyus, but of the whole world.

The Hindu male or chief canopied by the Naga, as shown in the lower bas-relief, occurs at least ten times at Sanchi, and must have occurred several hundred times at Amravati.

Mr. Fergusson asks, what are we to infer from these facts?

Is it that the Naga, or serpent, was the god of the aborigines, whom the conquering Hindus adopted as their own deity, and pretended that it was for *them* he reserved his patronage and support? We must recollect that the Topes were built and the sculptures carved by Hindus, and that there is no representation of a Hindu doing honour to a snake; on the contrary, the snake always does homage to the Hindu.

Shall we conclude, then, that the Hindus were the real Naga-worshipping people, and that it was they who enforced serpent-worship on the Dasyus? A conquered people have not infrequently imposed their language, laws, and religion on their conquerors.

It is, perhaps, impossible to answer these questions: a cloud of obscurity hangs over the whole subject of Snake-worship; but we take it to have been the old and prevalent faith of the aborigines of India prior to the Aryan immigration, and we believe that the Aryans adopted it more and more generally as they mixed more and more widely with the Hindus, and their blood became less and less pure. It is not mentioned in the Vedas; there is scarcely an allusion in the Râmâyana; in the Mahâbâhrata it occupies a considerable space; it appears timidly at Sanchi in the first century of the Christian era; is triumphant at Amravati in the fourth; and might have become the dominant faith of India had it not been elbowed from its pride of place by Vishnuism and Sivaism, which took its position when it fell together with the Buddhism to which it had allied itself so closely.

We turn to the celebrated Tope at Amravati, a town situated on the river Kishna. The dimensions of the Tope are 195 feet for inside diameter of the outer circle, and 165 feet for that of the inner. The procession path is paved with slabs 13 feet long, and the inner rail is 2 feet wide. It has four gateways, and projecting about 30 feet beyond the outer rail; but these are in so dilapidated a condition that their size cannot be accurately ascertained.

These circles, or circular bas-reliefs, from the intermediate rails of the outer enclosure are thus described:

In the upper circle on the right hand side a group of

Buddhist priests, in their yellow robes, may be seen worshipping. In front two supple women, such as so frequently occur in these sculptures, bend in attitudes of adoration, and on the left a chief in the ordinary Hindu costume—surrounded by the women of his family—presents his little son to the Buddha-emblem.

In the lower circle the same structural arrangements occur up to the Trisul (or emblem), but the whole is surmounted by the Chakra, or Wheel, which we know to be the symbol of Dharma or the Law. Here all the worshippers are men; it is, we are told, one of the very few scenes in these sculptures from which women are entirely excluded. Whether it was considered that the study of the Law was unsuited for women, or whether some other motive governed the designers, certain it is that, contrary to the usual rule, the whole of the worshippers are of one sex and one race. The only other noticeable peculiarity is the introduction of two antelopes, one on each side of the throne.

The second circle represents the Trisul ornament, or emblem, not on a throne, but behind an altar. The sacred feet of Buddha are depicted, but there are no relics. In the upper compartment the principal worshippers are two men with seven-headed snake-hoods, and two women with single snakes.

In the centre of the bas-relief sits the principal personage, with a nine-headed snake-hood, between two of his wives, and beyond, on both rims of the circle, stands a female figure, supporting herself by the branches of a tree. On each a young girl waits; one of these girls has a snake at the back of her head. In front are three musicians, also with snakes; and on their right a lady *without* a snake receives the assistance of a girl *with* a snake.

" This distinction," says Mr. Fergusson, "between people with snakes and those without is most curious and perplexing. After the most attentive study I have been unable to detect any characteristic either of feature or costume by which the races can be distinguished, beyond the possession or absence of this strange adjunct. That those with snakes are the Naga people we read of, can hardly be doubted; yet they never are seen actually worshipping the snake like the Dasyus, but rather as protected by it. The snake seems their tutelary genius, watching over, perhaps inspiring them; but whether they borrowed this strange emblem from the natives of the country, or brought it with them from the north-west, are questions we are hardly yet in a position to answer satisfactorily."

We have thus abundant evidence of the prevalence of Serpent-worship in India in "olden times;" the reader will, perhaps, be surprised to hear that it lingers still throughout the peninsula. Dr. Balfour, who had an intimate acquaintance with the habits and customs of the natives, asserts that the worship both of the sculptured form and the living creature, is general. The sculpture invariably represents the Nag or Cobra, and almost every hamlet owns its Serpent deity. Sometimes it is a single snake, with the hood spread open. Occasionally the sculptured figures are nine in number, forming the *Nao Nag*, which is designed to represent a parent snake and eight of its young, but the prevalent form is that of two snakes twining in the manner of the Esculapian rod of classical antiquity.

It is the opinion of some Hindus that the living snake is not worshipped as a devata, or deity, but simply reverenced in commemoration of some ancient event—possibly of some astronomical occurrences. Others, however, distinctly assert that it is worshipped as a devata. However this may be, there can be no doubt that the living snake is worshipped throughout all Southern India. On their feast days the worshippers resort to the snake's lair, which they bedaub with vermilion streaks and patches of turmeric and of wheat flour, and close at hand they suspend garlands of flowers, strung upon white cotton thread, and laid over wooden frames. During the rainy seasons occurs the great Nagpanchanic festival, when the Hindus go in search of snakes, or have them brought to their houses by the Sanpeli, the snake-charmers who ensnare them. The snakes are then worshipped, and offerings of milk are made to them, and in almost every house figures of snakes, drawn on paper, are affixed to the walls, and worshipped. Those who visit the snakes' abodes, or tents, plant sticks around the hole, and about and over these sticks wind white cotton thread. A bevy of Mahrathi women repair to the hût, and joining hands, wind round it in a circle five times, singing songs; after which they prostrate themselves. They pour milk into the hole; hang festoons of Chembela flowers and cucumber fruit, and sprinkle a mixture of sugar and flour.

In reference to this festival, Colonel Meadows Taylor writes:—

On this occasion, Nags or Cobras are worshipped by most of the lower classes of the people in the Dekhan, and more particularly in the Shorapore country. The ceremonies are very simple: the worshippers bathe, smear their foreheads with red colour, and in small parties,—generally families acquainted with one another,—resort to the places known to be frequented by snakes. In such places there are generally sacred stones, to which various offerings are made, and they are anointed with red colour and ground turmeric, and invocations are addressed to the local genius and to the serpents. Near the stones are placed small new earthen saucers, filled with milk; for cobras are fond of milk, and are believed to watch the ceremony, coming out of their holes and drinking the milk, even while the worshippers are near, or are lingering in the distance to see if their offerings be received. It is considered a fortunate augury for the worshippers if the snake should appear and drink. Should the snake *not* appear, the worshippers, after waiting awhile, return to the place next morning, to ascertain the result: if the milk have disappeared, the rite has been accepted, but not under such favourable auspices as if the reptile had come out at once. These ceremonies end with a feast.

Colonel Meadows Taylor (whose language we are partly adopting) continues:—

It is on behalf of children that Snake-worship is particularly practised; and the women and children of a family invariably accompany the male head, not only at the annual festival, but whenever a vow has been made to a Serpent Deity. The first hair shaved from a child which has passed teething, and gone through the other infantile ailments, is frequently dedicated to a Serpent. On such occasions the child is taken to the locality of the vow, the usual ceremonies are performed, and with the other offerings is included the child's hair. In every case a feast follows, served near the spot, and the attendant Brahmins receive alms and largess.

"In the Shakti ceremonies, Pooma-elhishék, which belong, I think, to aboriginal customs, the worship of the Snake forms a portion, as emblematical of energy and wisdom. Most of these ceremonies are, however, of an inconceivably obscene and licentious character. They are not confined to the lowest classes, though rarely perhaps resorted to by Brahmins; but many of the middle class sects, of obscure origin and denomination, practise them in secret, under the strange delusion that the divine energy of nature is to be obtained thereby, with exemption from earthly troubles.

"Although Snake-worship ordinarily belongs professedly to the descendants of aboriginal tribes, yet Brahmins never or rarely pass them over, and the Nagpanchani is observed as a festival of kindly greeting and visiting between families and friends—as a day of gifts of new clothes or ornaments to wives or children, &c.

"The worship of Gram Deotas, or village divinities, is universal all over the Dekhan, and indeed I believe throughout India. These divinities have no temples nor priests. Sacrifice and oblation is made to them at sowing time and harvest, for rain or fine weather, in time of cholera, malignant fever, or other disease or pestilence. The Nag is always one of the Gram Deota, the rest being known by local names. The Gram Deota are known as heaps of stones, generally in a grove or quiet spot near every village, and are smeared some with black and others with red colour.

"Nâg is a common name both for males and females among all classes of Hindus, from Brahmins downwards to the lowest classes of Sudras and Mléchhas. Nâgo Rao, Nâgoju, &c., are common Mahratta names, as Nagappa, Nagowa, and the like are among the Canarese and Telugu population.

"No Hindu will kill a Nag or Cobra willingly. Should any one be killed within the precincts of a village, by Mahomedans or others, a piece of copper money is put into its mouth, and the body is burned with offerings to avert the evil.

ZABIANISM AND SERPENT-WORSHIP.

"It is, perhaps, remarkable, that the Snake festival is held after the season or at the season of casting the skin, and when the Snake, addressed or worshipped, is supposed to have been purified. Some Brahmins always keep the skin of a Nag in one of their sacred books.

"In reference to the lower castes alluded to, I may mention those who practise Snake-worship with the greatest reverence :—1, Beydars. 2, Dhungars or shepherds, Ahens or milkmen, Waddiwars or stone-masons, Khungins or rope-makers, Brinjaras and other wandering tribes, Mangs, Dhérs, and Chennars, Ramorsers, Bhils, Ghonds, and Kohs, all which I believe, with many others, to be descendants of aboriginal tribes, partly received within the pale of Hinduism.

"Lingayots, who are schismatics from Hinduism, and who deny *in toto* the religious supremacy of the Brahmins, are nevertheless Snake-worshippers, many of them bearing the name Nag, both male and female.

"I cannot speak of the North of India, but in the whole of the South of India, from the Nerbudda to Cape Comorin, Snake-worship is now existent."[1]

[1] Col. Meadows Taylor, Appendix to Fergusson's "Tree and Serpent-worship," pp. 236, 237.

CHAPTER XII.

POLYNESIAN SUPERSTITIONS.

WHEN Captain Cook first visited those beautiful islands of the South Pacific which are now included under the general name of Polynesia, he found their inhabitants given over to the lowest and coarsest idolatry. Many of their rites and ceremonies were as lewd as any practised in ancient times under the auspices of the Paphian Venus. Gradually they were brought within the influence of the missionary work of the Christian Church; and though, if we may credit the testimony of recent observers, much heathenism still prevails, and gross superstitions are still secretly nourished, there cannot be a doubt, that, on the whole, their moral condition has been materially elevated.

Among the pioneers of the Cross in these "Summer-isles of Eden" one of the most eminent and successful was the Rev. John Williams; a missionary of the true type, of an enlightened mind and broad sympathies, who, after a long career of noble labour, sealed his witness to the truth with his blood, and lives in the Gospel record as the Martyr of Erromanga. From the plain, unvarnished, and effective chronicle of his "Missionary Enterprises" we glean much interesting information respecting the idolatrous ways of the islanders, revealing their identity with the superstitions that from all times have dominated over uncivilised man. In Rarotonga as in Mexico, for instance, the gods were supposed to be propitiated by human sacrifices; and in many of the islands cannibalism existed in its most disgusting form and under the sanction of a religious ordinance.

From the chief of Aitutaki Mr. Williams obtained some

curious relics of idolatry. As for example :—an idol named *Te-rongo*, one of the great deities, called a *Kaitangata*, or man-eater. The priests of this idol were supposed to be inspired by the shark.

Tangarou, the great national god of Aitutaki, and of almost all the adjacent islands. He holds the net with which he catches the spirits of men as they fly from their bodies, and a spear with which he kills them.

A rod, with snares at the end, made of the fibres of the cocoa-nut husk, with which the priest caught the spirit of the god. It was used in cases of pregnancy, when the female was ambitious that her child should be a son, and become a famous warrior. It was also employed in war-time to catch the god by his leg, to secure his influence on the side of the party performing the ceremony.

Ruanu; a chief from Raiatea, who, ages ago, sailed in a canoe from that island, and settled at Aitutaki. From him a genealogy is traced. He died at Aitutaki, and was deified as *Te atua taitai tere*, or the conductor of fleets.

Tanu; with his fan and other appendages; the god of thunder. The natives, when they heard a peal of thunder, were accustomed to say that this god was flying; and produced this sound by the flapping of his wings.

The Rarotongan idols were of a singular character. From their size they might have suited Swift's nation of Brobdingnagians, for the smallest seems to have been about fifteen feet high. Each was wrought out of a piece of *aito*, or iron wood, about four inches in diameter, carved with a rude imitation of the human hand at one end, and with an obscene figure at the other; round it were wrapped numerous folds of native cloth, until it measured two or three yards in circumference. Near the wooden image some red feathers were strewn, and a string of small pieces of polished pearl shells was regarded as the *manava*, or soul of the god.

An idol, somewhat resembling a Chinese joss, was placed in the fore-part of every fishing-canoe; and prior to their departure on a fishing excursion, the boatmen aways presented it with offerings, and invoked it to grant them a successful issue.

A striking scene was that when Papeiha, a converted

islander, lifted up his voice against idolatry, for the first time, among the banana-groves of Rarotonga.

The Rarotongans had assembled in great numbers at a *marae*, or sacred enclosure, for the purpose of making offerings of food to the gods. Many priests, pretending to be inspired, were filling the air with shouts and yells; whilst around them gathered the deluded worshippers, some with one side of their face and body blackened with charcoal; others were painted with stripes of various colours; others figured as warriors, wearing large caps adorned with white cowrie shells and birds' feathers. Breaking into their midst, Papeiha boldly addressed them on their folly in devoting such large quantities of food to a log of wood which they had carved and decorated and called a god. This challenge was immediately accepted by one of the priests, who springing to his feet, protested that their god was a real god, and a very powerful god, and that they were that day celebrating a very sacred feast.

Papeiha replied that the day was at hand when their folly would be revealed to them by the true GOD JEHOVAH, who would make their so-called gods "fuel for the fire." This strong declaration greatly perplexed the crowd, but they continued to listen attentively while Papeiha commented on the love of GOD in giving His SON to die for sinners. After he had ceased, the people asked him many questions; among others,—"Where does your GOD live?" He answered, that Heaven was His dwelling-place, but that both Heaven and Earth were filled with the majesty of His presence. They rejoined, in their inability to conceive of an Invisible but Omnipresent Deity;—"We cannot see Him, but ours are here before our eyes, and, if the earth was full of your GOD, He would surely be big enough to be seen." "And," said another, "why do we not run against Him?" To which Papeiha ingeniously responded :—"That the earth was full of air, but we did not run against it: that we were surrounded by light, but it did not impede our progress."

Five months later, a priest came to Papeiha and his associate missionary Tiberio, announcing his resolve to burn his idols; and he brought with him his eldest son, a boy of ten years old, to place under their care, lest the gods in their wrath should destroy him. Evidently, in spite of his iconoclastic purpose, the priest still cherished a belief in the power of his wooden deities. Leaving the child with the two teachers, he returned home, and next day at early dawn returned, staggering under the weight of his cumbrous idol. A crowd followed him, shouting at him as a madman, and looking upon him as one pre-doomed to destruction by his own folly; but he held fast to his resolve to embrace the word of JEHOVAH, and declared that he had no fear of the issue. He threw his idol at the feet of the teachers, one of whom fetched his saw to cut it up; but the crowd, as soon as they saw the instrument applied to the head of the god, were stricken with panic fear, and fled away. As no catastrophe occurred, they gradually returned impelled by curiosity, which is sometimes stronger than fear; and in their presence, amidst profound excitement, the first rejected idol of Rarotonga was committed to the flames.

To convince the people of the absurdity of their apprehensions, the teachers, as soon as the idol was converted into ashes, roasted some bananas upon them, of which they ate, and invited the spectators to partake. None however were brave enough to admit so dangerous a morsel into their mouths, and they waited, open-eyed, for the expected result of the profane audacity of the two teachers. But, like the inhabitants of Melita, "after they had looked a great while and saw no harm come to them, they changed their minds," and in less than ten days after this event no fewer than fourteen idols were destroyed. Soon afterwards, the chief Tinomana sent for the missionaries, and on their arrival at his mountain-home, informed them that after much deliberation, he had resolved to become a Christian, and to place himself under their direction. He therefore wished to know what was the first step he ought to take. They informed him that he must destroy his maraes and burn his idols; to which he immediately replied, "Come with me and see them destroyed." On reaching the place he desired some person to take a firebrand and set fire to the temple, the *ataraw*, or altar, and the *unus*, or sacred pieces of carved wood by which the marae was decorated. Four huge idols were then deposited at the feet of the teachers, who, having read a portion of the tenth chapter of S. Luke's Gospel, which was peculiarly appropriate, especially from verse 17 to 20, stripped them of their linen wrappings, which they distributed among the people, and threw them into the flames.

Some of the spectators waxed wroth with the chief, and expressed themselves with great violence, denouncing him as a fool and a madman for burning his gods, and listening to worthless fellows who "were drift-wood from the sea, washed on shore by the waves of the ocean." The women were specially vehement in their grief, and broke out into the loudest and dolefulest lamentations imaginable. Many of them inflicted deep gashes on their heads with sharp shells and shark's teeth, and ran wildly to and fro, smeared with the blood which streamed from their wounds, and crying in tones of the deepest melancholy, "Alas, alas, the gods of the madman Tinomana, the gods of the insane chief are given to the flames!" Others, blackened with charcoal, were not less demonstrative.

In the course of a few days a clean sweep was made of the idols of the district; never were Iconoclasts, not even our Puritan forefathers, more thorough or more resolute. The teachers then advised Tinomana and their other converts to prepare their food for the Sunday, and attend worship at the mission station. This they did,—but they came armed as for battle, with war-caps, slings, and spears, fearing lest the irate *Satanus* (as they called the idolaters) should attack them. Neither in coming nor going, however, were they molested.

"At this time," says Mr. Williams,[1] "a ludicrous circumstance occurred, which will illustrate the ignorance and superstition of this people. A favourite cat had been taken on shore by one of the teachers' wives on our first visit, and not liking his new companions, Tom fled to the mountains. The house of the priest Tiaki, who had just destroyed his idol, was situated at a distance from the settlement, and at midnight while he was lying asleep on his mat, his wife, who was sitting awake by his side musing upon the strange events of the day, beheld with consternation two fires glistening in the doorway, and heard with surprise

[1] John Williams, "Missionary Enterprises," p. 48.

a mysterious voice. Almost petrified with fear, she awoke her husband, and began to upbraid him for his folly in burning his god, who, she declared, was now come to be avenged of them. 'Get up and pray, get up and pray,' she said. The husband arose, and on opening his eyes beheld the same glaring lights, and heard the same ominous sound. Impelled by the extreme urgency of the case, he commenced, with all possible vehemence, vociferating the alphabet as a prayer to GOD to deliver them from the vengeance of Satan. On hearing this, the cat, as much alarmed as the priest and his wife, of whose nocturnal peace he had been the unconscious disturber, ran away, leaving the poor people congratulating themselves on the efficacy of their prayer."

Afterwards, in the course of his wanderings, Puss reached the district of the *Satanus;* and, as the marae was situated in a sequestered corner, and overshadowed by the luxuriant foliage of patriarchal trees, the graybeards of the wood, he was well pleased with the place. In order to keep the best of company, he took up his abode with the gods; and as he met with no opposition from within, he little expected any from without. But some few days after came the priest, accompanied by a number of worshippers, to present some offerings to the god; on his opening the door, Tom respectfully welcomed him with a *miaou*. At this unwonted salutation he rushed back in terror, shouting to his followers: "Here's a monster from the deep! here's a monster from the deep!"

Whereupon the whole party hastened home, assembled several hundreds of their companions, assumed their war-caps, equipped themselves with spear, club, and sling, blackened their bodies with charcoal, and in all this pomp and circumstance of Polynesian war, rushed, with yells, cries, and shouts, to attack poor Puss. He, however, daunted by their grim and strange array, did not await their approach. The moment the door was open, a leap and a bound—he was gone! *Abiit, evasit, erupit.* As he darted through the assembled warriors, they fled precipitately in all directions.

The religious system of the Samoans, according to Mr. Williams, differed in essential respects from that which prevailed at the Tahitian, Society, and other Polynesian groups.

They had neither maraes nor temples, nor altars nor offerings; and consequently none of the barbarous and sanguinary rites to which we have alluded. They shed no human blood; they strewed no maraes with the skulls and bones of their victims; they dedicated no sacred groves to brutal and sensual observances. Hence the Rarotongans denounced them for their impiety, and "a godless Samoan" was a proverbial phrase. Yet they were not without their superstitions; they had lords many and gods many; and their credulity was as marked as that of any other savage race on whom the light of Christianity and civilisation had never shone.

In considering the religion of the Polynesians, there are four points to be glanced at; 1, their gods; 2, their cultus; 3, their ideas of immortality; and 4, the means by which they hoped to secure future happiness.

1. Their gods consisted of three kinds: their deified ancestors, their idols, and their etus.

Some of their ancestors were deified, after the Greek fashion, for the supposed boons they had conferred upon mankind. For example, it was believed that the world was formerly in darkness; but that the sun, moon, and stars were created by one of their progenitors in a manner too absurd to be described. Also, that the heavens were of old so close to the earth that men could not walk erect, and were compelled to crawl; until a great man conceived the idea of elevating them to their present height; which he effected by the employment of almost Herculean energy. By his first effort he raised them to the top of a tender plant, called *teve*, about four feet high. There they remained until he had refreshed and rested himself. A second effort, and he upheaved them to the height of a tree called *kanariki*, which is as tall as the sycamore. His third attempt carried them to the summits of the mountains; and after a long period of repose, and another tremendous struggle, he raised them to their present altitude, at which they have ever since remained. This wonderful personage was appropriately apotheosized; and down to the date of the introduction of Christianity, was everywhere worshipped as "the Elevator of the Heavens."

The fisherman had his god; so had the husbandman, the

voyager, the warrior, the thief; mothers dedicated their offspring to one or other of these numerous Powers, and chiefly to Hero, the god of thieves, and to Oro, the god of war. " If to the former, the mother, while pregnant, went to the marae with the requisite offerings, when the priest performed the ceremony of catching the spirit of the god with the snare previously described, and infusing it into the child even prior to its birth, that it might become a clever and desperate thief. Most parents, however, were anxious that their children should become brave and renowned warriors. This appears to have been the very summit of a heathen mother's ambition, and to secure it, numerous ceremonies were performed before the child was born ; and after its birth it was taken to the marae, and formally dedicated to Oro. The spirit of the god was then caught, and imparted to the infant, and the ceremony was completed by numerous offerings and prayers. At New Zealand, stones were thrust down the throat of the babe, to give it a stony heart, and make it a dauntless and desperate warrior."

This dedication of the child to the sanguinary war-god points to a condition of society in which life was verily and indeed a battle, and every one had to hold his own by right of a strong arm and a reckless spirit. There was no room for the feeble in such a system ; they crawled aside to die ; or were trampled to death in the rush and press of the crowd. Civilisation has its victims ; but assuredly they are few in comparison to the thousands and tens of thousands destroyed by the merciless tyranny of Heathenism. Civilisation does at least teach us our duties towards our neighbours ; while Savage Man had little sentiment of compassion or affection for father or brother, daughter or wife.

The second class of objects regarded with religious veneration was *Idols*. In every island and district these were different ; but in every island and district they abounded. Some were large, some small ; some hideous in the extreme, others were almost comely. No fixed pattern appears to have been before the idol-makers ; each man followed his own fancy.

The third object of worship was the *Etu*,—that is, some bird, fish, or reptile, in which the natives believed that a spirit resided. This form of idolatry was more in vogue in the Samoas than in any other island-group. Among the Samoans, the objects regarded as *etus* were, indeed, almost innumerable, and frequently they were of extraordinary triviality. It was not unusual to see a chief, in other matters really intelligent, muttering his prayers to a fly, an ant, or a lizard, if such chanced to crawl or alight in his presence.

"On one occasion," says Mr. Williams, "a vessel from New South Wales touched at the Samoas, the captain of which had on board a cockatoo that talked. A chief was invited to the ship, and shortly after he entered the cabin the captain began a colloquy with the bird. At this he was struck with amazement, trembled exceedingly, and immediately sprang upon deck, leaped into the sea, and called aloud to the people to follow him, affirming the captain had his *devolo* on board, which he had both seen and heard. Every native dashed at once into the sea, and swam to shore with haste and consternation; and it was with much difficulty that they could be induced to revisit the ship, as they believed that the bird was the captain's *etu*, and that the spirit of the devil was in it."

Another illustration is given by Mr. Williams:—

"While walking," he says, "on one occasion, across a small uninhabited island, in the vicinity of Tongatabu, I happened to tread upon a nest of sea snakes. At first I was startled at the circumstance, but being assured that they were perfectly harmless, I desired a native to kill the largest of them as a specimen. We then sailed to another island, where a number of heathen fishermen were preparing their nets. Taking my seat upon a stone under a tou tree, I desired my people to bring the reptile, and dry it on the rocks; but as soon as the fishermen saw it, they raised a most terrific yell, and, seizing their clubs, rushed upon the Christian natives, shouting: 'You have killed our god, you have killed our god!' I stepped in between them, and with some difficulty stayed their violence, on the condition that the reptile should be immediately carried back to the boat."

The Polynesian islanders, or most of them, seem to have cherished a general idea of a Supreme Being, whom they regarded as the Creator of all things and the Author of their mercies. They called him Tangatoa; and at their great feasts, before the food was distributed, an orator would rise, and after enumerating each viand on the board, would say : " Thank you for this, great Tangatoa !"

The worship or *cultus* observed by the islanders included prayers, offerings of pigs, fish, vegetables, canoes, native cloth, and the like, and incantations. To these must be added the dread rite of human sacrifice. Of the style of their addresses to the gods one may form an idea from the formula with which they were accustomed to conclude it. Having presented the gift, the priest would say : " Now, if you are a god of mercy, come this way, and be propitious to our offering ; but if you are a god of anger, go outside the world,—you shall have neither temples, offerings, nor worshippers here."

As in other savage countries, they sought to propitiate the gods by inflicting physical injuries upon themselves. The Sandwich Islanders, in performing some of their rites, would knock out their front teeth ; the Friendly Islanders would cut off one or two of the bones of their little fingers. So common was the latter practice, that few were to be found who had not in this way mutilated their hands. One missionary relates that, on one occasion, a chief's daughter, —a fine young woman about eighteen years of age,—was standing by his side, when he observed by the condition of the wound that she had recently performed the ceremony. Taking her hand, he asked why she had cut off her finger ? There was a touch of pathos in her reply. Her mother was ill, and fearing lest she should die, she had mutilated herself in the hope the gods would preserve her life. " Well, and how did you do it?" " I took a sharp shell, and worked it about until the joint was separated, and then I allowed the blood to stream from it. This was my offering to persuade the gods to restore my mother." One cannot doubt the genuineness of the filial affection which could make such a sacrifice, though we may wish that it had been more wisely exercised.

When a second offering was required, the votary severed the second joint of the same finger. If a third or fourth were demanded, he amputated the same bones of the other little finger ; and when he had no more joints that he could conveniently spare, he would rub the stumps of his mutilated fingers with rough stones, until the blood again streamed from the wounds.

Human sacrifices, as we have said, were very numerous, especially in the Henry, the Tahitian, and the Society island groups. At the so-called Feast of Restoration (*Raumatavchi raa,*) no fewer than seven victims were required. It was always celebrated after an invading army had forced the inhabitants to retreat to the mountains, and had desecrated the maraes by cutting down the branches of the sacred trees, and cooking their food with them, and with the wooden altars and decorations of the sacred place.

At the inauguration of their greatest kings, the islanders used what was called *Maro ura*, or the red sash. This was a piece of network, about six feet long and seven inches wide, upon which the red feathers of the parroquet were neatly fastened. A chief could receive no more honourable appellation than that of *Arii maro ura*, "King of the Red Sash." A new piece, about eighteen inches long, was attached at every sovereign's inauguration; and on all such occasions several human victims were required. A sacrifice was made, first for the *mau raa tite*, or the extension of the network upon pegs, in order to attach to it the new piece. A second was necessary for the *fatu raa*, or actual attachment; and a third for the *piu raa*, or twitching the sacred relic off the pegs. These ceremonies not only invested the sash itself with peculiar solemnity, but also rendered the chiefs who wore it more important in the eyes of the people. Well might it be so, when the thing was dyed, as it were, in innocent human blood.

Human sacrifices were also offered on the breaking out of war. Mr. Williams remarks that a correct idea of the extent to which this system is carried may be obtained from a relation of the circumstances under which the last Tahitian victim fell, immediately prior to the introduction of Christianity. Pomare, king of Tahiti, was on the point of fighting a battle which would assure his supremacy or deprive him of his dominions. It became to him, therefore, a matter of the highest concern to propitiate the gods by the most valuable offerings he could command. For this purpose, rolls of native cloth, pigs, fish, and immense quantities of other food were presented at the maraes; but the gods (or their priests) would not be satisfied; a human victim was demanded. Pomare, therefore, sent two of his messengers to the house of the victim, whom he had marked for the occasion. On reaching the place they inquired of the wife where her husband was, and she, in her innocence, gave the required explanation. " Well," they continued, "we are thirsty; give us some cocoa-nut water." She had no nuts in the house, she replied, but they were at liberty to climb the trees, and take as many as they desired. They then requested her to lend them the *O*,—a piece of ironwood, about four feet long and an inch and a half in diameter, with which the natives open the cocoa-nut. She cheerfully consented, little suspecting that she was placing in their murderous hands the instrument which, in a few moments, was to inflict a fatal blow on her husband's head. Upon receiving the *O*, the men left the house, and went in search of their victim; and the woman, her suspicions being excited, followed them shortly afterwards, reaching the scene just in time to see the blow inflicted, and her husband fall.

She rushed forward to take a last embrace, but was immediately seized and bound hand and foot, while her husband's body was placed in a long basket made of cocoa-nut leaves, and carried from her sight. The sacrificers were always exceedingly careful to prevent the wife, or daughter, or any female relative from touching the corpse; for so polluting were females considered, that a victim would have been desecrated by a woman's touch or breath, to such a degree as to have rendered it unfit for an offering to the gods.

While the men were bearing their victim to the marae, he recovered from the stunning effect of the blow, and, bound as he was in the cocoa-nut leaf basket, said to his murderers: " Friends, I know what you are about to do with me; you are about to kill me, and offer me as a *tabu* to your savage gods; and I also know that it is useless for me to beg for mercy, for you will not spare my life. You may kill my body, but you cannot hurt my soul; for I have begun to pray to JESUS, the knowledge of Whom the missionaries have brought to our island: you may kill my body, but you cannot hurt my soul."

This address did not move the compassion of his murderers. Laying their victim on the ground with a stone under his head, they crushed it to pieces with another. It appears that he had been selected as a victim because he had "begun to pray for JESUS ;" and it is not unjust, therefore, to claim for this poor Tahitian savage a place in the noble army of martyrs.

"The manner in which human victims were sought," says Williams, "is strikingly illustrative of many passages of Scripture which portray the character of heathenism. As soon as the priest announced that such a sacrifice was required, the king despatched messengers to the chiefs of the various districts, and upon entering the dwelling they would inquire whether the chief had a *broken calabash* at hand, or a *rotten cocoa-nut*. These and sinister terms were invariably used, and well understood, when such applications were made. It generally happened that the chief had some individual on his premises whom he intended to devote to this horrid purpose. When, therefore, such a request was made, he would notify, by a motion of the hand or head, the individual to be taken. The only weapon with which these procurers of sacrifices were armed, was a small round stone concealed in the hollow of their hand. With this they would strike their victim a stunning blow upon the back of the head, when others who were in readiness would rush in and complete the horrid work. The body was then carried, amid songs and shouts of savage triumph, to the marae, there to be offered to the gods. At other times, the king's gang of desperadoes would arm themselves with spears, surround the house of their victim, and enjoy the sport of spearing him through the apertures between the poles which encircled the house. In these circumstances, the object of their savage amusement, frenzied with pain and dread, would rush from one part of the house to the other ; but wherever he ran he found the spear entering his body ; and at length, perceiving no possibility of escape, he would cover himself in his cloth, throw himself upon the floor, and wait until a spear should pierce his heart."

The Polynesian ideas of a future state were sufficiently curious. While believing in its existence, the natives had no conception of the value and immortality of the soul, no conception of the Everlasting. According to the Tahitians, there were two places of existence for separated spirits: one called *Roohutu noanoa*, or sweet-scented Roohutu, which in many points resembled the paradise of the Rarotongans; and the other was *Roohutu namu-namua*, or foul-scented Roohutu, of which it is impossible to furnish a description. According to the Rarotongans, paradise was a very long house, surrounded with beautiful shrubs and flowers, unfading, and of perpetual sweetness; its inmates enjoyed a beauty which never waned, and a youth which never waxed old, while passing their days, without weariness, in dancing, merriment, and festivity. This was the highest idea of Heaven and future blessedness to which they could attain, and was as materialistic as that of the Mohammedans.

It was not necessary that a man should live a pure, true, and noble life to gain admission to the Polynesian paradise, nor was he excluded from it on account of his sins. In order to pass the departed spirit into elysium, the corpse was dressed in the best attire the relatives could provide, the head was wreathed with flowers, and other decorations were added. A pig was then baked whole, and placed on the deceased's body, surrounded by a pile of vegetable food. After this, supposing the departed to have been a son, the father would deliver some such speech as the following:—
" My son, when you were alive I treated you with kindness, and when you were taken ill I did my best to restore you to health ; and now you are dead, there's your *momoe o*, or property of admission. Go, my son, and with that gain an entrance into the palace of Tiki, and do not come to this world again to disturb or alarm us." Body, pig, and food would then be buried; and, if the kinsman received no contrary intimation within a few days of the interment, they believed that the offerings had obtained for the departed the desired admission. But if a cricket were heard on the premises, it was considered an ill omen, and they would utter the dismalest howls, and such expressions as the following : " Oh, our brother! his spirit has not entered the Paradise; he is suffering from hunger, he is shivering with cold !" The grave would immediately be opened, and the offering repeated,—generally with success.

The sacrifices of the Fijians are of a costlier character.

The Fijian chiefs had from twenty to a hundred wives, according to their rank; and at the interment of a principal chief, the body was laid in state "upon a spacious lawn," in the presence of a great crowd of interested spectators. After the natives had exercised all the taste and skill at their command in adorning her person, the principal wife would walk out and take her seat near her husband's body. A rope was passed round her neck; eight or ten powerful men pulled at it with all their strength until she died of suffocation; and the body was then laid by that of the chief. This done, a second wife seated herself in the same place; the process of strangulation was repeated, and she, too, died. A third and a fourth became voluntary sacrifices in the same manner; and all were interred in a common grave, one above, one below, and one on either side of the husband. The motive of this barbarous practice was said to be, that the spirit of the chief might not be lonely in its passage to the invisible world, and that by such an offering its happiness might be at once secured.[1]

The Earl of Pembroke, in his light, gossipy book entitled, "South Sea Bubbles," describes a visit which he paid to one of the old sacrificial *maraes*, or inclosures, in the island of Raiatea.

"Strange places they were," he says; "built of enormous slabs of rock or coral, arranged in an oblong shape, and the space inside them filled with shingle and coral, so as to form a platform about eight feet high. I think the largest was about fifty yards long; we scrambled up on to it by help of a tree, and stood on the spot stained with so much blood shed in the *name* of religion. What horrible stories those stones could tell if they could speak! . . .

"What made the human sacrifices of the Society Islands so strangely ghastly and horrible, was the fact that the wretched victim was always chosen from one of certain families, set apart for that special purpose for generation after generation for ever. How this caste originated I do not know. Many of these families used to put to sea secretly in canoes, preferring an almost certain death by

[1] Rev. J. Williams, "Missionary Enterprises," pp. 143-146 (edit. 1841.)

drowning or starvation to the terribly uncertain fate that was always hanging over their heads.

"When a man came to the priests to beg some heavenly, or rather infernal, favour, they would tell him, either from whim, malice, or some reason best known to themselves, that the god required a human sacrifice, and naming the victim, present the supplicant with the death-warrant in the shape of a sacred stone. He hides this carefully somewhere about him, and collecting a few friends, seeks out the doomed man. At last they find him sitting lazily under a tree or mending his canoe, and squatting down round him begin talking about the weather, fishing, or what not. Suddenly a hand is opened—the death stone discovered to his horrified view. He starts up terror-stricken, and tries to escape—one short, furious struggle and he is knocked down, secured, and carried off to the merciless priests. Ugh! it is an ugly picture."

[1] "South Sea Bubbles," by the Earl and the Doctor, pp. 114-117.

CHAPTER XIII.

THE FIJI ISLANDERS.

THE annexation of the Fiji Islands to the British empire lends to the practices and beliefs of their inhabitants a peculiar interest, though to a great extent these have been abandoned since the establishment of Christianity.

Their creed is undiluted polytheism; their pantheon is full of all kinds of gods, differing in rank and power, and very widely represented on earth by some animate or inanimate object. Each Fijian has a god of his own, under whose care he supposes himself to be placed. They do not seem to have any religious teaching; but they have a priesthood, and that priesthood has, of course, its traditional formulas of worship. But nothing like regular worship, as Christians understand the phrase, is accepted or observed, and the Fijian religion is really a superstition, because its sole inspiring motive is fear. This motive the priests carefully develope, making it the basis of their claims and the source of their influence.

No man can gain access to the gods except through the priests; and the priests insist upon liberal offerings. When the worshipper comes upon questions of importance, the *Soro* or sacrifice consists of whales' teeth and large quantities of food. For matters of inferior moment, the god is content with a mat, a club, a spear, or a tooth, or even young nuts coated with turmeric powder. On one occasion, when the chief Tuikilakila solicited the help of the Somosomo gods in war, he built a large new temple to the war-god, and presented a quantity of cooked food, numerous turtles, and whales' teeth.

Part of the offering, or *sogaria*, is set apart for the god, and the rest forms a feast to which everybody is invited. The god's portion, as the reader will immediately conclude, is eaten by the priest and old men, but to the younger members of the community is strictly *tapu*.

Strangers who desire to consult a god begin by cutting a pile of firewood for the table. Sometimes only a whale's tooth and a dish of yams are presented. It is not necessary that the offering should be made in the temple. Mr. Williams speaks of priests to whom the inspiration came in a private house or in the open air.

He who designs to consult the oracle dresses and anoints himself, and, attended by his friends, goes to the priest, who, we will suppose, has been previously informed of the intended visit, and is lying near the sacred corner, preparing his response. When the votary arrives, the priest rises and sits so that his back is near the white cloth by which the god visits him, while the others occupy the opposite side. The votary presents a whale's tooth, states the object of his visit, and expresses a hope that the god will regard him with favour. Sometimes in front of the tooth is placed a dish of scented oil, with which the priest anoints himself, and then receives the tooth, eyeing it with deep and serious attention.

Unbroken silence follows. The priest, says Mr. Williams, grows absorbed in thought, and all gaze upon him with unwavering steadfastness. In a few minutes he trembles; his face appears slightly distorted, and twitching movements are seen in his limbs. These increase to a violent muscular action, which spreads until the whole frame is strongly convulsed, and the man shivers as with an ague fit. In some islands, adds Mr. Williams, this is accompanied with sobs and murmurs, the veins expand, and the circulation of the blood is quickened.

The priest is now possessed by his god, and all his words and actions are henceforth considered as the god's and not his own. Shrill cries of "Koi au! Koi au!" (It is I! It is I!) fill the air, and are supposed to indicate the deity's approach. While delivering the oracle, the priest's eyes stand out and roll, as if a frenzy had seized him; his voice is unnatural and his face pallid; his lips turn white; his breathing is laboured; and his whole appearance resembles that of "a furious madman." The perspiration streams from every pore; the tears start from his strained eyes. But by degrees the symptoms disappear, and the priest stares around with purposeless gaze. Then as the god says "I depart," he throws himself down violently on the mat, or suddenly beats the ground with a club; whereupon those at a distance are informed by blasts on the conch, or the discharge of a musket, that the deity has returned into the world of spirits.

It would be a mistake to conclude that in these scenes the priest-actor is always a conscious impostor; he is frequently the victim of his own imagination, which he stimulates into an excess of frenzy.

The Fijians conceive that the way to Buruto, or Heaven, is impeded by many difficulties, except for the great chiefs, and that, therefore, the only certain plan for a man of inferior rank is to impose upon the god with a lie,—declaring himself to be a chief with so much earnestness that the god believes him, and allows him to pass! Probably in no other creed is admission to heaven made to depend upon a lie! With his war club and a whale's tooth on his shoulder, the spirit journeys to the world's end. There grows the sacred pine, at which the spirit hurls his whale's tooth. If he miss the mark, his journey comes to an abrupt termination; if he hit it, he travels onward until he reaches the spot where the spirits of the women murdered at his death await his arrival.

With these faithful attendants he goes forward, but is opposed by a god called Ravuyalo, against whom he employs his club. If he be defeated, the god kills and eats him; if he conquer, he again goes forward until he falls in with a canoe. Embarking, he is conveyed to the celestial heights where dwells the supreme god, Ndengei. Over the brink of the cliff stretches the long-steering oar of the god's canoe. He is asked his name and rank, and to this inquiry he replies with a detailed and very imaginative recital of his greatness and opulence, the heroic deeds he has achieved, the devastation he has effected, and the realms over which he has ruled. He is then commanded to seat himself on the blade of the oar, and, if his story have met with credence, he is borne aloft into Buruto; if Ndengei disbelieves it, the oar is tilted up, and he is hurled down for ever into the watery depths of blackness.

Bachelors are not admitted into Buruto, because as we have stated, the spirit waits for his wives, to prove that he is married. And if an unmarried man venture on the journey, a goddess called the Great Woman, throws herself in his way. She bears towards bachelors an implacable hatred, and no sooner sees one than she springs upon him and tears him to pieces. In her haste she sometimes misses him; but even then he has to contend against another god, who conceals himself by the side of the path, and as the bachelor spirit passes by, leaps upon him, and dashes him against a stone.

There is a ghastliness about the funeral ceremonies of the Fijians which far surpasses even the dreary desolation of those in vogue among ourselves.

In common with several other savage tribes they hold that men and women who have grown decrepit and infirm have lived their lives, and should withdraw from this world of activity. Accordingly though they may be neither dead nor dying, preparations are made for their interment. And it seems that the moribund themselves do not object to this summary anticipation of the moment of dissolution; on the contrary, when they become sensible of infirmity, they invite their sons to strangle them. While the sons, far from objecting to an act of parricide, will intimate to their aged parents, if they delay the request, that they have lived long enough, and that it will be well for them to enjoy the rest of the grave. On both sides this singular conduct is due apparently to the Fijian belief that the condition of the spirit in the next world will exactly resemble that of the individual in this; and consequently everybody is desirous to cross the threshold while he retains some degree of activity of body.

Alone we must die, but we need not pass alone into the spirit-world! Such is the conviction of the Fijians, and accordingly they provide a dead chief with attendants, by strangling at his grave his favourite wives. And they slay a valiant warrior that he may precede him on his journey, and do battle for him with all evil spirits or demons. These victims are called "grass," and lie at the bottom of the chieftain's grave; the wives decked out in fleecy folds of the softest masi, the servants with their various implements in their hands, and the warrior equipped for the strife, with his favourite club by his side. No resistance is offered by any one of the sufferers; no attempt is made to escape; all seem to contend for the honour of escorting their chief into the other world.

Mr. Williams was present at the funeral of the King of Somo-somo in August, 1845. Age was beginning to tell upon him, but there was no immediately dangerous symptom, and on the 21st, when Mr. Williams visited him, he was better than he had been for two or three days before. Judge, then, of the missionary's surprise, when, on the 24th, he was informed that the king was dead, and that preparations were being made for his interment, he could scarcely believe the report. The ominous word "preparations" induced him to hasten at once to the scene of action, but his utmost speed failed to bring him to Nasima, the king's house, in time. The moment he entered it was evident that, as far as concerned two of the women, he was too late to save their lives. The effect of that ghastly scene was overwhelming. Scores of deliberate murderers in the very act surrounded him; yet was there no confusion, and the unearthly horrid stillness was broken only by an occasional word from him who presided. Nature seemed to lend her aid to enhance the impression of horror; there was not a breath in the air, and the half subdued light in that hall of death revealed every object with unusual distinctness.

"All was motionless as sculpture, and"—writes Mr. Williams—" a strange feeling came upon me, as though I was myself becoming a statue. To speak was impossible; I was unconscious that I breathed; and involuntarily, or rather against my will, I sank to the floor, assuming the cowering posture of those who were actually engaged in murder. My arrival was during a hush, just at the crisis of death, and to that strange silence must be attributed my emotions; and I was but too familiar with murders of this kind, neither was there anything novel in the apparatus employed. Occupying the centre of that large room were two groups, the business of whom could not be mistaken.

"All sat on the floor; the middle figure of each group

being held in a sitting posture by several females, and hidden by a large veil. On either side of each veiled figure was a company of eight or ten strong men, one company hauling against the other a white cord which was passed twice round the neck of the doomed one, who thus in a few minutes ceased to live. As my self-command was returning to me the group furthest from me began to move ; the men slackened their hold, and the attendant women removed the large covering, making it into a couch for the victim."

Mr. Williams now repaired to the hut of the deceased king, to intercede with his successor on behalf of the other intended victims. Judge of his surprise and horror to find the king still alive. He was very feeble, it was true, but he retained complete consciousness, and occasionally put his hand to his side as his cough shook and tortured him. The young king seemed overcome with grief, and embracing Mr. Williams, said : "See, the father of us two is dead." He regarded his father's movements, even his speaking and taking food, as mechanical; in his view, the spirit had departed, and nothing remained but an infirm, and, therefore, valueless body. The preparations for the funeral were not interrupted, and Mr. Williams could obtain no hearing for his expostulations. The young chief's principal wife and an attendant busily dusted his body with black powder, as if dressing him for the war-dance; and bound his arms and legs with long rolls of white masi, tied in rosettes, with the ends streaming on the ground. He was attired in a new masi robe, which fell about him in ample folds; his head was decorated with a scarlet handkerchief, arranged turbanwise, and ornamented with white cowrie-shells, strings of which flashed on his dusky arms ; while round his neck depended an ivory necklace, composed of long curved clawlike pieces of whale's teeth.

At the sound of a couple of conch-shells the chiefs present did homage, so to speak, to their new king, who was still deeply affected, and gazing on the body of one of the murdered women, his father's eldest and most loving wife, exclaimed : " Alas, Moalivu ! There lies a woman truly unwearied, not only in the day but the night also ; the fire consumed the fuel gathered by her hands. If we awoke in the still night, the sound of her feet reached our ears, and if harshly spoken to, she continued to labour only. Moalivu! alas, Moalivu!"

The bodies of the victims were then wrapped up in mats, placed on a bier, and carried out of the door; but the old king was borne through a gap purposely made in the wall of the house. On arriving at the seaside, they were deposited in a canoe, the old king reclining on the deck, attended by his wife and the chief priest, who fanned away the insects. The place of sepulture was at Weilangi. There, in a grave lined with mats, were laid as " grass" the murdered women. Upon them was stretched the dying king, who was stripped of his regal ornaments, and completely enveloped in mats. Lastly, the earth was heaped over him, though he was still alive. At the end of the ceremony the new king returned to his " palace," not unmindful of the fact that in the course of time a similar fate awaited himself.

Since the annexation of the Fiji Islands, such a scene as this has, of course, become impossible. Cannibalism, to which the Fijians were largely addicted, has also, been prohibited. Lord George Campbell, in his " Log of the Challenger," written in 1876, says that those who lived in the interior still cherished cannibalistic tendencies, and he seems to have been of opinion that cannibalism prevailed in those parts to which missionaries or civilisation had not yet penetrated. But under the firm rule of Sir Arthur Gordon it was doubtless extirpated.

Even in Lord George Campbell's time the change effected by the sacred influence of Christianity had been "great indeed." A party of English officers made a boat-excursion to the large island of Bau, where the king lived. They found him dressed in a waist-cloth, lying on his face in a hut, reading the Bible. Not far distant were the great stones against which they used to kill the sacrificial victims, battering their heads against them till dead. There too they saw a great religious " maki-maki," hundreds of men and women dancing, and singing New Testament verses before Wesleyan missionaries, who, sitting at a table, received the money-offerings of their converts as they defiled before them dancing and singing.

We have sketched a hideous scene belonging to the past,

and associated with the darkest superstitions of the Fijians. We shall adapt from Lord George Campbell a more pleasing picture, in which the past mingles with the present, and the old and the new are not unhappily blended.

The chronicler of the cruise of the "Challenger" was witness of a native dance or "maki-maki," given at Kandavu in honour of the English officers. When he landed the first "set" had already begun, and torches, consisting of bundles of palm branches tied together, threw a lurid light over the savage scene. On a strip of grass in front of the huts were gathered the dancers, and close around grouped picturesquely on the top of great piles of cocoa-nuts, or squatting on the ground, were the natives of Kandavu and the neighbouring villages, officiating as critics, but prepared in their turn to take part in the wild revelry.

"Glorious Rembrandt effects, as the torches' flames leapt and fell in the still night air, bathing with ruddy glow that strange scene around,—the semi-nude dusky natives chattering, laughing, glistening eyes and white gleaming teeth, on the reed-built huts, on the foliage above, and flushing redly up the white trunks of the cocoa-palms. Round a standing group of tawny-hued boys and girls who formed the band, some two dozen men, dressed in fantastic manner, their faces blackened, and skins shiny with cocoa-nut oil, were dancing. Wound round their waists they wore great rolls of tappa, or white cloth, falling nearly to the knees, and over these, belts fringed with long narrow streamers of brightly coloured stuff—red, yellow, and white, surging and rustling with every movement; on their heads turbans of finely-beaten tappa, transparent and gauzy, piled high in a peak; gaiters of long black seaweed or grass, strung with white beads; anklets and armlets of large bone rings, or of beads worked in patterns; tortoiseshell bracelets and bead necklaces, from which hung in front one great curled boar's tusk. Some are dressed better than others, but all in the same wild style. Moving slowly in a circle round and round the band, whose clapping and rollicking strain they accompanied by a loud droning kind of chant, at the end of each stave chiming in with the band with a simultaneous shout, a sudden swaying of the body, a loud hollow clap of the hands, once or twice repeated, and a heavy stamp, stamp of the feet; a moment's halt and silence, broken plaintively by one of the singers, quickly taken up by the remainder to a clapping, rattling, and vowely measure, and again the dancers circle slowly round, swinging their arms and bodies, clapping, shouting, and droning in faultless time together."

The first dances were dances of peace; pantomimic representations of the chief pursuits of a Fijian's life, as, for instance, fishermen hauling in their lines, or the tillers of the field planting tare and gathering in their crops.

Next came the war dances, which reproduced the incidents of the past, incidents never likely to be repeated under British rule. A solitary singer began the strain, and the others gradually joined in,—clappingly, jinglingly, bubblingly, slightly nasally, a strange ring audible throughout, and not less audible the stirring boom of a bamboo drum. Suddenly, from out the surrounding gloom, against which in strong contrast stood the white stems of the cocoa-trees, and into the red light of the torches, merged slowly one after another, in Indian file, a string of "mad, savage-looking devils." Crouching and bounding, now backwards, now forwards, from side to side, they gradually approached. Their hands carried great clubs, the tips of which were decked with white plumes of silvery "reva-reva," flashing whitely as they were whirled around; their fantastic finery rustling loudly with every wild movement, eyeballs glaring out from blackened faces, their motions sudden and simultaneous, their splendid stalwart forms swelling with muscles and shining with oil,—they looked "awfully savage and fine;" and to a captive bound and about to be eaten, one would imagine well that the whole performance would be thoroughly enjoyable.

"Now stealthily working their arms and clubs, as if feeling their victim, then with a shout bounding forward, brandishing aloft their clubs, suddenly, as if struck by some unseen hand, falling to the ground on bended knee, swaying first to the right, then to the left, and bringing their clubs down with an ominous thud; again leaping up, bounding back, from side to side, then to the right-about, and all over the place; it is impossible for me to attempt describing them, so I won't. They were, I suppose, braining enemies by the dozen, and as they worked themselves into mad excitement, so the more they bounded, smashed their enemies' heads, and were happy. Their drilling was admirable ; standing in line with the string, every club whirled as one, every bound and frantic motion went together, and we are told they make fine soldiers, as far as drill is concerned, from this idea of time that they have. In their dances they were led by a small boy—a chief's son, this function being their prerogative,—a lithe tawny little savage, with a great mop of frizzled yellow hair, and his face dabbed with charcoal. In his hands he carried an enormous palm-leaf fan, with which he directed the dancers. Going through all the movements of the dance, he at the same time careered over the ground, now shouting loud words of command to the singers, and now to the dancers, yards away on their flanks. He was simply splendid, flying about like a demented demon, here, there, and everywhere, the dancers, whether their backs were turned or not, all keeping exact time with him. As these men appeared, so, slowly, still bounding voicelessly, terrifically about, and whirling their clubs, they vanished into the darkness."

Out of darkness cometh light, and a future, irradiated by the light of Christianity, succeeds to the ghastly past of Fiji, with all its cruel and odious superstitions.

NOTE ON THE POLYNESIAN ISLANDS.

Exorcism.

When Captain Moresby, of H.M.S. Basilisk, visited Shepherd Isle, near the Torres group, he found himself compelled to submit to a curious process of exorcism before he was permitted to land.

A "devil-man," fantastically painted, and adorned with leaves and flowers, waded out to meet his boat, waving a bunch of palm leaves round his head, and as the captain jumped on shore, the devil-man rushed at him, and grasping his right hand, waved the palms round his head in the same manner. It was evident that he meant no harm, and the captain therefore offered no resistance. He placed the leaves in the captain's right hand and a small twig in his own mouth, and then, as if with a great effort, drew out the twig,—which was supposed to extract the evil spirit,—and blew violently, as if to hurry it away. Afterwards the captain held a twig between *his* teeth, and the devil-man repeated the process, all the while showing signs of strong excitement.

"He led me then," says Captain Moresby, "to the edge of the bush, and I began to feel rather reluctant, and doubtful as to how all was going to end, but thought I had better see it out. Here two sticks, ornamented with leaves, were fixed in the ground, and bent to an angle at the top, with leaves tied to the point, and round these sticks the devil-man and I raced in breathless circles till I was perfectly dizzy. He, however, did not seem to mind it at all, and presently flew off with me up a steep path into the bush, where at a short distance we came to two smaller sticks crossed; here he dropped my hand, and taking the bunch of palm leaves from me, waved them, and sprang over the sticks and back again. Then placing both his hands on my shoulders, he leaped with extraordinary agility, bringing his knees to the level of my face at each bound, as if to show that he had conquered the devil, and was now trampling him into the earth. When he had leaped for awhile, he made signs that all was over, and we walked back together to the officers, who had been rather anxiously watching these singular proceedings. The natives, who had kept quietly aloof, now came freely about us, and showed by their manner that they considered us free of the island."

CHAPTER XIV.

THE RELIGION OF THE MAORIES.

WE meet in New Zealand with that curious system of "taboo" or "tapu" which prevails throughout the greater part of the Polynesian Archipelago; a system evidently conceived in the interest of the priesthood, and forming, to a great extent, the basis of its power.

We meet also with a recognition of the two Principles of Good and Evil, whose antagonism colours the creed of almost every race.

The Good Spirit of the Maories is called Atua; the Evil Spirit, Wairua. All evil spirits, or all the objects representing them, are known as Wairuas, and all the emblems or types of the Good Spirit as Atuas; but there is one supreme Goodness, one great and overruling God, to which the name of Atua is also applied.

According to Mr. Angas, the *Kakariki*, or green lizard, is specially venerated as an Atua. On one occasion, during the early days of Christian mission work in New Zealand, a missionary was examining a phial of green lizards, and a Maori entering the room, the missionary showed it to him. Whereupon the Maori immediately exhibited all the signs of extreme terror, and exclaiming, "I shall die! I shall die!" proceeded to crawl away on his hands and knees. Any novel object, any object beyond the intelligence of the Maories, they convert into an Atua. Thus, a barometer is an Atua, because it indicates changes of weather; a compass, because it points to the north; a watch, because it mysteriously records the progress of time. Not to these typical atuas, however, does the Maori render the homage of prayer and praise; this he reserves for the supreme and unseen Atua, and offers through the agency of his priests or tohungas. It is to be feared that these prayers are often unintelligible to those on whose behalf they are offered, but the Maories do not the less heartily believe in them; and, indeed, the history of religion all over the world presents innumerable illustrations of the fact that faith is not incompatible with ignorance. It is the very essence and secret of Superstition. Whether they understand the prayers of the tohungas or not, they delight in their frequent repetition, and insist upon their use in almost every circumstance of life. They are generally accompanied by offerings of animal and vegetable food, which, of course, become the perquisites of the tohungas.

The Maori priesthood is hereditary, father transmits his office to son, after carefully educating him in its duties. Dr. Dieffenbach was present when an aged tohunga was giving a lesson to a neophyte. The old priest, he says, was sitting under a tree, with part of a man's skull, filled with water, by his side. At intervals he dipped a green branch into the water, and sprinkled the hand of a boy, who reclined at his feet, and listened attentively to his recital of a long string of words. Dr. Dieffenbach doubts the common statement that the prayers are often without meaning, while agreeing that they are unintelligible to the majority of the worshippers. He thinks they are couched in a language now forgotten; or, what is more probable, that among the Maories as among many of the nations of antiquity, the religious mysteries are carefully confined to a certain class of men, who conceal them from the *profanum vulgus*, or reveal only such portions as they think proper. The claims of the exponents of an artificial creed must necessarily depend in a great degree upon the amount of mystery in which they involve it. With the common people familiarity breeds contempt; they venerate that only which they do not understand; it is darkness and not light which moves their wonder, and excites their awe.

Devoid as it is of elevated attributes, the religion of the Maori rises above some of the Polynesian creeds in its acknowledgment of the immortality of man, though on this point its teaching is very vague.

The Maori believes that, after death, his soul enters the Reinga, or abode of departed spirits; and, with an unwonted touch of poetry, he looks upon shooting and falling stars as souls passing swiftly to this undiscovered bourne; the entrance to which he supposes to lie beneath a precipice at Cape Maria Van Diemen. The spirits in falling are supposed to rest momentarily, in order to break the descent, against an ancient tree, which grows about half way down. The natives were wont to indicate a particular branch as being the halting-place of the spirits; but a missionary having cut it off, the tree has of late diminished in sanctity.

The entrance to the Reinga is not accomplished by all spirits in the same manner. Those of the chiefs ascend in the first place to the upper heavens, where each chief leaves his left eye, this left eye becoming a new star. Hence the custom in Maori warfare for the victor to eat the left eye of a chief slain in battle, in the conviction that by this process he absorbed into his own system the skill, sagacity, and courage of the departed.

It is humiliating, perhaps, to record these illustrations of human folly; but they are valuable as proofs of the depths to which Humanity descends when unaided by the elevating influence of revealed religion.

According to the Maories, the soul is not confined absolutely within the limits of the Reinga, but may at its will revisit "the glimpses of the moon," and converse with its former friends and kinsmen,—of course, only through the medium of the tohungas. The latter are sometimes favoured with a view of the spiritual visitor, who takes the form of a sunbeam or a shadow, and speaks with a low whistling voice, like the sound of a light air passing through trees. This voice is occasionally heard by the uninitiated, but the language it speaks can be comprehended by none but the tohungas.

Respecting the wairuas, it is difficult to gather any satisfactory information. The word "wairua" means either "a dream," or "the soul," and Dr. Dieffenbach says it is chiefly used to signify the spirit of some dead man or woman who is supposed to cherish a malignant feeling towards the living. The wairuas frequent certain localities, such as mountain-tops, which the Maori consequently takes good care not to visit.

It is a necessary result of the Maori belief in atuas and wairuas that these should foster a belief in witchcraft. Individuals of bolder and stronger minds than the majority will always claim a special relationship to the unseen Powers, and avail themselves of this pretended relationship to work upon the popular imagination. Convince the ignorant of the existence of evil deities, and he will listen readily to any who tell him that they can shield him from their malignant influence. And then it naturally follows, "as the night the day," that all misfortunes arising from unseen or unintelligible causes, will be attributed to witchcraft. A vast—an almost boundless field is thus opened up to the practice of human unscrupulousness and the weakness of human incredulity.

Let a Maori chief lose some valued article, or suffer from an attack of illness, and he immediately concludes that he has been bewitched. Who has bewitched him? He fixes, as a matter of course, on the individual whom he conceives to be his enemy, and orders him to be put to death. Or he resorts to some potent witch, and bribes her to exercise her influence to remove the maleficent spell under which he is labouring.

According to Dr. Dieffenbach, the particular haunt of the witches is—or rather *was*, for Christianity has rapidly extended its blessed power over the population of New Zealand—a place called Urewera, in the North Island, between Hawkes Bay and Taupo. The natives of this wild and deserted district are reported to be the greatest witches in the country; are much feared and studiously avoided by the neighbouring tribes. When they come down to the coast, the natives there are almost afraid to oppose their most extravagant demands, lest they should incur their displeasure. It is said that they use the saliva of the people they design to bewitch, and, therefore, visitors carefully conceal it, so as to deprive them of the opportunity of working mischief. Yet, like the witches and sorcerers of mediæval England, they appear to be more sinned against than sinning, and by no means to deserve the ill reputation which attaches to them.

It is a curious fact, says Dr. Dieffenbach, which has been noticed in Tahiti, Hawaii, and the Polynesian islands generally, that the first intercourse of their inhabitants with Europeans produces civil war and social degradation, but that a change of ideas is rapidly effected, and the most ancient and apparently inveterate prejudices soon become a subject of ridicule, and are swept away. The grey priest, or tohunga, skilled in all the mysteries of witchcraft and native medical treatment, readily yields in his attendance on the sick to every European who possesses, or affects to possess, a knowledge of the science of surgery or medicine, and laughs at the former credulity of his patient. It is evident that, while deceiving others, he never deceived himself, and was well aware of the futility of his pretended remedies.

When a New Zealand chief or his wife fell sick, the most influential tohunga, or some woman enjoying a special odour of sanctity, was instantly called in, and waited night and day upon the patient, sometimes repeating incantations over him, and sometimes sitting in front of the house, and praying. The following is the incantation which the priests profess to be a cure for headache. The officiant pulls out two stalks of the *Pteris esculenta*, from which the fibres of the root must be removed, and beating them together over the patient's head, says this chant. It is entitled, "A prayer for the sick man, when his head aches : to Atua this prayer is offered, that the sick man may become well."

On the occasion of a chief's illness, all his kith and kin gather around his house, and give way to the loudest lamentations, in which the invalid is careful to join. When the weeping and wailing capacities of one village have been exhausted he is carried to another, and the process is repeated. But in New Zealand, as elsewhere, the common lot cannot be averted by sorrowing humanity; the sick man dies; and then all that remains to the survivors is to show their respect and regret by such funeral pomp as they are able to devise. They assemble round the dead body, after it has been equipped in its bravest attire, and indulge in the most violent demonstrations of grief,—partly feigned, no doubt, but partly sincere. This luxury of woe, however, is chiefly accorded to the women, who display that extravagance of passion we are accustomed to regard as characteristic of the Southern nations. They throw themselves upon the ground, wrap their faces and bodies in their mantles, shriek and sob aloud, wave their arms frantically in the air, and finally gash and scar their skin with long, deep cuts, which they fill in with charcoal until they become indelible records of the loss they have sustained. Funeral orations, full of the most vehement eulogies, and interrupted by complaints and reproaches against the dead man for his unkindness in going away from them, are incessantly delivered. These ceremonies completed, they place the corpse in a kind of coffin, along with various emblems of the rank of the departed, and leave it to decay.

The process of decomposition is completed in about seven or eight months; the ceremony of the *hahunga* then takes place. The friends and relatives assemble; the bones are removed from the coffin, and cleaned; a supply of provisions is passed around; a new series of funeral panegyric is spoken; and the *tiki*, *merai*, and other symbols of the departed chieftain's headship are handed over to his eldest son, who is thus invested with his father's power and privileges.

The place where the dead body lies while undergoing decomposition, the waki-tapu, as it is called, is frequently distinguished by peculiar signs, and the neighbourhood left uninhabited. Mr. Angas describes a visit which he paid to the village of Huriwonua. Its chief had died about six weeks before the visit, and Mr. Angas, on arriving there, found it entirely deserted. "From the moment the chief was laid beneath the upright canoe, on which were inscribed his name and rank, the whole village, he says, became strictly tapu, or sacred, and not a native, on pain of death, was permitted to trespass near the spot. The houses were all fastened up, and on most of the doors were inscriptions denoting that the property of such an one remained there. An utter silence pervaded the place. After ascertaining," says Mr. Angas, "that no natives were in the vicinity of the forbidden spot, I landed, and trod the sacred ground; and my footsteps were probably the first, since the desertion of the village, that had echoed along its palisaded passages.

"On arriving at the tomb, I was struck with the contrast between the monument of the savage and that of the civilised European. In the erection of the latter, marble and stone and the most durable of metals are employed, while rapidly-decaying wood, red ochre, and feathers form the decorations of the Maori tomb. Huriwonua having been buried only six weeks, the ornaments of the *waki-tapu*, or sacred place, as those erections are called, were fresh and uninjured. The central upright canoe was thickly painted with black and red, and at the top was written the name of the chief; above which there hung in clusters bunches of *kaka* feathers, forming a large mass at the summit of the canoe. A double fence of high palings, also painted red, and ornamented with devices in arabesque work, extended round the grave, and at every fastening of flax, when the horizontal rails were attached to the upright fencing, were stuck two feathers of the albatross, the snowy whiteness of which contrasted beautifully with the sombre black and red of the remainder of the monument."

We have entered at some length into an explanation of the system of Tapu, or Taboo, in our remarks on the religion of the Polynesians. It prevails, as we have already stated, in New Zealand; and though its disadvantages are many, and it is capable of great abuse, it serves nevertheless as a substitute for law, and to a large extent protects both life and property. For, supported and enforced as it is by the superstitious feelings of the people, it erects an insuperable barrier between possession and acquisition; it plays the part of a social police; it maintains the moral standard; it shields the feeble from the oppression of the strong. A man quits his dwelling for his day's work : he places the tapu mark on his door, and thenceforward his dwelling is inviolate. Or he selects a tree which will fashion into a good canoe; he distinguishes it with the tapu mark, and it becomes his own. Civilisation has designed no more effectual protection.

But like all restrictive and prohibitive systems, it is easily pushed to an inconvenient excess, and made an instrument of extortion or oppression in the hands of the chief or priest.

It is much in favour, says Mr. Williams, among the chiefs, who adjust it so that it sits easily on themselves, while they use it to gain influence over those who are nearly their equals; by means of it they supply their most important wants, and command at will all who are beneath them. If any object touch a chief's garment it becomes tapu; so, too, if a drop of his blood fall upon it; and, more particularly, it consecrates his head. To mention or refer to a chief's head is an insult. Mr. Angas says that a friend of his, in conversing with a Maori chief about his crops, inadvertently said: "Oh, I have some apples in my garden as large as that little boy's head!" pointing at the same time to the chief's son. This reference was felt and resented as a deadly insult, and it was only with the greatest difficulty that the incautious speaker obtained forgiveness. So very much *tapu* is a chief's head that, should he touch it with his own fingers, he must touch nothing else until he has applied the hand to his nostrils and smelt it, and thus restored to the head the virtue that departed from it when first touched. The hair is likewise sacred; it is cut by one of his wives, who receives every particle in a cloth, and buries it in the ground. The operation renders *her* tapu, for a week, during which time she is not allowed to make use of her hands.

The carved image of a chief's head is not less sacred than the head itself. Dr. Dieffenbach says: "In one of the houses of Te Puai, the head chief of all the Waikato, I saw a bust, made by himself, with all the serpentine lines of the aroko, or tattooing. I asked him to give it to me, but it was only after much pressing that he parted with it. I had to go to his house to fetch it myself, as none of his tribe could legally touch it, and he licked it all over before he gave it to me; whether to take the tapu off, or whether to make it more strictly sacred, I do not know. He particularly engaged me not to put it into the provision-bag, nor to let the natives see it at Rotu-rua, whither I was going, or he would certainly die in consequence."

Cannibalism is now extinct in New Zealand, having been crushed out by the strong arm of British authority, and the ever-increasing influence of British civilisation. But it was hard to die, and lingered down to a very recent date. As practised by the Maories, it lost few of its repulsive features. We must admit, however, that they did not indulge in it from a craving after human flesh, nor in time of peace, but after battles, from a belief that he who ate the flesh or blood, or even the left eye, of a slain warrior assimilated in his system all his martial and manly qualities. When the fight was at an end, the dead bodies were collected, and with much rejoicing carried into the villages, where they were roasted in the cook-houses, and duly eaten. But, first, the tohunga cut off a portion of the flesh, and with certain incantations and mystic gestures, suspended it upon a tree or pole, as an offering to the gods.

Mr. Angas describes one of the cooking-houses set apart for this horrid orgy. It was erected by a Maori chief in the Waitahanui Pah; and when visited by Mr. Angas, had happily ceased for some time to be used. The Pah stands on a low swampy peninsula, which is washed on one side by the river Waikato and on the other by the Taupo Lake. "The long façade of the Pah presents an imposing appearance when viewed from the lake; a line of fortifications, composed of upright poles and stakes, extending for at least half a mile in a direction parallel to the water. On the top of many of the posts are carved figures, much larger than life, of men in the act of defiance, and in the most savage postures, having enormous protruding tongues; and, like all the Maori carvings, these images, or waikapokos, are coloured with kokowai, or red ochre.

"The entire pah is now (1863) in ruins, and has been made tapu by Te Heuhen since its destruction. Here, then, all was forbidden ground; but I eluded the suspicions of our natives, and rambled about all day amongst the decaying memorials of the past, making drawings of the most striking and peculiar objects within the pah. The cook-houses, where the father of Te Heuhen had his original establishment, remained in a perfect state; the only entrances to these buildings were a series of circular apertures, in and out of which the slaves engaged in preparing the food were obliged to crawl.

"Near to the cook-houses stood a carved patuka, which was the receptacle of the sacred food of the chief; and nothing could exceed the richness of the elaborate carving that adorned this storehouse. . . . Ruined houses—many of them once beautifully ornamented and richly carved— numerous *waki-tapu*, and other heathen remains with images and carved posts, occur in various portions of this extensive pah; but in other places the hand of Time has so effectually destroyed the buildings as to leave them but an unintelligible mass of ruins. The situation of this pah is admirably adapted for the security of the inmates: it commands the lake on the one side, and the other fronts the extensive marshes of Tukanu, where a strong palisade and a deep moat afford protection against any sudden attack. Water is conveyed into the pah through a sluice or canal for the supply of the besieged in times of war.

"There was an air of solitude and gloomy desolation about the whole pah, that was heightened by the screams of the plover and the tern, as they uttered their mournful cry through the deserted coasts. I rambled over the scenes of many savage deeds."

Cannibalism, or to use the scientific term, anthropophagy, has its origin in different causes, and assumes different forms. Among some of the savage peoples it is, as among the Maories, simply the expression of a sanguinary instinct, of an atrocious sentiment of revenge. Among others it originates in a chronic condition of misery and famine. Yet, again, it is sometimes connected with the custom of human sacrifices, as among the Aztecs, and those who practise it come to esteem it a sacred duty, pleasing to their deities, or even to the *manes* of their hapless victims.

Unknown among the simple Eskimos, and, indeed, among all the hyperborean races, anthropophagy prevails with more or less intensity among peoples which have attained a rudimentary civilization.

Let us take, for example, the Khonds of Orissa, who keep up a system of human sacrifice, absolutely elaborate in its details. Its primary condition is that the victim, or Meriah, should be *bought*. Even if taken in war, he must be sold and purchased before the priest will accept him. No distinction is made as to age or sex; but the efficiency of the victim seems to depend on the sum he costs, and therefore the healthy are preferred to the feeble, and adults to children. The number consumed in a twelvemonth must be very considerable; as the Khonds do not believe in the success of any undertaking, or in the promise of their fields, unless a Meriah is first offered.

The victims are kindly treated during the period of their captivity, which is sometimes of considerable duration. In truth, a Meriah or dedicated maiden is sometimes allowed to marry a Khond, and to live until she has become twice or thrice a mother. Her children as well as herself are destined to the sacrificial altar; but must never be slain in the village in which they are born. To overcome this difficulty, one village exchanges its Meriah children with another.

There are various modes of accomplishing the sacrifice. In Goomten the offering is made to the Earth-god, Tado Pumor, who is represented by the emblem of a peacock. For a month previous to the day of doom, the people maintain an almost continuous revel, feasting and dancing round the Meriah, who seems to enter into the festivity with as much zest as they do. On the last day but one he is bound to a stout pole, the top of which carries the peacock emblem of the Tado Pumor; and around him wheel and wheel the revellers, protesting in their wild rude songs that they do not murder a victim, but sacrifice one who has been fairly purchased, and that, therefore, his blood will not be upon their heads. The Meriah, being stupefied with drink, makes no answer; and his silence is interpreted as a willing assent to his immolation. Next day he is anointed with oil, and carried round the village; after which he is brought back to the post, at the bottom of which a small pit has been dug. A hog is killed, and the blood poured into the pit, and mixed with the soil until a thick mud is formed. Into this mud the face of the Meriah is pressed until he dies from suffocation. It should be added that he is always unconscious from intoxication when brought to the post.

The zani, or officiating priest, cuts off a fragment of the victim's flesh, and buries it near the pit; as an offering to the earth; after which the spectators precipitate themselves upon the body, hack it to pieces, and carry away the fragments to bury in their fields as a propitiation to the rural deities.

In Sumatra exists a tribe, that of the Battas, which has not only a religion and a ceremonial worship, but a literature, a kind of constitution, and a penal code. This code condemns certain classes of criminals to be eaten alive. After the sentence has been pronounced by the proper tribunal, two or three days are suffered to elapse, to give the people time to assemble. On the day appointed, the criminal is led to the place of execution, and bound to a stake. The prosecutor advances, and selects the choicest morsel; after which the bystanders in due order choose such pieces as strike their fancy, and, terrible to relate! hack and hew them from the living body. At length the chief releases the poor wretch from his long agony by striking off his head. The flesh is eaten on the spot, raw or cooked, according to each man's taste.

We have seen that in some of the "sunny Eden-isles" of the Pacific, the natives consider that they render a service to their aged and infirm parents by putting them to death, and that, by eating them, they provide the most honourable mode of sepulture. In others, as in New Zealand, the belief prevails that a man, by devouring his enemy, gains possession of all the virtues with which the latter may have been gifted. This conviction is cherished by certain tribes on the river Amazon.

But it seems clear that in the majority of cases, anthropophagy originates in a constant scarcity of food, and in the lack of cattle and game; though in some it may be true that the cannibals are attracted by the delicious savour of human flesh, which they prefer to every other. Maury asserts that among the Cobens of the Uaupis, man is regarded as a species of game, and that they declare war against the neighbouring tribes solely for the purpose of procuring a supply of human flesh. When they obtain more than they require for their present need, they dry it and smoke it, and store it away for future use.

In Africa, Captain Richard Burton discovered, on the shores of Lake Tangauyika, a cannibal people, named the Worabunbosi, who fed upon carrion, vermin, larvæ, and insects, and even carried their brutality to such an extent as to eat raw and putrid human flesh. Although you may see on every countenance, says this enterprising traveller,[1] the expression of chronic hunger, the poor wretched, timid, stunted, degraded, foul, seem far more dangerous enemies to the dead than to the living.

We are speaking however of a barbarous custom which, from whatever cause it may have arisen, is rapidly dying out. Owing to the constant advance of the wave of civilisation, and to the vigorous efforts of our missionaries, the practice of cannibalism, against which our better nature instinctively rebels, is decaying even in the darkest and remotest regions of the globe. In Polynesia, for instance, as in New Zealand, it is almost extinct. And if we owed no other service to the heroic Soldiers of the Cross, this result would of itself entitle them to our gratitude, the extermination of Anthropophagy being the first step towards teaching man to reverence humanity.

[1] R. F. Burton, "Lake Regions of Equatorial Africa."

CHAPTER XV.

THE NORTH AMERICAN INDIANS.

THE general characteristics of the North American Indians, or the Red Men, have been made familiar to us through the writings of travellers, and the picturesque romances of Fenimore Cooper, the American novelist; though of the latter it may be said, perhaps, that he has used bright colours too uniformly, and introduced into his sketches too little shadow. The name by which they are popularly known is, of course, ethnologically incorrect. Just as, in speaking of the great Western Continent, our forefathers employed the expression "the West Indies," or the "Great Indies," from a mistaken conception of its geographical position, so they christened by the term "Indians" all its aboriginal races; and the term has survived in our common speech owing to its convenience.

Says De Maury: From the North Pole to Tierra del Fuego almost every shade of human colouring, from black to yellow, finds its representatives. According to their tribe, the Aborigines are of a brown-olive, a dark brown, bronze, pale yellow, copper yellow, red, brown, and so on. Nor do they differ less in stature. Between the dwarf-like proportions of the Changos, and the tall stature of the Patagonians, we meet with a great number of intermediary "sizes." The contours of the body present the same diversity. Some peoples, like those of the Pampas, are very long in the bust; others, like the inhabitants of the Peruvian Andes, are short and broad. So, too, with the shape and size of the head. Yet we recognize between the various American populations an air of kinship, or certain predominant and general features which distinguish them from the races of the old world. As, for example, the pyramidal form of the head and the narrowness of the forehead, characteristics of great antiquity among the American populations, having been found in skulls discovered by Mr. Lund in the caves of Brazil, in association with the bones of animals now extinct.

In spite of this variety of type, we may divide the Aborigines of America into two great races, of which one, at least, the Red Skins, is remarkable for its complete homogeneity. The Red Skins,—with whom alone we shall concern ourselves,—were formerly distributed over all the upper portion of the American Continent; that is, over the territory of Canada and the United States and the northern districts of Mexico. In the sixteenth century they numbered, it is said, a million and a half of souls. The "advance of civilisation,"—in other words, the greed and cruelty of the white man,—have reduced them now to a few thousand families. A few years more, and American rifles, brandy, poverty, and disease will have virtually effected the extermination of a race, which has assuredly merited the respect and recognition we are generally prone to render to courage and endurance. True it is that our estimate of the Red Skins must not be taken entirely from the imaginative pages of Chateaubriand and Fenimore Cooper. The Deerskins, the Hawkeyes, and the Leatherstockings of the novelist are ideal creations, the like of which have never been found in the wildernesses of the West. Yet we cannot deny to the Indians a character of true nobility and exceptional manliness. Their scorn of death and pain, their stoical composure under tortures, the mere description of which makes the blood of ordinary men run cold, their disdain of the allurements of civilisation, their stern refusal of foreign supremacy, their haughty pride, even their cold and calculated ferocity, are so many traits which raise them to a higher platform than that occupied by most savage races.

A hundred times in song, and romance, and drama have been portrayed the manners of this remarkable people, their subtle stratagems in war and the chase, the perseverance with which they hunt down their prey or enemy, their astuteness, their impassiveness, their brooding revenge. Who has not eagerly followed them in their unwearied wanderings across the rolling prairies, and through the interminable forests? Who has not listened eagerly, when seated round the watch-fire, with the calumet to their lips, they have meditated on the chances of peace and war,—chief after chief rising, with regal attitude and deliberate eloquence to take his part in the stern debate? Who has not watched them in their furious battle-charges, brandishing the dreadful tomahawk, and carrying off the scalps of their defeated enemies to hang up in their wigwams as the trophies of their prowess? Who has not breathlessly tracked them in their pursuit of a flying foe, or in their skilful escape through the thick brushwood from the pressure of some persistent antagonist? Assuredly this was a race well worthy of attentive study; and their history, or the narrative of their adventures, none can peruse without interest. There was a strain of poetry in their faith, in their customs, in their language at once laconic and picturesque, even in the names full of meaning which they bestowed on each tribe, and chief, and warrior. We can hardly suppress a feeling of regret that so much wild romance should have been swept off the earth, unless we bring our minds to dwell upon the deep dark shades of the picture, on their cruelty, perfidiousness, and lust. Even then our humanity revolts from the treatment they have received at the hands of the white man. Hunted from place to place like wild beasts, driven back from one hunting-ground to another, brutalised by misery or drunkenness, decimated by the diseases of civilisation, incapable of labour, the Red Skins have struggled in vain against the irresistible onward movement of a civilisation without bowels; a civilisation ill-adapted to attract and persuade them, and more anxious to destroy than to assimilate.

The treatment of the Indians is a dark chapter in the history of the United States. The great nations which were formerly the valued allies or dreaded enemies of the European settlers, the Hurons, the Algonquins, the Iroquois, the Natchez, the Leni-Lenapes, have entirely disappeared. The wrecks of other but less important tribes still linger on the shores of the great Northern lakes, in the woods and wildernesses of the Far West, at the base of the Rocky

Mountains, in Texas, in Arkansas, in California, and in the northern provinces and deserts of Mexico. Such are the Sioux, the Dacotahs, the Flatheads, the Big-Bellies, the Blackfoot, the Apaches, the Comanches. The two latter people have been the most successful in preserving their vitality. Their characteristics however are very diverse. The Comanches are of a mild gentle nature, and eager to live on peaceable terms with the whites. The Apaches, on the other hand, have vowed a relentless hatred against the Pale Faces; they are the terror of the *hacienderos* (or farm proprietors) and gold seekers of Upper Mexico, and the American journals to this day are full of their incursions, and their acts of cruelty and brigandage.

Physiologically, the distinctive features of the Red Men are, in addition to the colour of their skin and the pyramidal form of the head, the prominency and arched outline of the nose, the width of the nasal apertures, corresponding to a remarkable development of the olfactory nerve, and the absence of beard.

The superstitions, or religious customs, of the Red Men are in themselves a sufficiently interesting subject of study. We begin with an account of the ceremony through which every one of their youths has to pass before he is acknowledged to have entered upon manhood. Our knowledge of it is due to Mr. Catlin, who, as a reputed "medicine-man," lived for some time with the Mandan tribe, and became acquainted with their most secret customs.

The object of this rite, which for savage cruelty seems unparalleled, is, first, to propitiate the Great Spirit on behalf of the neophyte who undergoes it, so that he may become a successful hunter and a valiant warrior; and, second, to enable the leader and chief of the tribe, to watch his behaviour, and determine whether he will be likely to maintain its character and renown.

The Mandans, we must premise, cherish a legend of a flood which in times long past inundated the earth, and of which only one man, who escaped in a large canoe, was the survivor. In a large open space in the centre of the village a representation of this canoe, a kind of tub, bound with wooden hoops, and set up on one end, is carefully preserved.

s

The ceremony of initiation occurs once a year, at the season when the willow-leaves under the river-bank burst from their shade, and bloom in all their greenness. Early in the morning of the great day, a figure is seen on the distant ridge of hills, slowly approaching the village. Immediately the whole village is alive! The dogs are caught and muzzled; the horses are brought in from the meadows; the bravos paint their faces as if for battle, string their bows, feather their arrows, and grasp their pointed spears. Then into the central area strides the visitor, his body painted white, a plume of raven's feathers waving on his head, a white wolf's skin flung across his stalwart shoulders, and in his hand a mystery-pipe. The chief and his leading warriors immediately greet the new comer, Nu-mohk-muck-a-nah, or the First Man, as he is called,—and conduct him to the great medicine-lodge, which is open only on this occasion, and now reeks with the fragrant odours of various aromatic herbs. The skulls of men and bisons are solemnly laid on the floor; over the beams of the timber roof are hung several new ropes, with a heap of strong wooden skewers underneath them; and in the centre is raised a small daïs or altar, on which the First Man deposits the medicine or mystery of the tribe,—a profound, a sacred secret, known to none but himself.

To every hut in the village next stalks the First Man, pausing at the door of each to weep aloud, and when the owner comes out, relating to him the old, old story of the Flood, and of his own escape from it, and requiring axe or knife as an offering to the Great Spirit. The demand is never refused; and loaded with edged tools of various kinds, he returns to the medicine-lodge. There they remain until the conclusion of the ceremonies, when they are thrown into the river's deepest pool.

Thus passes the first day, during which, as during the whole period of the ceremony, an absolute silence prevails in the village. None know the place where he sleeps, but on the second morning he re-enters the village, and marches to the medicine-lodge, followed by a long train of neophytes, and carrying his bow and arrows, shield, and medicine-bag, and each painted in the most fantastic fashion. Hanging his weapons over his head, each man silently seats himself in front of the lodge, and for four days maintains his position, speaking to none, and neither eating, drinking, nor sleeping. At the outset, the First Man kindles his pipe at the fire that burns in the centre of the lodge, and harangues the neophytes, exhorting them to be brave and patient, and praying the Great Spirit to grant them strength to endure their trial.

Summoning an old medicine-man, he then appoints him to the charge of the ceremonies, and as a symbol of office hands him the mystery-pipe. After which he takes leave of the chiefs and their people, promising that he will return next year to re-open the lodge, and with slow and stately step passes out of the village, and disappears beyond the hills.

The master of the ceremonies hastens to put himself in the centre of the lodge, where he re-lights the pipe, and with every whiff of smoke utters a petition to the Great Spirit in behalf of the candidates.

During the three days' silence of the neophytes, the tribe indulge in a variety of pastimes.

First and foremost is the buffalo dance, in which eight persons are engaged, each wearing the skin of a bison, and carrying on his back a large bundle of faggots. In one hand they hold a mystery-rattle, in the other a small staff. In four couples they place themselves round the Big Canoe, each couple facing one of the cardinal points of the compass, and between them dances a young man,—two being got up in black, dotted with white stars, to represent day, and two in red, to represent night.

A couple of medicine-men, dressed in the hides of grizzly bears, sit beside the Big Canoe, and profess their intention of devouring the whole village. To satiate their voracity, the women convey to them abundant supplies of meat, which men, painted black all over, except their heads, which are white, in imitation of the bald-headed eagle, carry off immediately to the prairie, pursued by a number of little boys, painted yellow, with white heads, who are called antelopes. After a swift chase they overtake the eagle-men, seize the food, and devour it.

This rude frolic is repeated several times a day, the performers being summoned by the master of the ceremonies, who, followed by his assistants, issues from the medicine-lodge, and takes up his post against the Big Canoe, pouring forth many tears.

On the first day the dance is four times repeated, on the second eight times, on the third twelve times, and on the fourth sixteen; the dancers issuing from the hut in which they attire themselves immediately that the old man lifts up his head, and weeps.

During each performance, the old medicine-men keep up a rattle of drums, except when they pause to announce to the crowd that the Great Spirit is pleased with their offerings, and has given them peace; that even their women and children can hold the mouths of grizzly bears, and the Evil One does not appear to disturb them.

This bold declaration is repeated thirty-two times during the four days, and repeated without challenge; but at the thirty-third, the Evil Spirit makes his appearance, threads his way through the village, and breaks into the circle,—an uncanny creature, entirely naked, his body painted black, but with white rings, and his mouth blotched with white indentations like so many tusks. Carrying in his hand a long magic staff tipped with a red ball, which he slides before him on the ground, this Evil Spirit makes a rush at each group of females in the excited crowd. They shriek for assistance.

The master of the ceremonies straightway abandons his station by the Big Canoe, and presents his magic pipe to the intruder, who stands immediately as if petrified into stone, each limb quiescent, each muscle rigid,—a statue, rather than a man.

The women take advantage of this sudden pause to escape from the Evil Spirit's clutch; and as soon as they are out of danger, though their hearts still beat with excitement, they resume their ordinary quietude, only laughing loudly and gleefully at the sudden discomfiture of their antagonist, and at the awkward and ridiculous attitude in which he was surprised.

The old man stands upright by his side, with his eyeballs glaring him in the face, while the medicine-pipe holds under its mystic spell his Satanic Majesty, neutralises all the powers of his magic wand, and deprives him of the power of locomotion.

No two human beings, says Mr. Catlin, can ever present a more striking group than is presented by those two individuals, with their fierce eyes fixed in well-simulated hatred on each other; both contending for the supremacy, both relying on the potency of their mystery or medicine; the one, with dismal black body, pretending to be O-ku-hu-de, the Evil Spirit, and pouring everlasting vengeance on the other, who sternly gazes back with a look of contemptuous exultation, as he holds him bound by the influence of his sacred mystery-pipe. Truly, these Red-skinned Mandans are accomplished actors and pantomimists.

A repetition of this performance takes place until the power of the mystery-pipe has been sufficiently proved; and the women, gaining confidence in it, proceed to turn the tables on their persecutor, jeering him, and overwhelming him with shrieks of laughter. At last, one of the boldest dashes a handful of sand in his face; an insult which completely overwhelms him, so that he begins to weep abundantly. Another woman takes courage to seize his magic staff, and snaps it across her knee. Other women pick up the broken halves and break them into fragments, which they fling at O-ku-hu-de's head. Bereft of all his power, he incontinently turns tail, and dashes across the prairie, followed for half a mile or so by volleys of mud and stones and slates.

Thus ends the battle of Armageddon. The Evil Spirit has come, and fought, and been conquered. The next step is to remove the little altar and its mysterious deposit from the centre of the great medicine-lodge, and pass the hide ropes through openings in the roof to men stationed without. Then the master of the ceremonies and his assistants, together with the chiefs and bravos of the tribe, re-enter the lodge, and take up their positions.

Worn and wasted by four days of abstinence from food, drink, and sleep, the first neophyte enters the lodge, when called, and takes his stand in front of two of the executioners. One of them, with a blunt and jagged double-edged knife, pinches up an inch or so of the flesh of the breast or shoulder, inserts the knife, and through the incision thus accomplished, forces a wooden skewer; repeating the process on the other shoulder or breast, on each arm just below the shoulder and below the elbow, upon each thigh, and upon each leg just below the knee.

Painful as the operation must be, the neophyte bears it unflinchingly; not a sigh escapes him; his countenance remains as calm and unruffled as if he were wrapped in a pleasant dream.

Two of the hide ropes are now let down from the roof, and twisted round the skewers on the breast or shoulders. To the others are hung the neophyte's weapons, while the skulls of bisons depend from those of the lower arm or leg. At a given signal the neophyte is hauled aloft, and allowed to swing, at a height of six or eight feet from the ground, suspended only by the two skewers, while he sustains, not only his own weight, but that of the heavy skulls. With almost incredible fortitude, he endures this protracted agony, until exhausted nature gives way, and he falls into a swoon.

The bystanders seem no longer men, but demons intent on increasing his tortures. They surround him, a dozen or more at a time, and consider what new inventions can be adopted. At length, one advances towards the poor wretch, and begins to turn him round with a pole, which he has brought for the purpose. This is done very gently at first, but by degrees with more rapidity and increasing violence, until the neophyte breaks down in his self-control, and bursts forth into "the most lamentable and heart-rending cries that the human voice is capable of producing," imploring the Great Spirit to support and protect him in his agony, and repeatedly expressing his belief in that protection.

In this condition he revolves faster and faster, without the least hope of escape or relief, until he again falls into a swoon; his voice falters, his strugglings cease; he hangs a still and apparently lifeless thing. "When he is by turning gradually brought to this condition, which is generally done within ten or fifteen minutes, there is a close scrutiny passed upon him among his tormentors, who are checking and holding each other back as long as the least struggling or tremor can be discovered; lest he should be removed, before he is, as they term it, dead."

Having satisfied themselves that their victim is not feigning, they give a signal; he is lowered to the ground; the skewers which passed through his breast are removed, and the ropes attached to another candidate. He is allowed to lie where he fell; none dare to touch him; to do so would be a sacrilege, because he has placed himself under the protection of the Great Spirit.

After awhile he partially recovers, and crawls to another part of the lodge, where, with gleaming axe in hand and a bison's skull before him, sits a medicine-man. Holding up the little finger of his left hand as a sacrifice to the Great Spirit, the neophyte lays it upon the skull, and, in a moment, the medicine-man's axe severs it. Sometimes the fore-finger of the same hand is also offered, and only the thumb and two middle fingers, which are necessary in holding the bow, are left.

Then comes the last scene of this strange, eventful history, bringing the neophyte's sufferings to a climax. The skewers by which he is suspended to the roof are removed when he is lowered, but eight still remain; two in each arm, and two in each leg. To each is attached a heavy weight, such as a bison's skull, and they must not be *drawn* out, but must be *torn* out by sheer force. With this view he is required to run the last race,—which takes place in the open air, and in the presence of a concourse of excited spectators. Leaving the medicine-lodge, the master of the ceremonies leans his head against the Big Canoe, and fills the air with a loud long wail. Immediately a score or so of young men, all matched in height, wearing beautiful dresses of eagle-quills, and carrying in one hand a wreath of willow-boughs, issue from the dressing-hut. On arriving at the Big Canoe they assemble round it in a circle, holding on to each other's willow-wreath, and then race around it at their utmost speed, screaming and shouting until the air is filled with their uproar.

The candidates then come out of the medicine-lodge, dragging the heavy weights attached to their limbs, and are stationed at equal intervals outside the ring of runners. As each takes his place, two powerful young men take charge of him, who pass round each of his wrists a broad leathern strap, which they grasp very firmly, but without tying it.

When all the preliminaries are completed, a signal is given, and the neophytes begin to race round the Big Canoe, outside the inner circle, each man being dragged along by his custodians, until the skulls and other weights drag out the skewers to which they are fastened. The bystanders scream and yell and shout in a frenzy of excitement; eager, moreover, to drown the groans of the sufferers, should the instincts of nature prevail over their self-control, and desirous of encouraging them in their final trial.

Sometimes the neophyte's flesh proves to be so tough that the skewers cannot be dragged out, and in such cases their friends jump on the skulls as they rattle along the ground, so as to increase their weight.

Humanity cannot long endure a torture so horrible: the sufferers quickly faint, though they are still hauled round in the barbarous race, nor set free until the last weight is dragged from the quivering, bleeding body. Then the unconscious wretch is released, and left, for the second time, in the care and protection of the Great Spirit. In due time he recovers his senses, struggles to his feet, totters through the crowd, is received by his friends, and conducted to his own hut.

Mr. Catlin supplies two illustrations of the rigorous tenacity with which the Indians adhere to the rule that the skewers must be *dragged*, not *removed*, from the sufferer's flesh.

In one case the skewer had chanced to pass under a sinew, and the neophyte was dragged round and round the ring in vain. In vain his friends added their weight to that of the bison's skulls. The scene became so horrible that even the spectators could no longer endure it, and in sympathy with their cries the master of the ceremonies stopped the race, leaving the youth, unconscious, on the ground. As soon as he regained his senses, he crawled away to the prairie on his hands and knees, and there remained, without food or drink, for three hours longer, until suppuration took place, and he was enabled to get rid of the skewer. Then he crawled home, and strange to say, notwithstanding the agony he had undergone, and his loss of strength, recovered in a few days.

In the second case, two of the weights attached to the arms refused to yield, and the hapless neophyte crept as best he could to the steep bluff overhanging the river, where he drove a stake into the ground. Fastening the weights to this stake by a couple of ropes, he lowered himself about midway down the cliff, and so hung suspended for more than two days, until the obstinate flesh gave way, and allowed him to drop into the water. He swam to the side, crawled up the acclivity, and returned to his village. It gives one a vivid idea of the remarkable vitality and physical force of the Indian race, when one reads that this man, too, recovered!

The Indian has a vague idea of God and immortality. He believes in a Great Spirit, who, after death, admits the brave to his happy hunting-grounds, where game is inexhaustible, and the pleasure of the chase is ever open to the hunter. Beyond this dim and dubious conception, his imagination never carries him.

He is prone, as might be supposed, for such proneness is the cause of ignorance, and ignorance is the Red Man's bane, to the wildest and coarsest superstitions, and he is always at the mercy of the medicine-man of his tribe. One of his most potent superstitions is that connected with the "medicine-bag," which he firmly believes to be his sole "secret of success," his all-powerful charm and talisman, without which he would fail in every undertaking and be defeated and disgraced in battle.

At the age of fourteen or fifteen, the young Indian goes forth into the woods in search of his medicine. On a litter of leaves and twigs he lies for some days—as long, in fact, as his physical powers hold out—neither eating nor drinking; for in proportion to the duration of his fast will be the potency of his " medicine." His endurance at length gives way, and he goes to sleep. The bird, beast, or reptile of which he dreams becomes his " medicine." He returns home, and as soon as he has recovered his strength, he sallies forth in quest of the charm ; having found and killed the animal, he preserves the skin in such shape as his fancy suggests,—usually in the form of pouch or bag. If small, he slings it round his neck, and wears it concealed. In other cases, it hangs from his waist or shoulder.

However he may wear it, the Indian never parts from it. He would be disgraced and defeated in battle—he would fail in his undertakings—if it were absent from his person. Should he be deprived of it in battle, he is overwhelmed with shame, until he can kill an enemy, and take *his* medicine-bag to replace his own. If, without losing his own, he captures that of an enemy, he is entitled to assume a " double medicine," and with two medicine-bags about him he stalks to and fro, the observed of all observers. To take a medicine-bag is not less honourable than to take a scalp, and the successful bearer has all the advantage of the double protection afforded by the double charm.

It is seldom that an Indian will voluntarily part with his medicine-bag, and if he does, he forfeits his reputation almost irretrievably. Now and then he is persuaded by the white man to bury it, but its place of interment immediately assumes an air of sanctity in his eyes. He frequents the spot as if drawn thither by an irresistible influence, will throw himself on the sod, and talk to the buried treasure as if it were alive. Sometimes he will offer sacrifices to it, and if he be a rich man, will even offer a horse. On the latter occasion, the whole tribe take part in the ceremony, and march forth to the prairie in picturesque procession, led by the owner of the medicine-bag, who drives before him his most valued and valuable steed, decked with coloured devices. At the appointed spot, he delivers a long prayer or oration to the Great Spirit, and sets free the horse, which thenceforth enjoys the free life of the wild horses of the prairie, and if at any time recaptured is immediately released.

The position which in most savage tribes is held by the priest, among the American Indians is held by the "medicine-man." His influence is considerable, and his powers are supposed to be vast. He is called upon to heal the sick and save the dying, and, above all, to bring down the genial rain from heaven when it is needed for the growth of the crops.

We owe to Mr. Catlin an interesting description of the

rain-making ceremony. A drought had withered the maize-fields for some weeks, and application for help having been made to the medicine-men they duly set to work. On the first day one Wah-ku, or the Shield, came to the front; but failed—that day an equally unsuccessful experiment was made by Om-pah, or the Elk. The third day was devoted to Wa-rah-pa, or the Beaver, and on the fourth recourse was had to Wak-a-dah-ha-ku, the White Buffalo Hair, who was strong in the possession of a shield coloured with red lightnings, and in the arrow which he carried in his hand.

Taking his station by the medicine-lodge, he harangued the people, protesting that for the good of his tribe he was willing to sacrifice himself, and that if he did not bring the much-desired rain, he was content to live for the rest of his life with the old women and the dogs. He asserted that the first medicine-man had failed, because his shield warded off the rain-clouds; the second, who wore a head-dress made of a raven's skin, because the raven was a bird that soared above the storm, and cared not whether the rain came or stayed; and the third, because the beaver was always wet, and required no rain. But as for him, Wak-a-dah-ha-ku, the red lightnings on his shield would attract the rain-clouds, and his arrow would pierce them, and pour the water over the thirsty fields.

It chanced that, as he ended his oration, a steamer, the first that had ever ploughed the Missouri river, fired a salute from a twelve-pounder gun, as she passed the Mandan village. To the Indians the roar of the cannon was like the voice of thunder, and their joy knew no bounds. The successful medicine-man was loaded with valuable gifts; mothers hastened to offer their daughters to him in marriage; and the elder medicine-men issued from the lodge, eager to enrol him in their order. But, from the roof of the lodge, where he had taken his stand, Wak-a-dah-ha-ku discovered the steamer, as she dashed up the river, and discharged her gun again and yet again. He hastened to address the chiefs and people, explaining that the sounds they heard were not those of thunder, but that his potent medicine had brought a thunder-boat to the village. To the river-bank rushed the wondering population, and the rest of the day was spent in a fever of excitement, in which the rain-maker was forgotten.

Just before sunset his quick eyes discovered a black cloud, which, unobserved by the noisy multitude, swiftly came up from the horizon. At once he assumed his station on the roof of the lodge; strung his bow and made ready his arrow; arrested the attention of his fellows by his loud and exultant speech; and as the cloud impended over the village, shot his arrow into the sky. Lo, the rain immediately descended in torrents, wetting the rain-maker to the skin, but establishing in everybody's mind a firm and deep conviction of his power.

All night raged the storm; but unhappily a flash of lightning penetrated one of the wigwams, and killed a young girl. The newly-made medicine-man was sorely terrified by this catastrophe, which he feared the chiefs would impute to him, making him responsible for the girl's death, and punishing him accordingly.

But he was a man of much astuteness, and early in the morning, collecting three of his best horses, he mounted the lodge-roof again, and for a third time addressed the people of his tribe.

"Friends," he said, "my medicine was too strong, I am young, and I did not know where to stop. I did not regulate its power. And now the wigwam of Mah-sish is laid low, and many are the eyes that weep for Ko-ka, the antelope. Wak-a-dah-ha-ku gives three horses to rejoice the hearts of those who sorrow for Ko-ka. His medicine is great. His arrow pierced the black cloud, and the lightning came, and with it the thunder-boat. Who says that the medicine of Wak-a-dah-ha-ku is not strong?"

This artful address was received with much favour, and thenceforward Wak-a-dah-ha-ku was known as the "Big Double Medicine."

Of the medical practices of these medicine-men Mr. Kane, in his "Wanderings of an Artist," furnishes a striking illustration.

"About ten o'clock at night," he says, "I strolled into the village, and on hearing a great noise in one of the lodges, I entered it, and found an old woman supporting one of the handsomest Indian girls I had ever seen. She was in a state of nudity. Cross-legged and naked, in the middle of the room, sat the medicine-man, with a wooden dish of water before him; twelve or fifteen other men were sitting round the lodge. The object in view was to cure the girl of a disease affecting her side. As soon as my presence was noticed, a space was cleared for me to sit down.

"The officiating medicine-man appeared in a state of profuse perspiration, from the exertions he had used, and soon took his seat among the rest, as if quite exhausted; a younger medicine-man then took his place in front of the bowl, and close beside the patient.

"Throwing off his blanket, he commenced singing and gesticulating in the most violent manner, whilst the others kept time by beating with little sticks in hollow wooden bowls and drums, singing continually. After exercising himself in this manner for about half an hour, until the perspiration ran down his body, he darted suddenly upon the young woman, catching hold of her side with his teeth, and shaking her for a few minutes, while the patient seemed to suffer great agony. He then relinquished his hold, and cried out he had got it, at the same time holding his hands to his mouth; after which he plunged them in the water and pretended to hold down with great difficulty the disease which he had extracted, lest it might spring out and return to its victim.

"At length, having obtained the mastery over it, he turned round to me in an exulting manner, and held up something between the finger and thumb of each hand, which had the appearance of a piece of cartilage; whereupon one of the Indians sharpened his knife, and divided it in two, having one in each hand. One of the pieces he threw into the water and the other into the fire, accompanying the action with a diabolical noise which none but a medicine-man can make. After which he got up perfectly satisfied with himself, although the poor patient seemed to me anything but relieved by the violent treatment she had undergone."

A considerable amount of superstition attaches to the calumet, or medicine-pipe, by which all the great questions of peace and war are settled. This pipe is borne by an individual specially selected for the honour, who, during his term of office, is not less sacred than the pipe he carries.

His seat is always on the right side of the lodge, and no one is suffered to interpose between him and the fire. He is not even allowed to cut his own food, but his wives cut it for him, and place it in an official food-bowl, specially reserved for his use. As for the calumet, it is hung outside the lodge in a large bag, which is picturesquely and gaily embroidered. Much ceremony attends its uncovering. Whatever the weather, or the time of year, the bearer begins by stripping off all his garments except his cloth, and he then pours upon a red-hot coal some fragrant gum, which fills the air with perfumed smoke. Removing the different wrappers, he fills the bowl with tobacco, and blows the smoke to the four points of the compass, to the earth, and to the sky, with each breath uttering a prayer to the Great Spirit for assistance in war against all enemies, and for bison and corn from all parts. With equal ceremony the pipe, which no woman is allowed to see, is restored to its bag. The whole proceeding takes place in the deepest silence.

The bowl of the calumet is made of a peculiar stone, found in the Red Pipe-stone Quarry, on the Citeau des Prairies, a place to which the following tradition attaches. We give it as related by Mr. Catlin :

Here, he says, according to the Indian traditions, happened the mysterious birth of the red pipe, which has blown its fumes of peace and war to the remotest corners of the continent, which has visited every warrior, and passed through its reddened stem the irrevocable oath of war and desolation. And here, also, the peace-breathing calumet was born, and fringed with the eagle's quills, which has shed its thrilling fumes over the land, and soothed the fury of the relentless savage.

At a remote period the Great Spirit here called the Indian nations together, and, standing on the precipice of the red pipe-stone rock, broke from its wall a piece, and made a huge pipe by turning it in his hand, which he smoked over them, to the north, the south, the east, and the west, and told that this stone was red,—that it was their flesh,—that they must use it for their pipes of peace,—that it belonged to them all,—and that the war-club and scalping-knife must not be raised on its ground. At the last whiff of his pipe his head went into a great cloud, and the whole surface of the rock for several miles was melted and glazed. Two great ovens were opened beneath, and two women (guardian spirits of the place) entered them in a blaze of fire; and they are heard there yet, (Tso-mec-cos-tu and Tso-me-cos-te-won-du,) answering to invocations of the high priests or medicine-men, who consult them when they are visitors to this sacred place."

The reader will remember, perhaps, the allusion to the Peace-pipe in Longfellow's " Hiawatha,"—

> "On the mountains of the Prairie,
> On the great Red Pipe-stone quarry,
> Gitche Manito, the Mighty,
> He the Master of Life, descending,
> On the red crags of the quarry
> Stood erect, and called the nations,
> Called the tribes of men together.
> From his footprints flowed a river,
> Leaped into the light of morning,
> O'er the precipice plunging downward,
> Gleamed like Ishkoodah, the comet.
> And the Spirit, stooping earthward,
> With his finger on the meadows,
> Traced a winding pathway for it,
> Saying to it, 'Run in this way!'
> From the red stone of the quarry
> With his hand he broke a fragment,
> Moulded it into a pipe-head,
> Shaped and fashioned it with figures;
> From the margin of the river
> Took a long reed for a pipe-stem,
> With its dark green leaves upon it;
> Filled the pipe with bark of willow;
> With the bark of the red willow;
> Breathed upon the neighbouring forest,
> Made its great boughs chafe together,
> Till in flame they burst and kindled;
> And erect upon the mountains,
> Gitche Manito, the mighty,
> Smoked the calumet, the Peace-pipe,
> As a signal to the nations."

Some of the legends of the Indian tribes are of a very picturesque, and even poetical character, as may be seen in Mr. Schoolcraft's " Algic Researches." Take, as an example, the graceful tradition of the Red Swan.

Three brothers went out to the chase, excited by a wager

to see who would carry home the first game. But the binding and limiting condition was, that each was to shoot no other animal than those he was in the habit of killing.

They set out in different directions. Odjebwa, the youngest, had not gone far before he saw a bear, an animal which by the agreement he had no right to kill. He followed him close, however, and drove an arrow through him, which brought him to the ground. Although contrary to the bet, he immediately began to skin him, when suddenly something red tinged all the air around him. He rubbed his eyes, thinking he was perhaps deceived, but without effect, for the red hue continued. At length he heard a strange noise in the distance. It first resembled a human voice; but after following it up for some time, he reached the shores of a lake, and then discovered the object he was in search of. Far out on the shining waters sat a most beautiful Red Swan, whose plumage glittered in the sunshine; and ever and anon he made the noise which had before attracted Odjebwa's attention. He was within long-bow range, and pulling the arrow from the bow-string up to his ear, he took deliberate aim, and shot. The arrow took no effect, and he shot again and again until his quiver was empty. Still the swan remained statelily circling round and round, stretching its long neck, and dipping its bill into the water, indifferent to the missiles aimed at it. Odjebwa ran home, secured all his own and his brother's arrows, and these too, ineffectually shot away: then stood and gazed at the beautiful bird.

While thus standing, he remembered a saying of his brother's, that in their deceased father's medicine-bag were three magic arrows. Off he started, his anxiety to kill the swan overcoming every scruple. At any other time he would have deemed it a sacrilege to open his father's medicine-bag, but now he hastily violated it, seized the three magic arrows and ran back. The swan was still floating on the lake. He shot the first arrow with great precision, and came very near his mark. The second flew still nearer; and as he took the third and last arrow, he felt his arm strengthen, and drawing it up with vigour, sent the shaft right through the neck of the swan, a little above the breast. Still even this death-stroke did not prevent the bird from flying off,—which it did very slowly, flapping its wings, and rising gradually into the air, until it passed far away into the sunset.

Quoting again from Longfellow, we place before the reader his allusion to this pretty legend :—

> " Can it be the sun descending
> O'er the level plain of water?
> Or the Red Swan, floating, flying,
> Wounded by the magic arrow,
> Staining all the waves with crimson,
> With the crimson of its life-blood,
> Filling all the air with splendour,
> With the splendour of its plumage?
> Yes ; it is the sun descending,
> Sinking down into the water ;
> No ; it is the Red Swan floating,
> Diving down beneath the water ;
> To the sky its wings are lifted,
> With its blood the waves are reddened!"

The Indians regard the maize, or Indian corn, with almost superstitious veneration,—which is not wonderful, perhaps, when its immense importance to them is taken into consideration. They esteem it, says Schoolcraft, so important and divine a grain, that their story-tellers invented various tales, in which this idea is symbolised under the form of a special gift from the Great Spirit. The Odjebwa-Algonquins, who call it Mon-da-min, or the Spirit's grain or berry, cherish a legend, in which the stalk in full tassel is represented as descending from the sky, under the guise of a handsome youth ; in response to the prayers of a young man offered at his fast of virility, or coming to manhood.

> " All around the happy village
> Stood the maize-fields, green and shining,
> Waved the green plumes of Mondamin,
> Waved his soft and sunny tresses,
> Filling all the land with plenty."

CHAPTER XVI.

AMONG THE ESKIMOS.

THE success which has attended the labours of the Lutheran and Moravian Missionaries among the Eskimos has been well deserved by their self-denying devotedness. Few of the Arctic tribes are now outside the pale of Christianity; and all have been more or less directly influenced by its elements of purification and elevation. But prior to the coming of the pioneers of the Cross, the moral code of the Eskimo was curiously imperfect, and did not recognise murder, infanticide, incest, and the burial of the living among its crimes. Woe to the unfortunate vessel which touched upon the coast! The Eskimos were not less treacherous than the Polynesians of the Eastern Seas. And Krantz relates the story of a Dutch brig that was seized by the natives at the port of Disco in 1740. The whole crew were murdered. Two years later a similar fate befell the crew of another vessel that had accidentally stranded.

The religion or creed of the aborigines seems to have been very vague and imperfect. It is certain, however, that they believed in the immortality of the spirit, and in a heaven and a hell. It was natural enough that their conception of the latter should be affected by the conditions under which they lived; that their experience of the miseries of an Arctic climate should lead them to think of hell as a region of darkness and of ice, traversed by endless snow-storms, and without any seals.

They placed implicit confidence in their angekoks, or angekos, or "medicine-men," ascribing to them almost unlimited powers over the things of earth and sea, this world and the next. When setting out for the chase, or prostrated by illness, they always sought the assistance of the angekoks, who, on such occasions, indulged in a variety of strange ceremonies. The nature of these may be inferred from what was witnessed by Captain Lyon, who, during his famous Arctic voyage, bribed an angekok, named Toolemak, to summon a Tomga, or familiar demon, in the cabin of his ship.

All light having been carefully excluded from the scene of operations, the sorcerer began by vehemently chanting to his wife, who, in her turn, responded with the Amna-aya, the favourite song of the Eskimo. This lasted throughout the ceremony. Afterwards, Toolemak began to turn himself round very rapidly, vociferating for Tomga, in a loud powerful voice and with great impatience, at the same time blowing and snorting like a walrus. His noise, agitation, and impatience increased every moment, and at length he seated himself on the deck, varying his tones, and making a rustling with his clothes.

Suddenly the voice seemed smothered, and was so managed as to give the idea that it was retreating beneath the deck, each moment becoming more distant, and ultimately sounding as if it were many feet below the cabin, when it ceased entirely. In answer to Captain Lyon's queries, the sorcerer's wife seriously declared that he had dived and would send up Tomga.

And, in about half a minute, a distant blowing was heard approaching very slowly, and a voice differing from that which had first been audible was mixed with the blowing, until eventually both sounds became distinct, and the old beldame said that Tomga had come to answer the stranger's questions. Captain Lyon thereupon put several queries to the sagacious spirit, receiving what was understood to be an affirmative or a favourable answer by two loud slaps on the deck.

A very hollow yet powerful voice, certainly differing greatly from that of Toolemak, then chanted for some time ; and a singular medley of hisses, groans, shouts, and gobblings like a turkey's, followed in swift succession. The old woman sang with increased energy, and as Captain Lyon conjectured that the exhibition was intended to astonish "the Kabloona," he said repeatedly that he was greatly terrified. As he expected, this admission added fuel to the flame, until the form immortal, exhausted by its own might, asked leave to retire. The voice gradually died away out of hearing, as at first, and a very indistinct hissing succeeded. In its advance it sounded like the tone produced by the wind upon the bass cord of an Æolian harp; this was soon changed to a rapid hiss, like that of a rocket, and Toolemak, with a yell, announced the spirit's return. At the first distant sibilation Captain Lyon held his breath, and twice exhausted himself; but the Eskimo conjuror did not once respire, and even his returning and powerful yell was uttered without previous pause or inspiration of air.

When light was admitted, the wizard, as might be expected, was in a state of profuse perspiration, and greatly exhausted by his exertions, which had continued for at least half an hour. Captain Lyon then observed a couple of bunches, each consisting of two strips of white deerskin and a long piece of sinew, attached to the back of his coat. These he had not seen before, and he was gravely told that they had been sewn on by Tomga while he was below.

During his absence, the angekok professes to visit the dwelling-place of the particular spirit he has invoked, and he will sometimes astonish his audience with a description of the nether-world and its inhabitants. For instance, there is a female spirit called Aywilliayoo, who commands, by means of her right hand, all the bears, whales, seals, and walruses. Therefore, when a lack of provisions is experienced, the angekok pays a visit to Aywilliayoo, and attacks her hand. If he can cut off her nails, the bears are immediately released; the loss of one finger-joint liberates the small seals; the second joint dismisses the larger seals; the knuckles place at liberty the whole herds of walruses, while the entire hand liberates the whale.

Aywilliayoo is tall, with only one eye and one pigtail, but as this pigtail is as large as a man's leg, and descends to her knee, she may well be contented with it. She owns a splendid house, which, however, Toolemak refrained from entering, because it was guarded by a huge dog, with black hindquarters and no tail. Her father, in size, might be mistaken for a boy of ten years old; he has but one arm, which is always encased in a large bear-skin mitten.

Dr. Kane considers it a fact of psychological interest, as it shows that civilised or savage wonder-workers form a single family, that the angekoks have a firm belief in their own powers. "I have known," he says, "several of them personally, and can speak with confidence on this point. I could not detect them in any resort to jugglery or natural magic: their deceptions are simply vocal, a change of voice, and perhaps a limited profession of ventriloquism, made more imposing by the darkness." They have, however, like the members of the learned professions everywhere else, a certain language or jargon of their own, in which they communicate with each other.

While the angekoks are the dispensers of good, the issintok, or evil men, are the workers of injurious spells, enchantments, and metamorphoses. Like the witches of both Englands, the Old and the New, these malignant creatures are rarely submitted to trial until they have suffered punishment—the old "Jeddart justice"—*castigat auditque*. Two of them, in 1818, suffered the penalty of their crime on the same day, one at Kannonak, the other at Upernavik. The latter was laudably killed in accordance with the "old custom" . . . custom being everywhere the apology for any act revolting to moral sense. He was first harpooned, then disembowelled; a flap let down from his forehead "to cover his eyes and prevent his seeing again"—he had, it appears, the repute of an evil eye; and then small portions of his heart were eaten, to ensure that he should not come back to earth unchanged.

When an Eskimo has injured any one of his countrymen,—has cut his seal-lines, or lamed his dogs, or burned his bladder-float—or perpetrated some equally grievous offence—the angekok summons him to meet the countryside before the tribunal of the hunapok. The friends of the parties, and the idlers for miles around, assemble about the justice-seat; it may be at some little cluster of huts, or, if the weather permit, in the open air. The accuser rises, and strikes a few discords with a seal-rib on a tom-tom or drum. "He then passes to the charge, and pours out in long paragraphic words all the abuse and ridicule to which his outrageous vernacular can give expression. The accused meanwhile is silent ; but, as the orator pauses after a signal hit, or to flourish a cadence on his musical instrument, the whole audience, friends, neutrals, and opponents signalise their approval by outcries as harmonious as those we sometimes hear in our town meetings at home. Stimulated by the applause, and warming with his own fires, the accuser renews the attack, his eloquence becoming more and more licentious and vituperative, until it has exhausted either his strength or his vocabulary of invective. Now comes the accused, with defence, and counter-charge, and retorted abuse ; the assembly still listening and applauding through a lengthened session. The Homeric debate at a close, the angekoks hold a powwow, and a penalty is denounced against the accused for his guilt, or the accuser for his unsustained prosecution."

CHAPTER XVII.

A MEDIÆVAL SUPERSTITION: THE FLAGELLANTS.

AMONG the extraordinary delusions of the human mind, none is more hateful than the conviction cherished among so many sects, that the Supreme Being can be propitiated by the self-imposed torture of His worshippers. And nothing more vividly illustrates the difference between the GOD of the Christian religion and the stern deity of so many human creeds, than the aspect of the former as man's Heavenly FATHER, Who requires from him no other offering than that of a contrite and humble heart,—Who asks not that the Indian Fakir should cramp his limbs and lacerate his body, or that S. Simeon Stylites should stand night and day, in the scorching sun of summer, and the freezing cold of winter, on his lonely pillar. It is a proof of our wider and deeper knowledge of GOD that we are beginning to emancipate ourselves from the thraldom of this evil idea, and to recognise in Him a tender, compassionate Guide and Friend, Who, unto them that love Him, causeth all things to work for the best. In modern Calvinism the superstition still lingers, and it is supposed that a gloomy life, unrelieved even by the most innocent pleasures, must needs be acceptable to the Almighty Love; but this shadow in the Christian's faith is rapidly receding before the growing and broadening light. We are sons of GOD, and heirs; and what He asks from us, what alone He will receive, is the offering of affection and the sacrifice of fear. And the greatest claim which Christianity puts forward to the hearts and minds of men is that it has delivered, or will deliver them, when rightly understood, from the degrading superstition of the ascetic solitary and the self-torturer. "Its true dignity is, that unseen it has ever gone about doing good. Link after link has it struck from the chain of every human thraldom; error after error has it banished; pain after pain has it driven from body or from mind; and so silently has the blessing come, that (like the sick man whom the SAVIOUR made to walk) 'he that was healed wist not who it was.'"

But error is slow to die; and long after the introduction of Christianity men continued to think that GOD would not hear them, unless, like the priests of Baal, they approached Him in blood and tears. At the bottom of it lay, no doubt, a truth, that the spirit could be exalted and purified only by contempt of the flesh:—and not perceiving that what was demanded of them was a moral and spiritual victory, they sought, by sore treatment of the body, to conquer its sinful appetites. They forgot that CHRIST had spoken of the body as "a temple,"—the temple of the HOLY GHOST; that it was as much the creation of GOD as the immortal soul, and as His wondrous handiwork should be treated with the reverence due to all that He has made. And they came to look upon the body as a deadly enemy, the slave and accomplice of the devil, which could be subdued only by a regimen of pain and terror. And so, when an evil suggestion tempted them, they scourged themselves until the blood ran from their mangled flesh, or they plunged naked into the deep winter snow, or barefooted they trod the flinty soil, or they fasted until the exhausted brain sank into the stupor of delirium.

Thus we read of S. Hilarion :—

Covering his limbs only with a sackcloth, and having a cloak of skin, he wandered forth into the desert that lies beyond Gaza, and enjoyed the "vast and terrible solitude," feeding on only fifteen figs after the setting of the sun; and because the region was of ill repute from robberies, no man had ever before stayed in that place. The devil, seeing what he was doing, and whither he had gone, was tormented. And he who of old boasted, saying: "I shall ascend into heaven, I shall sit above the stars of heaven, and shall be like unto the Most High," now saw that he had been conquered by a boy, and trampled under foot by him, who, on account of his youth, could commit no sin. He therefore began to tempt his senses; but he, enraged with himself, and beating his breast with his fist, as if he would drive out thoughts by blows, "I will force thee, mine ass," said he, "not to kick; and feed thee with straw, not barley. I will wear thee out with hunger and thirst; I will burden thee with heavy loads; I will hunt thee through heat and cold, till thou thinkest more of food than of play." He therefore sustained his sinking spirit with the juice of herbs and a few figs, after each three or four days, praying frequently, and singing psalms, and digging the ground with a mattock, to increase the labour of fasting by that of work. At the same time, by weaving baskets of rushes, he imitated the discipline of the Egyptian monks, and the Apostle's saying, " He that will not work, neither let him eat," till he was so attenuated, and his body so exhausted, that his flesh scarce clung to his bones.

"From his sixteenth to his twentieth year," says Kingsley, "he was sheltered from the heat and rain in a tiny cabin, which he had woven of rush and sedge. Afterwards he built a little cell, four feet wide and five feet high,—that is lower than his own stature, and somewhat longer than his small body needed,—so that you would believe it a tomb rather than a dwelling. He cut his hair only once a year, on Easter Day, and lay till his death on the bare ground and a layer of rushes, never washing the sack in which he was clothed, and saying that it was superfluous to seek for cleanliness in hair-cloth. Nor did he change his linen until the first was utterly in rags. He knew the Scriptures by heart, and recited them after his prayers and psalms as if GOD were present."

Of S. Simeon Stylites we read that, having gone to the well one day to draw water, he took the rope from the bucket, and wound it round his body from his loins to his neck, and going in, he adventured an audacious falsehood, for he said to his brethren, " I went out to draw water, and found no rope on the bucket." And they said, " Hold thy peace, brother, lest the Abbot know it, till the thing has passed over." But the tightness and roughness of the rope wore grievous wounds in his body, as the brethren at last discovered. Then with great trouble they took off the rope, and his flesh with it, and attending to his wounds, healed them.

For twenty-eight years of his life he was continually experimenting in long fasts—forty days at a time. Custom gradually made it comparatively easy to him. For on the first days he used to stand and praise GOD; after that, when through emptiness he could stand no longer, he would sit and perform the divine office, and on the last day even lie down. For when his strength failed slowly, he was forced to lie half dead. But after he stood on the column he could not bear to lie down, but invented another way by which he could stand. He fastened a beam to the column, and tied himself to it by ropes, and so passed the forty days. But afterwards, when endued with greater grace from on high, he did not need even that assistance, but stood for the whole forty days, dispensing with food, but strengthened by eagerness of soul and the divine help.

At length he caused a pillar to be built, first of six cubits, then of twelve, next of twenty-two, and finally of thirty-six, and upon the top of this he took his station. The sun beat upon his bare head in the summer, and the winter snows fell upon him, and the pitiless rains soaked him to the skin,—but still he endured his self-imposed penance. He bowed himself frequently, offering adoration to GOD; so frequently that a spectator counted 1244 adorations, and then missing gave up counting; and each time he bowed himself, he touched his feet with his forehead. And ever in spirit he deprecated the wrath of an offended GOD, to Whom, as a meet sacrifice, he offered up his poor, wounded, tortured, emaciated body.

> "I will not cease to grasp the hope I hold
> Of saintdom, and to clamour, mourn and sob,
> Battering the gates of heaven with storms of prayer.
> Have mercy on me, LORD, and take away my sins,
> Let this avail, just, dreadful, mighty GOD,
> This not be all in vain, that thrice ten years
> Thrice multiplied by superhuman pangs . . . .
> A sign between the meadow and the cloud,
> Patient on this tall pillar I have borne
> Rain, wind, frost, heat, hail, damp, and sleet, and snow;
> And I had hoped that ere this period closed,
> Thou wouldst have caught me up into Thy rest,

Denying not these weather-beaten limbs
The meed of saints, the white robe, and the palm.
O take the meaning, LORD: I do not breathe
Nor whisper any murmur of complaint."[1]

We turn from these pictures of human error,—error based, it must be owned, on a substratum of truth,—to put together a few particulars of the Sect of the Flagellants, which practised on a curiously elaborate scale the science of self-punishment.

This sect first made its appearance in Italy in 1210. The following account of its origin is taken by Mr. Cooper from the " Chronicon Ursitius Basiliensis" of the monk of Padua, S. Justin :[2]

" When all Italy was sullied with crimes of every kind, a certain sudden superstition, hitherto unknown to the world, first seized the inhabitants of Perusa, afterwards the Romans, and then almost all the nations of Italy. To such a degree were they affected with the fear of GOD, that noble as well as ignoble persons, young and old, even children five years of age, would go naked about the streets without any sense of shame, walking in public, two and two, in the manner of a solemn procession. Every one of them held in his hand a scourge, made of leather thongs, and with tears and groans they lashed themselves on their backs till the blood ran : all the while weeping and giving tokens of the same bitter affliction, as if they had really been spectators of the passion of our SAVIOUR, imploring the forgiveness of GOD and His Mother, and praying that He, Who had been appeased by the repentance of so many sinners, would not disdain theirs. And not only in the daytime, but likewise during the nights, hundreds, thousands, and ten thousands of these penitents ran, notwithstanding the rigour of winter, about the streets, and in churches, with lighted wax candles in their hands, and preceded by priests who carried crosses and banners along with them, and with humility prostrated themselves before the altars : the same scenes were to be seen in small towns and villages ; so that the mountains and fields seemed to resound alike the voice of men who were crying to GOD.

[1] Tennyson. [2] Cooper, pp. 102, 104.

"All musical instruments and love-songs ceased to be heard. The only music that prevailed both in town and country was that of the lugubrious voice of the penitent, whose mournful accents might have moved hearts of flint: and even the eyes of the obdurate sinner could not refrain from tears. Nor were women exempt from the general spirit of devotion we mention; for not only those among the common people, but also matrons and young ladies of noble families, would perform the same mortifications with modesty in their own rooms.

"Then those who were at enmity with one another became again friends. Usurers and robbers hastened to restore their ill-gotten riches to their right owners. Others, who were contaminated with different crimes, confessed them with humility, and renounced their vanities. Gaols were opened; prisoners were delivered; and banished persons permitted to return to their native habitations. So many and so great works of sanctity and Christian charity, in short, were then performed by both men and women, that it seemed as if an universal apprehension had seized mankind, that the divine power was preparing either to consume them by fire, or destroy them by shaking the earth, or some other of those means which Divine justice knows how to employ for avenging crimes. Such a sudden repentance, which had thus diffused itself all over Italy, and had even reached other countries, not only the unlearned, but wise persons also admired. They wondered whence such a vehement fervour of piety could have proceeded: especially since such public penances and ceremonies had been unheard of in former times, had not been approved by the sovereign pontiff, nor recommended by any preacher or person of eminence; but had taken their origin among simple persons, whose example both learned and unlearned alike had followed."

In 1260, the sect was reconstituted by Rainer, a hermit of Perugia, and it sprang up with such vigour and alacrity, that its members soon numbered 10,000, who marched in procession, carrying banners and crosses. The folly soon crossed the Alps into Germany, and found its disciples in Bohemia and Poland, Alsatia and Bavaria. It was sternly repressed by the different governments, but in 1349, when the plague broke out in Germany, it again lifted up its head. Albert of Strasburg relates[1] that two hundred came from Schwaben to Speier, under one chief and two lieutenants, whom they almost slavishly obeyed. Their form of proceedings was always the same : placing themselves within a circle drawn on the ground, they removed their clothing, until nothing was left but a covering for the loins. Then they walked, with arms outstretched like a cross, round and round the circle for a time, finally prostrating themselves on the ground. Springing to their feet, each struck his neighbour with a scourge, armed with knots and four iron points, regulating his blows by his singing of psalms. At a given signal the discipline ceased, and the fanatics threw themselves first on their knees, then flat upon the ground, groaning and sobbing. The leader, on rising, gave a brief address, exhorting them to ask the mercy of GOD upon their benefactors and enemies, and also on the souls in purgatory. This was followed by another prostration, and then another discipline. Those who had taken charge of the clothes now came forward, and performed the same ceremonies.

"Penance took place twice a day : in the morning and evening the flagellants went abroad in pairs, singing psalms amid the ringing of bells, and when they arrived at the place of flagellation they stripped the upper part of their bodies, and took off their shoes, wearing only a linen dress from the waist to the ankles. Then they lay down in a large circle in different positions, according to the nature of their crime : the adulterer with his face to the ground ; the perjurer on one side, holding up three of his fingers, &c., and were then castigated, more or less severely by the master, who gave the order to rise in the words of a prescribed formula :

> ' Stant uf durch der reinen Martel ere ;
> Und hüte dich vor der Sünden mere.' "

After which they scourged themselves, chanting psalms and uttering prayers for deliverance from the plague.

[1] Cooper, p. 105.

Hecker, quoted by Mr. Cooper, thus describes the resuscitation of the sect:

"While all countries were filled with lamentations and woe, there first arose in Hungary, and afterwards in Germany, the Brotherhood of the Flagellants, called also the Brotherhood of the Cross, or Cross-Bearers, who took upon themselves the repentance of the people for the sins they had committed, and offered prayers and supplications for the averting of this plague. The order consisted chiefly of the lowest class, who were either actuated by sincere contrition, or joyfully availed themselves of this pretext for idleness, and were hurried along with the tide of distracting frenzy. But as these brotherhoods gained in repute, and were welcomed by the people with veneration and enthusiasm, many nobles and ecclesiastics ranged themselves under their standard, and their bands were not unfrequently augmented by children, honourable women, and nuns, so powerfully were minds of the most opposite temperaments enslaved by this infatuation. They marched through the cities in well-organised processions, with leaders and singers; their heads covered as far as their eyes, their looks fixed on the ground, accompanied by every token of the deepest contrition and mourning. They were robed in sombre garments with red crosses on the breast, back, and cap, and bore triple scourges tied in three or four knots, in which points of iron were fixed. Tapers and magnificent banners of velvet and cloth of gold were carried before them; wherever they made their appearance they were welcomed by the ringing of bells, and crowds of people came from great distances to listen to their hymns and to witness their penance with devotion and tears. In the year 1349, two hundred flagellants first entered Strasburg, where they were received with great joy and hospitality, and lodged by the citizens. Above a thousand joined the brotherhood, which now assumed the appearance of a wandering tribe, and separated into two bodies for the purpose of journeying to the north and to the south."

The Flagellants, however, did not secure the favour of the ecclesiastical authorities; who discerned only too clearly the demoralising effect of their practices and pretensions. Pope Clement VI. issued a bull against them, and their influence gradually waned and seemed on the point of dying out, when, in 1414, it was revived by one Conrad, who, of course, professed to have received a Divine commission. The terrors of the Inquisition were now hurled against the sect, and ninety-one deluded wretches were burned alive at Sangerhausen, besides numbers at other places. It continued, however, to exhibit occasional signs of vitality; and in the sixteenth century broke, in France, into three great branches, the White, Black, and Grey Penitents, companions of whom were scattered over the whole kingdom, but chiefly in the southern provinces. Catherine de Medicis, at Avignon, in 1574, assumed the lead of the Black Penitents, and took part in their disgusting ceremonies. Henry III., in 1585, established a White Penance brotherhood, which paraded in public procession through the streets of Paris. The better members of the clergy preached against the fanaticism; the wits of Paris levelled their ridicule at it; and finally, in 1601, the Parliament of Paris passed an act to abolish a fraternity of Flagellants, called the Blue Penitents, in the town of Bourges, and afterwards against all whipping brotherhoods without distinction, declaring the members to be not only heretics, traitors, and regicides, but unchaste. The fraternity thereafter declined, and finally disappeared from France.

CHAPTER XVIII.

SCOTTISH SUPERSTITIONS: HALLOWEEN.

THE imaginative element in the character of the Celtic race naturally predisposes them to the reception and retention of fanciful ideas in connection with our relations to the unseen. Keenly sensible of the existence of supernatural influences, they are morbidly curious as to the mode in which they act upon humanity, and ever desirous to propitiate or guard against them. There is something in the presence of the sea and the mountains which fosters a habit of reverie; and the mind, awed and perplexed by the vastness of the forces of Nature, is led to give them an actual and definite embodiment, and to associate them directly with the incidents of our mortal life. Granted the existence of invisible creatures, there is no reason why man, who looks upon the universe as a circle of which he is the centre, should not suppose them to be interested in all that interests himself; and when this is once admitted, it follows as an inevitable result, that he will endeavour to make them the agents of his inclination or his will, unless he fears them as powers whose anger must be reverently deprecated. It will be found that most of the popular superstitions to which we refer are based upon these motives; that most of them originate in the desire to bribe and cajole Fortune, or to command and defeat it. Others will be found to have had their rise, as we have hinted, in the feelings of awe and wonder awakened by the mystery or the grandeur of Nature. The wail of waters against a rocky coast has suggested the cries of the ocean maiden who seeks to lure the mariner to his destruction; the wreathing mists floating in fantastic shapes across the mountain valleys, has peopled their depths with a world of spirits or friendly or inimical to mortals. The imagination, which has been quickened by Nature, proceeds in turn to breathe into Nature a new life.

To some of the superstitions which haunt the glens, and peaks, and torrents of the Scottish Highlands, the poet Collins has alluded in one of his most beautiful odes. He speaks of the North as fancy's land, where still, it is said, the fairy people meet, beneath the shade of the graceful birches, upon mead or hill. To the belief in a tribe of hobgoblins, tiny creatures, visiting the peasant's hut in the silence of the night, he also refers :—

> " There, each trim lass, that skims the milky store,
> To the swart tribes their creamy bowls allots ;
> By night they sip it round the cottage door,
> While airy minstrels warble jocund notes."

The malicious disposition of the elves is thus insisted upon :—

> " There every herd, by sad experience, knows
> How, wing'd with fate, their elf-shot arrows fly,
> When the sick ewe her summer food foregoes,
> Or, stretch'd on earth, the heart-smit heifers lie."

To superstitions of higher import the poet alludes in the following noble lines :—

> " 'Tis thine to sing, how, framing hideous spells,
> In Skye's lone isle, the gifted wizard seer,
> Lodged in the wintry cave with fate's fell spear,
> Or in the depth of Uist's dark forest dwells :
> How they, whose sight such dreary dreams engross,
> With their own vision oft astonished droop,
> When, o'er the watery strath, or quaggy moss,
> They see the gliding ghosts' unbodied troop.
> Or, if in sports, or on the festive green,
> Their destined glance some fated youth descry,
> Who now, perhaps, in lusty vigour seen,
> And rosy health, shall soon lamented die.
> For them the viewless forms of air obey ;
> Their bidding heed, and at their beck repair :
> They know what spirit brews the stormful day,
> And heartless, oft like moody madness, stare
> To see the phantom train their secret work prepare."

We may allow ourselves one more quotation, in which the poet accumulates instances of the "second sight," or power of divination, to which the Highland seers laid claim :—

> "To monarchs dear, some hundred miles astray,
>   Oft have they seen fate give the fatal blow !
>   The sea, in Skye, shrieked as the blood did flow,
>   When headless Charles warm on the scaffold lay !
> As Boreas threw his young Aurora forth,
>   In the first year of the first George's reign,
> And battles raged in welkin of the North,
>   They mourned in air, fell, fell rebellion slain !
> And as, of late, they joyed in Preston's fight,
>   Saw, at sad Falkirk, all their hopes near crowned !
> They raved, divining through their second sight,
>   Pale-red Culloden where these hopes were drowned."

This same power of second sight forms the groundwork of Campbell's poem of "Lochiel's Warning," in which the poet represents the aged seer or soothsayer in the act of warning the ferocious Highland chieftain against the consequences of joining Prince Charles Edward's expedition of the '45 :—

> "Lochiel, Lochiel, beware of the day
>   When the Lowlands shall meet thee in battle array.
> The sunset of life gives me mystical lore,
>   And coming events cast their shadows before !"

A curious superstition respecting "the non-giving of fire" lingers still in some parts of Scotland, more particularly in the North, and seems to be connected with the old sun-worship : a survival of the Pagan past which is strange enough in this matter-of-fact and prosaic Present of ours. "At Craigmillar, near Edinburgh, a woman, not long ago, refused to give a neighbour 'a bit peat' to light her fire, because she was supposed to be uncanny. The old woman muttered, as she turned away, that her churlish neighbour might yet repent of her unkindness. This speech the other repeated to her husband on his return from work, whereupon he went straight to the old woman's house, and gave her a sharp cut on the forehead, for which he was duly called to account, and pleaded his belief that scoring the witch above the breath would destroy her glamour."

On certain days, such as Beltane (or S. John's Eve,) Midsummer, Halloween, and New Year's Day, it is regarded as most unlucky to allow a neighbour to take a brand from your hearth, or even to light his pipe.

Evil-disposed persons, desirous of doing their neighbours an ill turn, will apply to them for "a kindling." Thus, in Ross-shire, an old beldame repaired to a neighbour's house with this intent. There was only a child of eight years old at home, but she was thoroughly acquainted with the popular superstition, and stoutly refused the applicant tinder, match, or lighted stick. When the old woman had departed, the girl fetched two friends, who straightway followed her home, to find there a blazing fire and a boiling pot. "See you," exclaimed the lassie, "gin the *cailliach* had gotten the kindling, my father would not get a herring this year."

A poor tinker's wife walked one morning into a house in Applecross—this was as late as July, 1868—and snatched a live peat from the hearth to kindle her own fire. Before she had gone any distance, she was observed, and the gudewife sped after her, overtook her, and snatched away her prize. To a stranger who remonstrated with her for the unkindness, the gudewife exclaimed, " Do you think I am to allow my cow to be dried up? If I allowed her to carry away the fire, I would not have a drop of milk to-night to wet the bairns' mouths." And she flung the peat into a pail of water in order to undo the evil charm so far as possible.

Allusions to this "non-giving of fire" abound in the old legends, but a single illustration will suffice. Of old two brother giants, Akin and Rhea, who dwelt on the Scottish mainland, were wont to pay frequent visits to the Isle of Skye by leaping across the Straits. They reared for themselves two strong towers in the Glenelg country, and there they lived in peace and good fellowship, until one day, the younger brother, returning from one of his excursions, found his hearth dark and cheerless, and passed on therefore, to his brother's castle. Stirring the smouldering fire into a hearty blaze, he warmed himself luxuriously, and then returned to his own tower, carrying with him a burning peat.

Unhappily, at this moment, his elder brother came in from the chase, and discovering the theft, broke out into a violent passion. Off sped the culprit, and after him went his brother, hurling rock after rock in his rage, until he perceived that further pursuit was useless. The truth of this story is attested by the boulders which to this day lie strewn all over the valley-side.

A survival of the old Paganism is, undoubtedly, this apprehension of ill-luck connected with the giving or stealing of fire; and it recalls to us the days when every mountain-peak was as an altar raised to Baal, and Sun and Moon were worshipped with solemn mysterious rites. On the great Fire-festival the priests kindled fire by friction, and the people carried it to their cottages, where it was kept alive all round the year and extinguished only when a new supply was ready. "As the purchase of the fire was a source of profit to the priests, it would naturally be considered criminal for one neighbour to give it to another at the seasons when every man was bound to purchase it for himself. Of course, though the old customs are still retained, their original meaning is utterly forgotten; and the man who throws a live peat after a woman who is about to increase the population, or he who on Halloween throws a lighted brand over his own shoulder without looking at whom he aims, little dreams whence sprang these time-honoured games." It is said that in many parts of the remote glens of Perthshire there are women still living who on Beltane morn always throw ashes and a live peat over their heads, repeating a certain formula of words to bring them back. But the strictest secrecy is observed, lest such practices should reach the ear of "the minister:" so the stronger their belief, the less willing are they to confess to any knowledge of such matters.

We cannot pass from this subject without an allusion to the Fire-Churn or Need-Fire, which is held a sovereign charm against cattle-plague. When in a Highland district an invasion of murrain was apprehended, a small shanty or hut was erected near loch or river, and in it were placed various wooden posts, vertical and horizontal: the horizontal were provided with several spokes, and being rapidly turned round against the upright, quickly generated a flame by the friction. Then all other fires upon the farm were extinguished, to be re-lighted from the Need-fire, which all the cattle were afterwards made to smell, until the charm was complete.

It was on Halloween, or All Hallows' Eve—the evening of the 31st of October—that Superstition ran riot, because on that particular evening the supernatural influences of the other world were supposed to be specially prevalent, and the power of divination was likewise believed to be at its height. Spirits then walked about with unusual freedom, and readily responded to the call of those armed with due authority. In the prehistoric past, the Druids at this time celebrated their great autumn Fire-Festival, insisting that all fires, except their own, should be extinguished, so as to compel men to purchase the sacred fire at a certain price. This sacred fire was fed with the peeled wood of a certain tree, and that it might not be polluted, was never blown with human breath.

Needless to say that the sacred fire has vanished with the Druids, but the Halloween customs which still survive may be traced back to a hoar antiquity. For instance, various kinds of divination are practised, and chiefly with apples and nuts. Apples are a relic of the old Celtic fairy lore. They are thrown into a tub of water, and you endeavour to catch one in your mouth as they bob round and round in provoking fashion. When you have caught one, you peel it carefully, and pass the long strip of peel thrice, *sunwise*, round your head; after which you throw it over your shoulder, and it falls to the ground in the shape of the initial letter of your true love's name.

As for the nuts, they would naturally suggest themselves to the dwellers in mighty woods, such as covered the land of old. Brand says it is a custom in Iceland, when the maiden would know if her lover be faithful, to put three nuts upon the bar of the grate, naming them after her lover and herself. If a nut crack or jump, the lover will prove faithless; if it begin to blaze or burn, it's a sign of the fervour of his affection. If the nuts named after the girl and her swain burn together, they will be married.

This lover's divination is practised in Scotland, as everybody knows who has read Burns's poem of "Halloween :"—

> "The auld guidwife's weel hoordet nits
>   Are round and round divided,
> An' monie lads and lasses' fates
>   Are there that night decided :
> Some kindle, couthie, side by side,
>   An' burn thegither trimly ;
> Some start awa wi' saucy pride,
>   And jump out-owre the chimlie
>   Fu' high that night.

> "Jean slips in twa wi' tentie e'e ;
>   Wha 'twas, she wadna tell ;
> But this is *Jock*, an' this is *me*,
>   She says in to hersel' :
> He bleez'd owre her an' she owre him,
>   As they wad never mair part ;
> Till, fuff! he started up the lum,
>   An' Jean had e'en a sair heart
>   To see't that night."

In some places, on this mystic night, a stick is suspended horizontally from the ceiling, with a candle at one end, and an apple at the other. While it is made to revolve rapidly, the revellers successively leap up and endeavour to grasp the apple with their teeth—the hands must not be used—if they fail, the candle generally swings round in time to salute them disagreeably. The reader will note the resemblance between this pastime and the game of quintain, to which our forefathers were partial.

Another amusement is to dive for apples in a tub of water.

In Strathspey, a lass will steal away from the kitchen fire, make her way to the kiln where the corn is dried, throw a ball of thread into it, and wind it up slowly, while uttering certain words. The form of her future lover will take hold of the end of the thread, and reveal itself to her. The most arduous part of this charm is, that no speaking is allowed either on the outward journey or the return.

Another mode of lover's divination is for the young people, after being duly blindfolded, to go forth into the kailyard, or garden, and pull the first stalks they meet with. Returning to the fireside, they determine, according as the stalk is big or little, straight or crooked, what the future wife or husband will be. The quantity of earth adhering to the root is emblematic of the dowry to be expected ; and the temper is indicated by the sweet or bitter taste of the *motoc* or pith. Lastly, the stalks are placed in order, over the door, and the Christian names of persons afterwards entering the house signify in the same order those of the wives and husbands *in futuris*.

Burns describes another custom :

> " In order on the clean hearth-stane,
> The luggies[1] three are ranged,
> And every time great care is ta'en
> To see them duly changed :
> And uncle John wha wedlock's joys
> Sin' Mar's-year did desire,
> Because he gat the toom-dish[2] thrice,
> He heav'd them on the fire
> In wrath that night."

For this amusement three dishes are taken : one filled with clean and one with dirty water, and the other empty. They are set upon the hearth, and the parties, blindfolded, advance in succession to dip their fingers. If they chance upon the clean water, it is understood that they will marry a maiden ; if upon the foul, they will marry a widow ; if upon the empty dish, they will not marry at all.

Again : if a damsel eat an apple in front of a looking-glass, she will shortly see her future husband peeping over her shoulder. So Burns :

> " Wee Jenny to her Grannie says,
> 'Will ye go wi' me, Grannie?
> I'll eat the apple at the glass
> I gat frae uncle Johnie.'
> She fuff't[3] her pipe wi' sic a lunt,
> In wrath she was sae vap'rin',
> She notic't na an aizle[4] brunt,
> Her braw new worset apron,
> Out thro' that night.

> " 'Ye little skelpie limmer's[5] face !
> How daur you try sic sportin',

[1] Dishes.   [2] Empty.   [3] Puffed.
[4] Ash, or cinder.   [5] Saucy child.

> As seek the foul thief ony place,
>   For him to spae your fortune :
>   Nae doubt but ye may get a sight !
>   Great cause ye hae to fear it ;
>   For mony a ane has gotten a fright,
>   An' liv'd an' di'd deleeret,
>   On sic a night.'"

A shirt-sleeve may be wetted, and hung before the fire to dry : then if *he* or *she* lie in bed and watch it until midnight, *he* or *she* will behold *his* or *her* future partner's phantasm come in and turn it !

Children born on Halloween were formerly supposed to be gifted with certain mysterious endowments, such as the power of perceiving and conversing with the " dwellers on the threshold," the inhabitants of the World Invisible.

Once upon a time, all over Scotland a bonfire was lighted on every farm ; and often the bonfire was surrounded by a circular trench, symbolical of the sun. Every year these bonfires decrease in number ; but within the recollection of living men no fewer than thirty could be seen on the high hill-tops between Dunkeld and Abergeldy. And a strange weird sight it was, worthy of the pencil of a Rembrandt,—the dusky figures of the lads and lasses dancing wildly around them, to the hoarse music of their own voices ! Miss Cumming writes that in the neighbourhood of Crieff, the balefires, as the people call them, still blaze as brightly as ever; and from personal observation we can assert that they are still lighted in many parts of Argyllshire.

A remarkable Halloween story is recorded in Dr. Robert Chambers's valuable miscellany, "The Book of Days." Mr. and Mrs. M., we are told, were a happy young couple, who, in the middle of the last century, resided on their own estate, in a pleasant part of the province of Leinster. Possessed of a handsome fortune, they spent their time in various rural avocations, until the birth of a child, a little girl, seemed to crown their felicity. On the Halloween following this notable event, the parents retired to rest at their usual hour, Mrs. M. cradling her infant on her bosom that she might be roused if it showed the least sign of uneasiness. From teething or some other ailment, the child, about midnight, became very restless, and not receiving the usual attention from its mother, woke up Mr. M. by its cries. He at once called his wife, and told her the baby was unwell; she made no answer. She seemed in an uneasy slumber, and in spite of all her husband's efforts continued to sleep on, until he was compelled to take the child himself and endeavour to soothe it to rest. From sheer exhaustion it at last sank into silence, while the mother slumbered until a much later hour than usual. When she at last awoke, her husband told her of what had happened, and of the extent to which his night's rest had been disturbed. "I, too," she replied, "have passed the most miserable night I ever experienced : I now see that sleep and rest are two different things, for I never felt so unrefreshed in my life. How I wish you had been able to awake me—it would have spared me some of my fatigue and anxiety ! I thought I was dragged against my will into a strange part of the country, where I had never been before, and, after what appeared to me a long and weary journey on foot, I arrived at a comfortable looking house. I went in longing to rest, but had no power to sit down, although there was a nice supper laid out before a good fire, and every appearance of preparations for an expected visitor. Exhausted as I felt, I was only allowed to stand for a minute or two, and then hurried away by the same road back again ; but now it is over, and after all it was only a dream."

Her husband listened with deep interest to this strange narrative, and then, sighing deeply, said, "My dear Sarah, you will not long have me beside you ; whoever is to be your second husband played last night some evil trick, of which you have been the victim."

Shocked as she naturally was by this assertion, she sought to subdue her own emotion, and to rally her husband's spirits, hoping that the impression would pass from his mind as soon as he entered into the every-day work of life.

Months passed away, and both husband and wife had almost forgotten the Halloween dream, when Mr. M.'s health began to fail, and to fail so rapidly, that in spite of loving care and the best medical skill, he sank into a premature grave. His wife mourned him sincerely, but her natural energy and activity prevented her from yielding to a hopeless sorrow. She continued to farm her husband's estate, and in this employment, and in the education of her little girl was able to divert her thoughts. Not less admired for her conspicuous ability, than beloved for her benevolence and amiability, she was more than once solicited to lay aside her widow's weeds; but she persisted in a calm refusal. Her uncle, a man of much kindness of heart and clearness of judgment, frequently visited her, inspected her farm, and gave her advice and assistance. He had a nephew, whom we will call C., a prudent and energetic young man, in whom he had every confidence, and whenever they met, he would strongly recommend him to take to himself a wife, and "settle." On one occasion C. replied that it was not his fault he still remained a bachelor, but he had never yet met with any woman whom he would care to call his wife. "Well, C.," said his uncle, "you seem difficult to please, but I think I know a lady who would approve herself even to *your* fastidious taste." After a good-humoured exchange of quip and repartee, the uncle invited the nephew to ride over with him next day, and be introduced to his niece, whom C. had never yet seen.

The invitation was accepted; the two friends set out early on the following morning, and after a pleasant ride drew near their destination. At a short distance they caught sight of Mrs. M. retiring towards her house after her usual daily inspection of her farm. Mr. C. started violently, and displayed a considerable agitation. Pointing towards the lady, he exclaimed, "Uncle, we need go no further, for if ever I am to be married, yonder goes my wife!" "Well, C.," replied his uncle, "that is fortunate, for yonder lady is my niece, to whom I am about to introduce you. But tell me," he continued, "is this what you call love at first sight? Or what do you mean by such a sudden decision in favour of a lady with whom you have never exchanged a word?" "Well, sir," was the reply, "as I have betrayed myself, it is well that I should make full confession. A year or two ago, I was foolish enough to try a Halloween spell,—and sat up all night to watch the result. I declare to you most solemnly that the figure of that lady, as I now see her, entered my room, and looked at me. She stood a minute or two by the fire, and then disappeared as suddenly and as silently as she had entered. I was wide awake, and felt considerable remorse at having thus ventured to tamper with the powers of the Unseen World; but I assure you that every particular of her features, dress, and figure have been so present to my mind ever since, that I could not possibly make a mistake, and the moment I saw your niece I was convinced that she was indeed the woman whose image I saw on that never-forgotten Halloween."

It is unnecessary to say that the uncle was considerably astonished at this extraordinary narrative, but he forbore to comment upon it, as by this time they had arrived at Mrs. M.'s house. The lady was delighted to see her uncle, and made his friend heartily welcome, discharging the duties of hostess with a simplicity and grace that fascinated her guest.

After her visitors had rested and refreshed themselves, her uncle walked out with her to inspect the farm, and seized the opportunity, in the absence of Mr. C., to bespeak for him his niece's favourable consideration. Many words were unnecessary, for the impression produced had been mutually agreeable. Before leaving the house Mr. C. obtained Mrs. M.'s permission to visit her in the character of a suitor for her hand,—and after a brief courtship they were married. The story ends, as all such stories *should* end, with the affirmation that they lived long and happily together, and it was from their daughter that Dr. Chambers's informant derived his knowledge of the preceding remarkable episode in their career.

Dr. Chambers assures us that the leading incidents of the narrative may be relied on as correct; but we think the reader will exercise a wise incredulity: that at all events his belief will not go beyond the admission of some possible resemblance, entirely accidental, between Mrs. M. and the lady whom the imaginative Mr. C. had seen in his Halloween dream, and whose image he had so carefully treasured in his memory.

CHAPTER XIX.

SECOND SIGHT: DIVINATION: UNIVERSALITY OF CERTAIN SUPERSTITIONS: FAIRIES IN SCOTLAND.

THERE are many aspects of the Past which have an interest for the psychological student as well as for the antiquary, and there are not a few to which everybody may occasionally direct their attention with advantage. We are too much inclined to put it aside as a " sealed book," which none but the scholar can open,—which, when opened, is hardly worth the reading. Or we are attracted only by its picturesque and romantic side, and take no heed of the valuable lessons which may be deduced upon a careful examination. Yet, as all history is more or less the history of human error and human folly, those chapters which treat of the credulities and superstitions of the Past, must surely embody many warnings and much counsel for the present.

Our glance at Halloween superstitions in Scotland reminds us of other old Scottish practices, which serve to point a moral, if not to adorn a tale. We have met with a volume by a Mr. Walter Gregor, which furnishes some curious illustrative instances. On his vivid picture of the gloom and desolation of a Scottish Sabbath, we will not dwell, for our readers will probably have gathered from other sources, or even from personal experience, an idea of the dreariness of that sombre institution in the days when bigotry was mistaken for zeal, and the spirit was killed outright by the letter. It is pleasanter to read of the strong yearning for knowledge that then possessed the hearts of our Scottish youth ; and how, in the age before School Boards were conceived of, the parish school supplied for twenty shillings per annum an education which fitted the scholar for entering the University. No Royal Road to Learning had as yet been discovered; and with much sweat of brain did the aspiring student brood over his Homer or Virgil by the flickering light of the peat-fire. When the time came for his removal to Glasgow or Aberdeen, thither he trudged afoot with his little "all" in a knapsack slung from his sturdy shoulders; and during the "sessions" it was a hard hand-to-hand fight with poverty which he stoutly fought, while delving deep into classical and mathematical lore; not forgetting occasional excursions into that vague metaphysical region which has always had so keen an attraction for the strong Scotch intellect. Our "present-day" students would too often shrink, we suspect, from the sacrifices demanded of their forefathers, and give way under the hardships which they endured, when a few potatoes and a salt herring served for dinner, and all the expenses of the academical year were covered by some twelve to sixteen pounds! We are by no means sure that knowledge was not more valued when it was attainable only at such a cost of self-denial and rigid effort; and we certainly believe that it was more thorough, more entirely a man's own, because it was wrung, so to speak, from the reluctant goddess by strenuous, steadfast work and sheer mental travail. To the Age of Gold and the Age of Iron has succeeded the Age of Veneer; and we trouble ourselves too little now-a-days, in spite of the teaching of Ruskin and Carlyle, about the solidness and durability of the material, so long as it will take a ready polish.

But what a strange world was that of the Scotch peasant in those far off days—far off at least they *seem*, on account of the immense social revolution that has taken place, and set between the *now* and the *then* a profound chasm. Men often speak of the hard-headedness and matter-of-fact stolidity of the Scotch nature; but is it not true that below the surface lies an abundant fountain of wild, quaint, original fancy? And how, in the olden time, it surrounded itself with signs and omens and wonders! How it loved to put itself in communion, as it were, with that *other* world which lies beyond and yet around us, which perplexes us with its subtle intelligence, which we cannot discern, though of its presence we are always sensible! From the cradle to the grave the Scotch peasant went his way attended by the phantoms of this mysterious world; always recognising its warnings, always seeing the shadows which it cast of coming events, and so burdening himself with a weight of grim and eëry superstition, that we marvel he did not stumble and grow faint, seeing that his dreary Calvinistic creed could have brought him little hope or comfort. Nay, it is a question whether his superstition did not partly grow out of, or was fostered by, his hard, cold religion. Superstition is the shadow of Religion, and from the shadow we may infer the nature of the substance or object that casts it.

But of these darker things we shall not speak. Let us trace a few of the common traditions and customs of the people, though in doing so we digress, perhaps, from the main lines of the present volume. While less impressive than the mere mystical practices, they proceeded from the same source,—an imagination haunted by the formidable presence of Nature, by the forms of lofty mountains, by the mysteries of pine-clad ravines, and the murmurs of storm-swept lochs and falling waters. For it has been truly said that the Scotch people have been made what they are by Scotland; that the Land has moulded and fashioned the People; and that in their literature, their religion, their manners, their history, the influence is seen of the physical characteristics of the country.

On the birth of a child—to begin at the beginning—we read that both mother and offspring were "sained," a lighted fir-candle being carried three times round the bed, and a Bible, with a bannock or bread and cheese being placed under the pillow, while a kind of blessing was indistinctly uttered. Sometimes a fir-candle was set on the bed to keep off fairies. If the new-born showed any symptoms of fractiousness, it was supposed to be a changeling; and to test the truth of the supposition, the child was placed suddenly before a peat-fire, when, if really a changeling, it made its escape by the "lum," throwing back words of scorn as it disappeared. Great was the eagerness to get the babe baptised, lest it should be stolen by the fairies. If it died unchristened, it wandered in woods and solitary places, bewailing its miserable fate. In Ramsay's "Gentle Shepherd," Bauldy, describing Manse the witch, says of her :—

"At midnight hours o'er the kirkyard she raves,
And howks unchristened weans out of their graves."

It was considered "unlucky" to mention the name of an "unchristened wean;" and even at baptism the name was commonly written on a slip of paper, which was handed to the officiating minister. What care was taken that the consecrated water should not enter the child's eyes! For if such a mishap occurred, his future life, wherever he went and whatever he did, would be constantly marred by the presence of wraiths and phantoms. If the babe remained quiet at the font, it was supposed to be destined to a brief career; and hence, to extort a cry, the woman who received it from the father would handle it roughly or even pinch it. If a boy and girl were baptised together, much anxiety was evinced lest the girl should first receive the rite. And why? In the "Statistical Account of Scotland," the minister of an Orcadian parish says : "Within these last seven years the minister has been twice interrupted in administering baptism to a female child before the male child, who was baptised immediately after. When the service was over, he was gravely told he had done very wrong, for, if the female child was first baptised, she would, on her coming to the years of discretion, most certainly have a strong beard, and the boy would have none."

Following up the course of human life through the honeyed days of "wooing and wedding," we find it darkened still by the clouds of Superstition. If a maiden desired to call up the image of her future husband, she read the third verse, seventeenth chapter of the Book of Job after supper, washed the supper dishes, and retired to bed without uttering a single word, placing before her pillow the Bible, with a pin thrust through the verse she had read. It is curious to observe the use of the Bible in these wild and foolish customs : was it not an indirect testimony to the reverence, not always intelligent, perhaps, but certainly sincere, in which the holy book was held? Nor are we certain that it is not sometimes turned to worse purposes in these "enlightened days," when a pseudo-science seeks to convert it into the battle-field of audacious theories, and an ignorant intolerance too often professes to discover in its bright and blessed pages an excuse for its uncharitable follies.

But we must continue our *resumé*. It is curious to read that the wedding-dress might not be "tried on" before the wedding-day, and if it did not fit, it might not be cut or altered, but was adjusted in the best manner possible. The bride, on the way to church, was forbidden to look back, for to do so was to ensure a succession of disasters and quarrels in the married state. It was considered inauspicious, moreover, if she did not "greet" or weep on the marriage-day; a superstition obviously connected with the wide-spread idea of the necessity of propitiating the Fates which inspired the advice of Amasis to the too fortunate Polycrates,[1] that he should fine himself for his success by throwing some costly thing into the sea. It was thought well to marry at the time of the growing moon, and among fisher-folk a flowing tide was regarded as "lucky." These customs were puerile enough, undoubtedly, but before we censure them too severely we may ask whether our modern bridals are wholly free from superstitious observances; whether we do not still pretend to "bribe" the fickle Fortune by showers of rice and old slippers rained on the departing couple!

It is needless to say that the "last scene of all" was invested with all the attributes of grotesque terror the wayward popular imagination could invent. Before it took place the light of the "death-candle"—the Welsh call it the "corpse-candle"—might be seen hovering from chamber to chamber; or the cock crowed before midnight; or the "dead-drap," a sound as of water falling monotonously and lingeringly, broke the silence of the night; or three dismal and fatal knocks were heard, at regular intervals of one or

---

[1] The unbounded good fortune of Polycrates, King of Samos, awakened the fear of his friend, Amasis, King of Egypt, who wrote to warn him of the jealousy of the gods :—

"This counsel of thy friend disdain not—
Invoke Adversity !
And what of all thy worldly gear,
Thy deepest heart esteems most dear,
Cast into yonder sea !"

two minutes' duration; or over the doomed person fluttered the image of a white dove. And when the spirit had departed, the doors and windows were immediately opened wide; the clocks were stopped; the mirrors were covered; and it was held to disturb the rest of the dead, and to be fatal to the living, if a tear fell upon the winding sheet. And thus, from the cradle to the grave, Superstition dogged the steps of life; nor even at the grave did it cease to vex and worry the minds of men with the fancies and visions born of excited imaginations.

That such fancies, that customs so wild and grotesque, should have existed in Scotland, and among a well-educated people, down to a comparatively recent date, might be matter of wonder, if we were not aware of the tenacity with which the heart clings to the "use and wont" of the Past. Nor trivial as some, and inexcusable as all of them seem to the philosophic eye, is it wise to regard them too contemptuously. They seem to us to show how difficult man found it to realise to himself the idea of a living, personal GOD,—of a GOD, a FATHER, ever watching over the welfare of His children, chastening them in His mercy, but never refusing them the light of His countenance when they have sought Him with faith in the hour of sorrow and darkness. For want of this strengthening, consoling, elevating idea, he has endeavoured to support himself by the feeble prop of superstitious credulity, and instead of yielding wholly and trustfully to the love of GOD the FATHER, has vainly striven to secure some glimpse or foreshadowing of the Future, and to avert evil by puerile practices and idle traditions.

We may next be allowed to point out the kinship in superstition which prevails all over the world; so that the observance or custom which seems peculiar to England or Scotland, is found in India or Tartary. This remarkable similarity indicates a certain general tendency to attach an "ominous significance" to particular things and events. Take as an illustration, the act of sneezing. In Asia as well as Europe, among Semitic peoples as well as among Aryan, it is usual to connect with the act some form of blessing. Sometimes the sneezer is blessed by the bystander; sometimes he blesses himself; if a Mohammedan, he blesses GOD. In Italy, for example, the salutation ad-

x

dressed to him runs : "May GOD preserve you !" or "May you have children !" In Hindi it takes the form of "Sadàji's" (May you live for ever !) and a similar salutation is used by the Jews of Austria.

But in different places and at different times sneezing has been made to carry a very different meaning. Among the Arabs, if, while a person is making an assertion which some may think hazardous or dubious, another sneezes, the speaker appeals to the omen as a confirmation of what he is saying. A writer in the "Calcutta Review" thinks this notion as old as the Greeks of the time of Xenophon, as appears from a well known passage in Chap. ii. Book iii. of the Anabasis : Ἐπεὶ περὶ σωτηρίας ἡμῶν λεγόντων οἰωνὸς τοῦ Διὸς τοῦ σωτῆρος ἐφάνη. Sneezing among the Hindus, if it occur behind your back, is regarded as so unfavourable an omen, that they at once abandon the work on which at the time they may have been engaged.

Various but not satisfactory attempts have been made to explain these customs. Thus, the Mohammedan accounts for his "Al hamdu-l Allah" by the tradition that, when the breath of life was breathed into the nostrils of Adam, he sneezed, and immediately uttered those words. While in Europe the custom of blessing the sneezer has been traced to the occurrence in Italy in the middle ages of some fatal epidemic, of which one of the symptoms was sneezing.

The superstition which regards as a favourable omen the throbbing of the eye, was well known to the ancient Greeks, is common in England, and flourishes all over India. In England, it is the man's right eye and the woman's left that is auspicious ; and so it was in the Greece of Theocritus, and so it is in India and Persia.

The curious superstition that ghosts are visible to dogs, to which we find an allusion in Homer's Odyssey, still flourishes in India. It may have originated in the place given to the dog in the mythology of both Greek and Hindu, or in the position enjoyed by the watch-dog among all the shepherd peoples of the world. The belief belongs to the Semitic as well as the Aryan races ; and its true origin after all may be the apparently causeless howling of the dog at night,—the time when "spirits walk abroad." Whatever the ground of the belief, it is probably in itself the cause of the superstition that the howling of dogs presages death or misfortune.

Another singular coincidence of this kind is furnished "by the custom of spitting on the breast as a charm against fascination." In his "Greek Antiquities," Potter notes that it was an ancient Greek custom to spit three times on the breast at the sight of a madman; and Theocritus has,—

τοιάδε μυθίζοισα τρὶς εἰς ἑὸν ἔπτυσε κόλπον.

" Precisely the same effect is attributed to the act among the Aryan inhabitants of India, where its threefold repetition is also insisted on. No sort of reason that we can imagine, can be found for this belief; and in this case the idea is a complex one.

" The notion of a hiccough being an indication that some one is thinking of the person affected, is equally common in Europe and in India.

" The same may be said of the superstition regarding an itching of the palm of the hand; and further the idea that the palm should be rubbed against something to make the event the more sure, prevails both in India and in England. In England it should be 'rubbed against wood,' in India on the forehead."[1]

We supply but one more illustration, and that shall be in folk lore; a nursery story which presents virtually the same features in the East as in the West. The following is the Hindu parallel to the old Saxon nursery tale of "The Woman that found a Silver Penny." The coincidence will be seen to be complete.

"Once upon a time, a little bird, on its way through the woods, picked up a pea, and took it to the *barbhunja* to be split; but, as ill luck would have it, one half of it stuck fast in the mill-handle, and the *barbhunja* being unable to get it out, the little bird went off to the carpenter, and said, 'Carpenter, carpenter, come and cut the millhandle; my pea is in the mill-handle; what shall I eat, what shall I drink, and what shall I take to foreign countries?' 'Be off,' said the carpenter, 'is it likely I shall come and cut the mill-handle for the sake of a single pea?'

[1] Calcutta Review, LI. iii.

"Then the little bird went to the king, and said, 'King, king, chide the carpenter; the carpenter won't cut the mill-handle; my pea has stuck in the mill-handle; what shall I eat, what shall I drink, and what shall I take to foreign countries?' 'Be off with you,' said the king, 'do you think that for the sake of a single pea I am going to chide the carpenter?'

"Then the little bird went to the queen, and said, 'Queen, queen, speak to the king; the king won't chide the carpenter; the carpenter won't cut the mill-handle; my pea is in the socket of the mill-handle; what shall I eat, what shall I drink, and what shall I take to foreign countries?' But the queen said, 'Be off with you, do you think that for the sake of a single pea I am going to talk to the king?'

"Then the little bird went to the snake, and said, 'Snake, snake, bite the queen; the queen won't talk to the king; the king won't chide the carpenter; the carpenter won't cut the mill-handle; my pea is in the socket of the mill-handle; what shall I eat, what shall I drink, and what shall I take to foreign countries?' But the snake said, 'Be off with you, do you think that for the sake of a single pea I am going to bite the queen?'

"Then the little bird went to the stick, and said, 'Stick, stick, beat the snake; snake won't bite queen; queen won't talk to king; king won't chide carpenter; carpenter won't cut mill-handle; my pea is in the socket of the mill-handle; what shall I eat, what shall I drink, and what shall I take to foreign countries?' But the stick said, 'Be off with you, do you think that for the sake of a single pea I am going to beat the snake?'

"Then the little bird went to the fire, and said, 'Fire, fire, burn stick; stick won't beat snake; snake won't bite queen; queen won't talk to king; king won't chide carpenter; carpenter won't cut mill-handle; my pea is in the socket of the mill-handle; what shall I eat, what shall I drink, and what shall I take to foreign countries?' But the fire said, 'Be off with you, do you think that for the sake of a single pea I am going to burn the stick?'

"Then the little bird went to the sea, and said, 'Sea, sea, quench fire; fire won't burn stick; stick won't beat snake;

UNIVERSALITY OF SUPERSTITIONS. 309

snake won't bite queen; queen won't talk to king; king won't chide carpenter; carpenter won't cut mill-handle; my pea is in the socket of the mill-handle; what shall I eat, what shall I drink, and what shall I take to foreign countries?' But the sea said, 'Be off with you, do you think that for the sake of a single pea I am going to quench the fire?'

"Then the little bird went to the elephant, and said, 'Elephant, elephant, dry up the sea; sea won't quench fire; fire won't burn stick; stick won't beat snake; snake won't bite queen; queen won't talk to king; king won't chide carpenter; carpenter won't cut mill-handle; my pea is in the socket of the mill-handle; what shall I eat, what shall I drink, and what shall I take to foreign countries?' But the elephant said, 'Be off with you, to dry up the sea would take the whole host of elephants; do you think that for the sake of a single pea I am going to assemble all of my kith and kin?'

"Then the bird went to the *bhaunr*, (a tangled creeping plant,) and said, '*Bhaunr, bhaunr*, snare the elephant; elephant won't drink up sea; sea won't quench fire; fire won't burn stick; stick won't beat snake; snake won't bite queen; queen won't talk to king; king won't chide carpenter; carpenter won't cut mill-handle; my pea is in the socket of the mill-handle; what shall I eat, what shall I drink, and what shall I take to foreign countries?' But the *bhaunr* said, 'Be off with you, do you think that for the sake of a single pea I am going to snare the elephant?'

"Then the bird went to the mouse, and said, 'Mouse, mouse, cut *bhaunr; bhaunr* won't snare elephant; elephant won't drink up sea; sea won't quench fire; fire won't burn stick; stick won't beat snake; snake won't bite queen; queen won't talk to king; king won't chide carpenter; carpenter won't cut mill-handle; my pea is in the socket of the mill-handle; what shall I eat, what shall I drink, and what shall I take to foreign countries?' But the mouse said, 'Be off with you, do you think that for the sake of a single pea I am going to cut the *bhaunr?*'

"Then the bird went to the cat, and said, 'Cat, cat, eat mouse; mouse won't cut *bhaunr; bhaunr* won't snare elephant; elephant won't drink up sea; sea won't quench fire;

fire won't burn stick; stick won't beat snake; snake won't bite queen; queen won't talk to king; king won't chide carpenter; carpenter won't cut mill-handle; my pea is in the socket of the mill-handle; what shall I eat, what shall I drink, and what shall I take to foreign countries?' And the cat said, 'By all means; the mouse is my natural prey, why should I not eat it?'

"So the cat went to eat the mouse; and the mouse went to cut the *bhaunr*, saying,—

'Hamko khao, a o, mat koi,
Ham bhaunr ko katat loi.'

'Oh, oh, eat, oh! eat me no one, I will take and cut the *bhaunr*.' And the *bhaunr* went to snare the elephant, saying, 'Oh, cut, oh! cut me no one, I'll take and snare the elephant.' And so on with each one, till it came to the carpenter, who extracted the pea, and the bird took it, and went away rejoicing."

The close resemblance between this fable and the English one of "The Silver Penny," attests a common origin. For it cannot be supposed that either was conveyed by means of oral communication from one country to the other; and the only feasible conclusion seems to be that they are different versions of a nursery tale which belonged to our common Aryan forefathers. There can be no doubt as to its antiquity.[1]

Among the earlier superstitions of Scotland was a belief in the efficacy of charms, or metrical incantations; a belief prevailing in almost every country and period, and indirectly attesting man's strong inward conviction of the existence of another world. That communications could be maintained with the unseen creatures that live in the air, and "the ooze;" above, beneath, and around us; that they could be made to assume a bodily form and presence; that storms could be raised or dispelled, evil prevented, secrets discovered, diseases cured, love engendered,—and that all this was possible by the utterance of certain words arranged in metrical form, though generally perfectly mean-

[1] Calcutta Review, LI., 118. In the Gaelic we find a similar story, called "Moorochug and Meenachug."

ingless, was never doubted. Many of those used in Scotland evidently had their origin in the reputed efficacy of verses among the ancients; and being of an early date, they are often "intermixed with the formula of the Roman Catholic ritual." Thus we read that one Elspeth Reoch (in 1616) had been supernaturally instructed to cure distempers by resting on her right knee while pulling a certain herb " betwixt her midfinger and thumb, and saying of, *In nomine Patris, Filii, et Spiritus Sancti.*" An old and popular charm for curing cattle (1607), is given by Dalyell as follows :—[1]

> "I charge thee for arrow shot,
> For deer shot, for womb shot,
> For eye shot, for tongue shot,
> For liver shot, for lung shot,
> For heart shot,—all the most :
> In the Name of the FATHER, the SON, and HOLY GHOST.
> To wind out of flesh and bone,
> Into oak and stone :
> In the Name of the FATHER, the SON, and HOLY GHOST.
> Amen."

Sometimes these invocations were accompanied by the administration of medicinal herbs which had been gathered before sunrise. A woman accused of witchcraft, in 1588, declared that she saw "the guid nychtbours makand thair sawis with pains and fyres, and gadderit thair herbis before the sone rysing as sche did." Among the various remedies prescribed for "the trembling fever," or ague, by Katharine Oswald, one related to plucking up a nettle by the root, three successive mornings, before sunrise. A favourite time for this herb-gathering rite was Midsummer; a relic of the old Pagan superstition connected with the sun's position in the Zodiac. The metrical charm then made use of was popular also in England,—

> "Haile be thou, holie hearte,
> Growing on the ground ;
> All in the Mount Calvarie
> First wast thou found.
> Thou art good for manie a sore,
> And healest manie a wound ;
> In the Name of Sweet JESUS,
> I take thee from the ground."

[1] We have Anglicised Mr. Dalyell's version. See his "Darker Superstitions of Scotland," p. 22. (Edit. 1835.)

"Bleeding at the touch," has been accepted in several countries as a revelation of guilt. A man suspected of murder was brought to the side of the murdered man's body, and forced to touch it; if the suspicions were just, blood immediately oozed from the wound, or at the mouth, or nose. Even at the man's approach this sign of crime would appear. It is easy to see how precarious and dangerous a test was this; how readily it might release the guilty, and betray the innocent. Naturally therefore it was not accepted without reluctance. A man and his sister had quarrelled; he died suddenly, and his body was found in his own house, naked, and with a wound on the face, but bloodless. "Although many of the neighbours in the town came into the house to see the dead corpse, yet she, the sister, never offered to come, howbeit her dwelling was next door, nor had she so much as any seeming grief for his death. But the minister and bailiffs of the town taking great suspicion of her in respect of her carriage, commanded that she should be brought in. But when she came, she came trembling all the way to the house; she refused to come nigh to the corpse, or to touch, saying, that she never touched a dead corpse in her life. But being earnestly entreated by the minister and bailiffs, and her brother's friends, who was killed, that she would but touch the corpse softly, she granted to do it. But before she did it, the sun shining in at the house, she expressed herself thus: 'Humbly desiring, as the LORD made the sun to shine and give light into that house, that also He would give light in discovering that murder.' And with these words, she touching the wound of the dead man very softly, it being white and clean, without any spot of blood or the like, yet immediately, while her finger was upon it, the blood rushed out of it, to the great admiration of all the beholders, who took it as one discovery of the murder, according to her own prayer."

It will seem astonishing to readers of the present day that a poor creature's life could be taken away on such fanciful and uncertain evidence.

We read that a Sir James Standsfield was found lying dead in a stream. His body was interred precipitately. Two days afterwards it was exhumed and partially dissected, the neck in particular being laid open, in order to ascertain the cause of death. After being well cleansed, blood burst from that side supported by his son Philip, on returning the body to the coffin for re-interment—not an unlikely result from the straining of the incisions—and it deeply stained his hand. He was arraigned, on this slight ground, for parricide; and in the course of the trial it was gravely argued that it was the will of Providence to disclose by this peculiar incident a secret crime.

The preservation of health and the prolongation of life are necessarily objects of interest to all mankind, and it was natural enough that around them should flourish a rank growth of superstitions.

To ailing or diseased persons all kinds of potions, pills, and powders were administered in the past as they are in the present; but whereas we are now content with the mystic characters endorsed on his formula by the physician, our ancestors were not satisfied unless certain mystical words, numbers, or ceremonies accompanied them. The sign of the cross was in constant requisition; or the medicine was to be taken according to mystical numbers—thrice or nine times, as the case might be. For hooping-cough was prescribed a draught from the horn of a living ox, nine times repeated. The patient was also put "nine several times" in the miller's hopper.

The importance ascribed to the figure of a circle is probably a relic of the influence of the old sun-worship. Consumptive invalids, or children suffering from hectic fever, were thrice passed through a circular wreath of woodbine, cut during the increase of the March moon, and let down over the body from head to foot. We read of a sorceress who healed sundry women by "taking a garland of green woodbine, and causing the patient to pass thrice through it." Afterwards, the garland was cut in nine pieces, which were cast into the fire—generally an indispensable particular in ceremonies of this kind. Another passed her patient through a heap of green yarn, which the nurse shook, and then divided it into nine pieces, which were buried in the lands of three owners. A certain Thomas Grieve directed a patient to pass thrice through a heap of yarn, which he duly burned. He also cured the wife of a Michael Glanis by having a hole broken on the north side of the chimney, and putting a hoop of yarn thrice through it, and taking it back at the door; and thereafter compelling the patient to go nine times through the said hoop of yarn.

White of Selborne tells us of a custom, prevalent in his time in the south of England, of stripping feeble and diseased children, and transmitting them head foremost through an artificial cleft in a young tree, the several parts of which were held forcibly asunder. The wound was then bound up carefully, and it was expected that the child would recover as the tree healed. If the cleft did not unite, the remedy proved abortive; and if the tree were cut down, the patient relapsed or died.

Borlase speaks of a similar custom in Cornwall, except that a perforated stone was used instead of a cleft tree.

In Persia, according to Alexander, passage through a long fissure or crevice in a rock, by crawling on hands and knees, is employed as a test of legitimate birth. And in the Church of the Holy Sepulchre at Jerusalem, to pass between the pillars supporting an altar and the neighbouring wall, was practised as a like test. It has been suggested, as the meaning of these various transmissions through cleft, aperture, skein of yarn, and garland, that they are symbolical of regeneration; a second birth, whereby a living soul is cleansed from its former impurities and imperfections. Wilford speaks of a sanctified fissure in a rock in the East, to which pilgrims resort "for the purpose of regeneration, by the efficacy of a passage through this sacred type."

The faculty of divining events, passing at a distance from the seer, or of passively receiving a knowledge that such events are taking place, is the well-known "second sight," which plays so important a part in many Scottish stories. "In the stricter acceptation of this faculty," we are told, "contemporary objects and incidents are beheld at the time, however remote their locality, but neither those which have passed, nor those which have yet to come. If extending to futurity, the subject of the vision is about to be realised. Therefore the second sight borders only on prognostication. It is affirmed to be more peculiar to

Scotland, for very faint analogy to such a property has been claimed for other countries : and that the highlanders chiefly, together with the inhabitants of the insular districts, or that portion of the kingdom less advanced, have enjoyed it in the highest perfection. Marvellous to be told, they have said that their cattle are gifted with it as well as themselves."

The faculty was one which knew no distinction of age or sex, or class; it was enjoyed by man and woman, young and old, rich and poor, high-born and plebeians, and in many cases was inherited. It might occasionally be imparted by a gifted person, or acquired by study and preparation. It is a proof, were proof needed, of the living influence of the imagination, that the vision beheld by one individual only, might be revealed to a companion visionary, thus confirmed in his belief in the value of his new prerogative; simply by the pressure of the seer's right foot on the novice's left, holding one hand on his head, while he was admonished to look over the master's right shoulder. Thus, Lilly, the astrologer—Butler's "hight Sidrophel"— relates how one John Scott desired William Hodges, an astrologer in Staffordshire, to show him the person and features of the person he should marry. Hodges carried him into a field not far from his home; pulled out his magic crystal; bade Scott set his foot against his, and after awhile desired him to inspect the crystal, and observe what he saw there. Of course he saw exactly what his fevered wishes were resolved to see.

Ceremonies of a more fantastic character were sometimes involved, and round the novice's body was coiled a hair rope with which a corpse had been bound to its bier. He was then required to look through a hole left by the removal of a fir knot; and, on stooping, he was instructed to look back between his legs, until an advancing funeral procession should cross the boundary of the estates of two different owners. The inconvenience of this complicated performance is obvious; it might also be dangerous; for if the wind changed while the novice was girded with the mystical cord, he was liable to the penalty of death.

A seer gifted with this wonderful faculty could not divest himself of it, though often he would fain have done so.

However acquired, it was a perilous endowment, fraught with physical and mental suffering, and reputed to be no gift from on high, but to have come from the Father of Evil.

The objects seen were generally sad and sorrowful; calamities to persons or nations. Woodrow says that before the Marquis of Argyll went to London in 1660, he was playing "at the bullets," or bowls, with some Scottish gentlemen; when one of them, as the Marquis stooped down to lift the bullet, "fell pale," and said to those about him: "Bless me, what is this I see? my lord with his head off, and all his shoulder full of blood?"

On one occasion, a gentleman joined a company, all of whom were very frank and cheerful. He had no sooner entered than one of the guests, who had not previously known him, showed much depression of spirit. Without taking any notice of it the new-comer quickly rose, and went his way. The other thereupon showed great concern, and wished he would remain; for he saw him, he said, with a shroud up to his neck, and he knew that this sign foreboded his death. In vain some of the company would have persuaded the doomed man to take warning, but he departed, and having ridden a short distance, he and his horse fell, and he broke his neck.

On the morning of the battle of Bothwell Bridge, that sore defeat to the Covenanters—so vigorously described by Scott in his "Old Mortality"—Mr. John Cameron, minister at Lochhead in Kintyre, fell into a fit of melancholy, so that Mr. Morison, of his elders, observing him through his chamber door, sore weeping and wringing his hands, knocked until he opened to him. Then he asked what was the matter? Were his wife and children well? "Little matter for them," he answered; "our friends at Bothwell are gone." Mr. Morison told him it might be a mistake, and the offcome of his gloomy thoughts: "No, no," said he, "I see them flying as clearly as I see the wall." As near as they could calculate by the accounts they afterwards obtained, this incident at the Lochhead of Kintyre was contemporaneous with the flight of the Covenanters at Bothwell.

Munro, the Scotch soldier of fortune, who bore himself so gallantly in the wars of Gustavus Adolphus, tells a story of a vision that was seen by a soldier of his company on the morning of the storm of Stralsund in 1628. One Murdo Macleod, born in Assen, a soldier of tall stature and valiant courage, being sleeping on his watch, awoke at break of day, and "jogged" two of his comrades lying by him, much to their indignation at his "stirring them." He replied: "Before long, you shall be otherwise stirred." A soldier called Allan Tough, a Lochaber man, recommending his soul to GOD, asked him what he had seen: "That you shall never behold your country again." The other replied, the loss was but small, if the rest of the company were well. He answered: "No, for there was great hurt and dearth of many very near." The other again asked, what others he had seen who would perish. He then told by name sundry of his comrades who would be killed. The other asked, what would become of himself. Eventually, he described by their clothes all the officers who would be hurt. "A pretty quick boy near by," asked him, what would become of the Major (that is, Munro himself?) "He would be shot, but not deadly," was the answer,—and so it proved.

A good deal is said of this *Taisch*, or "Second Sight," in Dr. Johnson's "Journey to the Hebrides," and some striking anecdotes are told. It was just the thing to interest his moody temperament, with its terrible dread of death and its longing to lift the curtain that hides from us the Unseen. He seems, however, to have been unable to convince himself of the actual existence of such a power; all the evidence he could collect failed to advance his curiosity to conviction, so that he could not believe, while remaining willing to believe. To use the noble words of Goethe, nobly rendered by Coleridge:

> "As the sun,
> Ere it is risen, sometimes paints its image
> In the atmosphere, so often do the spirits
> Of great events stride on before the events,
> And in To-day already walks To-morrow."

This it is not difficult to accept. It seems fitting that presages should herald the death of kings and the revolutions of nations; but the mind cannot convince itself that the spirits of the dead will cross the shadowy borders to foretell the trivial accidents that chequer ordinary lives.

Yet, as Johnson says: "A man on a journey far from home falls from a horse; another who is perhaps at work about the house, sees him bleeding on the ground, commonly with a landscape of the place where the accident befalls him. Another seer, driving home his cattle, or wandering in idleness, or musing in the sunshine, is suddenly surprised by the appearance of a bridal ceremony or funeral procession, and counts the mourners or attendants, of whom, if he knows them, he relates the names, if he knows them not he can describe the dresses."

Woodrow tells of "a popish lady," living near Boroughbridge, who dreamed that she saw a coach, and a lady in it, almost lost in the river. She directed her servants to watch during two nights, to guard against an accident, but nothing happened. "On the third night, pretty late, the Lady Shawfield came, and of a sudden the coach was overturned, and filled with water. The coachman got upon one of the horses, to save his life. The good and religious Lady Shawfield was for some time under water: and upon the cry rising, the popish lady's servants came to their assistance. With much difficulty, the coach and lady in it were got out of the water." And the Lady Shawfield, being laid upon the bank, gradually recovered her senses.

In the early months of the Commonwealth, while Mackenzie of Tarbat, afterwards Earl of Cromarty, was riding in a field among his tenants, who were manuring barley, a stranger "called that way on his foot, and stopped likewise, and said to the countrymen, 'You need not be so busy about that barley, for I see the Englishmen's horses tethered among it; and other parts mowed down for them.' Tarbet asked him how he knew them to be Englishmen, and if he had ever seen any of them? He said, 'No; but he saw them strangers, and heard the English were in Scotland, and guessed it could be no other than they.' In the month of July, the thing happened directly as the man said he saw it."

The influence exercised on the imagination by events in which we are deeply interested, and the manner in which our hopes or fears are mistaken for predictions, may be illustrated by two examples from antiquity. On the day that Cæsar and Pompey contended at Pharsalia for the mastery of the world, Cornelius, a priest and patrician of

Padua, declared, under a sudden impulse of passion, that he beheld the eddies and currents of a desperate battle, and the fall and flight of many of the combatants, eventually exclaiming : " Cæsar has conquered !" His hearers laughed at him, but his words were afterwards verified, and it appeared that he had foretold not only the day, but the incidents, and the result of the famous battle in Thessaly. The anecdote is related on the authority of the " Noctes Atticæ" of Aulus Gellius.

Dio Cassius tells a similar story about the assassination of the Emperor Domitian at Rome, by his freedman Stephanus. " It is to be admired," he says, " that, as accurately proved by persons in either place, Apollonius Thyanæus, ascending an eminence at Ephesus or elsewhere, cried out before the multitude : 'Well done, Stephanus, well done ! Strike the murderer ! thou hast struck him, thou hast wounded him, he is slain !'" But it may well be supposed that a secret understanding existed between Apollonius and the murderer.

From " second sight" we pass on to " prediction" or " divination," another of the superstitious modes by which humanity has endeavoured to read the book of the Future. In the north this power of prophecy was largely assumed by women, a circumstance of which Scott has made ample and picturesque use in more than one of his admirable fictions.

A woman foretold the tragical end of James I. of Scotland, in 1436. In the early stage of a journey from Edinburgh to Leith, and in the midst of the way, arose a woman of Ireland, who claimed to be a soothsayer, and as soon as she saw the king, she cried with a loud voice, saying, " My lord king, an ye pass this water, ye shall never turn again to live." The king was astonished at her words, for but shortly before he had fallen in with a prophecy, that in the self-same year the King of Scots should be slain. And as he rode onward, he called to him one of his knights, and commanded him to return and speak with this woman, and ask of her what she would, and what she meant by her loud crying : and she began and told him what would befall the king if he passed that water. The king asked her how she knew so much, and she said that Huthart told her so. "Sire," quoth the knight, "men may gallantly talk, nor take heed of yonder woman's words, for she is but a drunken fool, and wots not what she saith." And so with his folk he passed the water called the Scottish Sea, towards S. John's town [Perth,] about four miles from the country of the wild Scots, and there, in a convent of Black Friars, outside the town, he held a great feast. In the course of the revel came "the said woman of Ireland, who called herself a divineress," and made several vain attempts to gain access to the king. Meanwhile the conspirators matured their plot, removed the king's guards, attacked him, and slew him.[1]

All the predictions which come true are preserved; we hear nothing of those which fail, for no one has an interest in recording or repeating them; hence an undue importance is gradually attached to what are nothing more than remarkable coincidences. Many others are prophecies "after the event." Others are based on a careful calculation of probabilities. As in the following example: An Orkney warlock, full of displeasure with James Paplay, a proud and haughty chief, with whose character, doubtless, she was well acquainted, broke forth into a torrent of predictive utterances: "Thou art now the highest man that ever thou shalt be! Thou art gone to shear thy corn, but it shall never do you good! Thou art going to set house with thy wife,—ye shall have no joy of one another. Oil shall not keep you and her; ye shall have such a meit-will [craving,] and shall have nothing to eat, but be fain to eat grass under the stones and wair (sea-weed) under the rocks." It was seriously asserted that not only were these predictions—or menaces—uttered, but that they were all fulfilled; and it is possible that the prophet may have had something to do with their fulfilment.

A curious anecdote is related of a Scottish minister, who, on the day of the battle of Killiecrankie, was preaching at Anworth, and in his preface before his prayer, according to his usual mode of homely expression, began to this purpose: "Some of you will say, What news, minister? What news

[1] This is the subject of D. G. Rossetti's fine poem, "The King's Tragedy."

about Clavers, who has done so much mischief in this country? That man sets up to be a young Montrose, but as the LORD liveth, he shall be cut short this day. Be not afraid," added he, " I see them scattered and flying : and as the LORD liveth, and sends this message by me, Claverhouse shall no longer be a terror to GOD's people. This day I see him killed—lying a corpse." And on that day, and at that hour, Claverhouse fell[1] (July 27th, 1689.)

In their anxiety to obtain a glimpse of the dread writing in the Book of Fate, men have resorted to divers strange expedients, applying to warlocks and witches, or seeking to wring a response to their questionings from the creatures of the Invisible World. The ceremony known as *Taghairm*, or " Echo," seems to have been peculiar to Scotland. The inquirer was wrapped in a cow's hide, his head being left free, and was carried by assistants to a solitary spot, or left under the liquid arch formed by the " sheeted column's silvery perpendicular" in waterfall or cataract : there he remained during the watches of the night, with phantoms fluttering round about him, from whence he was supposed to derive the burden of the oracular response he delivered to his comrades on the following day.

It is probable that this ceremony is the relic of some ancient form of ritual. At all events, the skins of animals played an important part in the old worship. When the

---

[1] At the beginning of the action he had taken his place in front of his little band of cavalry. He bade them follow him, and rode forward. But it seemed to be decreed that, on that day, the lowland Scotch should in both armies appear to disadvantage. The horse hesitated. Dundee turned round, stood up in his stirrups, and, waving his hat, invited them to come on. As he lifted his arm, his cuirass rose, and exposed the lower part of his left side. A musket ball struck him : his horse sprang forward, and plunged into a cloud of smoke and dust, which hid from both armies the fall of the victorious general. A person named Johnstone was near him, and caught him as he sank down from the saddle. "How goes the day?" said Dundee. "Well for King James," answered Johnstone ; " but I am sorry for your lordship." "If it is well for him," answered the dying man, "it matters the less for me." He never spoke again : but when, half an hour later, Lord Dunfermline and some other friends came to the spot, they thought that they could still discover some faint remains of life. The body, wrapped up in two plaids, was carried to the Castle of Blair.— *Macaulay*, chap. xiii.

Thebans slew a cow on the festival of Jupiter Ammon, his image was clothed with the skin : all present in the temple then struck the carcase, which was buried in a consecrated place.

Pausanias records that a temple in honour of the soothsayer Amphiaraus, the reputed son of Apollo, stood in the territory of Oropus in Attica. Votaries who resorted thither for the purpose of divination, underwent certain lustrations, or purifying rites, sacrificed a ram, and, in expectation of seeing visions, slept upon its skin.

Virgil, in one of the most elaborate scenes of the Æneid, represents to us a similar oblation as being offered at a consecrated fountain, where the priest, to prepare himself for the delivery of responses, slept on the skin :—

> "Et cæsarum ovium sub nocte silenti
> Pellibus incubuit stratis, somnosque petivit ;
> Multa modis simulacra videt volitantia miris
> Et varias audit voces."[1]

It seems to have been an important part of the heathen ritual to make use of the skin of the sacrificed animal for the purposes of clothing. Lucian, describing the ceremonies practised in the temple of Hierapolis, says that, on his arrival, the head and eyebrows of the novice were shaved ; a sheep was then sacrificed; he knelt on the skin, and covering his own head with the head and feet of the animal, prayed that his offering might be accepted while promising a worthier one.

The Spanish invaders of the New World discovered that the religion of its most civilised race, the Aztecs, was founded upon human sacrifices. The number of victims offered up to the Aztec gods is stated in figures which seem almost incredible. Peculiar to the Aztec kingdom was the horrid ceremony entitled "the flaying of men." The Aztecs having demanded the daughter of some neighbouring potentate as their queen, she was flayed on the very night of her arrival by command of their deity, and a young man clothed in her skin. In this originated the custom that a captive slave, distinguished by the name, the honours, and the ornaments of the divinity, should be sacrificed after a certain

[1] Æneid. lib. vii. l. 87.

time; and another, clothed with his skin, then exacted contributions for the service of the gods, which no one, says Acosta, dared to refuse.

We have no space to dwell on the various forms of divination that were wont to prevail. Almost everything in nature, from the stars of heaven to the clods of earth, was made to give indications of coming events. The historian of the darker Superstitions of Scotland brings together a few striking illustrations.

If a certain worm in a medicinal spring on the top of a hill in Strathdon, were found alive, it was a sign that the patient would live; and in a well of Ardwacloich, in Appin, if the patient were to die, a dead worm was found in it, and a live one, if he were to recover. In the district of Lorn, the figures assumed by an egg dropped into water were supposed to indicate the appearance of a future spouse. "Also, one of four vessels being filled with pure, and another with muddy water, the third with milk, and the fourth with meal and water; if the diviner blindfold dips his hand in the first, it augurs that his spouse shall be led to the nuptial couch in all her pristine purity; but otherwise if dipping in the second: if finding his way to the milk, a widow shall fall to his lot; and an old woman awaits him from the meal and water. Three vessels are used in the south of Scotland; one of them empty; and should fate direct the diviner hither, it augurs perpetual celibacy."

A belief in Fairies was widespread, and has survived, in remote districts, down even to our own time:

"Oft fairy elves
Whose midnight revels by a forest side
Or fountain, some belated peasant sees,
Or dreams he sees, while overhead the moon
Sits arbitress, and nearer to the earth
Wheels her pale course, they on their mirth and dance
Intent, with jocund music charm his ear:
At once with joy and fear his heart rebounds."[1]

It is not easy to reconcile the conflicting details of the disposition, manners, habits, and influence of these lilipu-

[1] Milton.

tian spirits which we meet with in the early writers. But on a general survey it appears that they were very diminutive; in their intercourse with mortals sometimes good-tempered, sometimes malignant; that they loved and married, and had offspring; that they were very merry, and loved to dance upon the green, and fill the air with choral music; that they possessed stores of gold and silver, which they distributed freely; that they were invisible, but could at will present themselves to mortals; that they were very timid, and would inflict a summary punishment upon intruders. Their influence was at its highest on Friday, at noon, and at midnight.

Kirk, the Scotch minister of Aberfoyle, who died in 1688, relates some other particulars of the "good people." Their substance, he says, is denser than air; too subtle to be pierced, and, like that of Milton's angels, reuniting when divided, or when any attempt is made to cleave it asunder. Their voice is like unto whistling. They change their places of abode every quarter of the year, floating near the surface of the earth; and persons gifted with the second sight have often had fierce encounters with them. The Highlanders, to preserve themselves and their cattle against them, went regularly to church on the first Sunday of every quarter, though they might not return during the interval. At the name of GOD or JESUS they vanished into thin air. They were of both sexes, and like mankind, they were mortal.

"Some meagre allusions appear to the Queen of the Fairies, and especially by King James, whose immediate knowledge may have been derived from the vignettes in Olaus Magnus, and the words of his own unhappy subjects, who perished on account of their credulity. Alexoun Perisoma was convicted, on her confession, of repairing to the 'queen of Elfame,' with whom she was familiar. Jean Wire (1670) declared that, while she taught a school at Dalkeith, a woman desired to be employed 'to speik to the Queen of Fairie, and strike ane battell in hir behalf with the said Queen.'" The name of Titania is familiar enough to all lovers of English literature. There was a necromancer or wizard, in the reign of Charles I., who affirmed he had an incantation—"O Micol, Micol, regina Pigmiorum, veni,"— that Titania could not resist. Lilly tells us that when it was tested at Hurst wood, first a gentle murmurous sound was heard; then rose a violent whirlwind, which swelled into a hurricane; and lastly the Fairy Queen appeared in all her radiance.

Fairies generally dwelt in subterraneous abodes; in the interiors of grassy hillocks, whence issued dulcet sounds and flashes of weird light; sometimes the side of a hill opened, and exposed them to the gaze of the belated wayfarer. No doubt they were seen everywhere by the potent gaze of imagination; on the meads and in the groves, or curled up among the bending flowers; for

"Visions as poetic eyes avow,
Hang from each leaf, and cling to every bough."

They were reputed to be well skilled in the medical art, and to favoured mortals they sometimes imparted their knowledge. It is difficult to understand why they were credited with the abstraction of children, and with the substitution of other beings in their place. For this curious kind of theft was commonly attributed to them. A "wise woman"—a dealer in simples and herbal potions—having failed to cure a child, declared that "the bairn had been taken away, and an elf substituted."

Besides the fairies, Scotland could boast of its spirits of the waters, just as Germany had its Loreleys and Ondines.

We can gather, however, no definite information respecting the water-kelpie, the water-horses, or the water-bull, or of another anomalous animal called shelly-coat. Describing Lochlomond, Graham says:—"It is reported by the countrymen living thereabouts, that they sometimes see the hippopotam or water-horse, where the river Cudrie falls into it, a mile west of the church of Buchanan." A river known as the Ugly Burn, in the county of Ross, springing from Loch Glaish, was regarded with awe by all the countryside, as the retreat of the water-horse and other spiritual beings. Shetland is represented as having possessed a handsome water-horse which, when mounted, carried the rider into the sea. Mr. Dalyell, writing in 1835, says, that the water-bull is still believed to reside in Loch Awe and Loch Rannoch, nor, he adds, are witnesses wanting to bear testimony to the fact. It was reputed to be invulnerable against all except silver shot; though no one had put it to the proof. In the Isle of Man certain persons who saw the water-bull in a field were unable to distinguish him from one of the ordinary terrestrial species, nor did the cows show any disposition to avoid him. But his progeny always turned out to be a rude lump of flesh and skin, without bones.

The spirit of the sea was believed to be malicious, and capable of inflicting injury. Allusions are frequent to "sea-trowis, meermen, meermaids, and a number of little creatures coming from the sea" in response to spell and charm. Nor must we forget the practice of pouring out libations to the aquatic divinities. A century ago, in Crawford Muir, when a tenant was evicted and another took his place, he cut the throat of a black lamb and threw it into a stream, with a malediction both upon stream and lamb.

To this futile department of human error we can, however, devote no more space. To treat it adequately we should need at least a couple of volumes as closely printed as the present.

INDEX.

Aborigines, the, of North America, 254.
African Superstitions, 171.
Ahetas, the, 153.
Ancestors, Worship of, 220.
Anecdotes of Khandikya and Kesidhwaja, 114.
Apples, Halloween, 293.
Ark-festival, an Indian, 90.
Ashi, the Rabbi, 72.
Asia, savage races of, 155.

Babylonian Talmud, the, 72.
Bouru, 146.
Brahman Religion, the, 14, 84.
Buddhism, 16.
Buddhists, Prayer-wheels of the, 1.
Buffalo-dance, the, 259.

Cannibalism, 250.
Caste, Brahman, 14.
Cat, adventures of a, 218.
Ceremonies, Hindu, 6; Eskimo, 275.
Chandu, Palace of, 163.
Charms, Scottish, 310.
China, in, 119.
Chinese offerings to gods, 139.
Chinese temples, 132.
Chunda Sen, Babu Keshub, 97.
Chung-Yung, 123.
Confucianism, 119.
Confucius, Life of, 120.
Court of Justice, an Eskimo, 277.
Cumming, Miss Gordon, Experiences of, 1; quoted, 3.

Daksha, sacrifice of, 103.
Debendunath Tagore, 97.

Devil-dancing, 91.
Divination, 319.
Dorians, the, 147.
Dyaks, the, 145.

Egg-trick, the, 169.
Equatorial Savage, the, 172.
Eskimos, the, 274.
Etu, the, 221.

Fairies, belief in, 323.
Feast of Lanterns, the, 129.
Fetich-man, the, 174.
Fiji-islanders, the, 230.
Fire-superstitions, 290.
Fish-charmers, Brahman, 87.
Flagellants, the, 279.

Gemara, the, 69.
Gods, belief in, 12.

Halloween, 288.
Health-superstitions, 313.
Hilarion, S., 280.
Hindu Mythology, the, 99.
Hindus, the, 203.
Hindu Temples, Ceremonies of the, 6.
Hiouen-thsang, Career of, 26.

Idol Worship, 221.
Indians, North American, 254.

Jerusalem Talmud, the, 72.
Jewish Superstitions, 68.
Jugglery, 163.

Khudas, the, 89.

INDEX.

King, or, the Five Canonical Works, 125.
Lao-tsze, the Chinese Philosopher, 129.
Lun-Yu, the, 124.

Magianism, 43.
Maize, Indian reverence for the, 273.
Malays, among the, 142.
Maories, the, 241.
Medicine-bag, the Indian, 265.
Medicine-man, the Indian, 174; the Eskimo, 274.
Meng-tze, the, 124.
Mishna, the, 68.
Mongols, the, 157.
Müller, Max, quoted, 10.

Nâgpanchanic Festival, the, 210.
New Zealand, 241.
North American Indians, the, 254.
Nursery tale, a Hindu, 307.

Old age, African veneration of, 172.
Orang-lauts, the, 152.
Ormuzd and Ahriman, 191.
Ostiaks, the, 158.

Paharis, the Customs of, 87.
Papeiha's witness to Christianity, 215.
Papuan Tribes, the, 147.
Parsees, the, 43.
Peace-pipe, the Indian, 270.
Polo, Marco, 161.
Polynesian Sacrifices, 228.
Polynesian Superstitions, 214.
Prayer-Wheels of the Buddhists, 1.
Public Games, 109.
Puranas, the, 99.

Rammohun Roy, Life of, 92.
Red Men, the, 257.
Religion, Brahman, 14, 84; Buddhism, 16; Parsee, 43; Chinese, 119; among the Malays, 142; the Dyaks, 145; in Bouru, 146; among the Papuan tribes, 147; the Orang-lauts, 152; Savage nations of Asia, 155; in Tibet, 161; Zabianism, 186; in Polynesia, 214; among the Fiji-islanders, 230; the Maories, 241; North American Indians, 254.
Rudra, Origin of, 103.

Samoans, the, 219.
Samojedes, 155.
San-tsing, the Chinese deity, 131.
Scottish Superstitions, 288.
Second Sight, 290, 300, 314.
Serpent-worship, 186.
Shae-tung, the, 129.
Shamanism, 91.
Shang-te, the, of the Chinese, 131.
Slamatan Bromok, the, 142.
Snake-charmers, 87.
Stylites, S. Simeon, 281.
Sun-worship, 8, 200.
Superstitions, African, 171.
Supreme Being, belief in a, 11.

Taboo, or Tapu, 241.
Tadibe, the, 156.
Ta-heo, the, 123.
Talmud, the, 68.
Taossi, the, 132.
Taouism, 129.
Tchu-Chor, the, 3.
Thibetan Prayer or Litany, the, 4.
Tibet, in, 161.
Topes, the, 203.
Typhon and Osiris, 173.

Vishnu Purana, the, 100.

Weather-conjuring among the Mongols, 159.
Williams, Rev. John, 214.

Yadageri, 160.

Zabianism, 186.
Zendavesta, the, 43.
Zoroaster, 45.
Zulu Witch-finders, 180.

www.ingramcontent.com/pod-product-compliance
Lightning Source LLC
Chambersburg PA
CBHW021201230426
43667CB00006B/505